The New Religious Right

The New Religious Right:

Piety, Patriotism, and Politics

by Walter H. Capps

University of South Carolina Press

Published in Columbia, South Carolina, by the
University of South Carolina Press

Manufactured in the United States of America

Library of Congress Cataloging-in-Publication Data

Capps, Walter H.
    The new religious right : piety, patriotism, and politics / by
Walter H. Capps.
        p.   cm.
    Includes bibliographical references.
    ISBN 0-87249-607-4 (alk. paper)
    ISBN 0-87249-741-0 (pbk.)
    1. Evangelicalism—United States—History—20th century.
2. Fundamentalism—History. 3. Christianity and politics.
4. Conservatism—United States—History—20th century.
5. United States—Politics and government—1977– 6. United
States—Church history—20th century. I. Title.
BR1642.U5C36   1990
277.3'0825—dc20   90-39818

For Carl and Ruth Segerhammar,
and Bob and Florence Michaelsen—
even in these days
there are giants in
the earth

Contents

Preface

New Right religion is a reluctant and unforgiving subject for a scholar in religious studies. By training and temperament, a scholar who approaches subjects from this vantage point is quite prepared to consider all fundamentalisms as probable exhibits of the sort of mental rigidity a more compelling human nature is obliged to overcome. New Right religion is "true believer" religion, which, as everyone knows, is sometimes beguiled into dogmatic militancy, and carries the ability, in some circumstances, to work pathological mischief on its devotees.

I did not undertake this project, I confess, as an advocate or out of deep personal empathy for the subject. It was simply that my curiosity had been aroused by the fact that the rise of a New Religious Right seemed demonstrably out of touch with the real needs and deeper challenges of our time. I wondered how this could be, and how its proponents could respond to the course of human events in such a peculiar fashion. Along the way, of course, I discovered that there was much more to the story than I had anticipated, and that the movement's advocates were quite able to explain their convictions on grounds they believed to be intellectually defensible. I also came to recognize just how easy it is to dismiss Religious Right theology even before considering it or trying to comprehend it.

Thus I was caught in an unexpected place. I had not yet determined why a religious right movement should have come to prominence in the late 1970s and early 1980s, but I was developing confidence that there are such reasons. However, even to acknowledge this possibility is to ascribe a degree of seriousness to the subject that is inconsistent with the disposition to dismiss the matter out of hand. Therefore, I was motivated not only to understand and interpret a subject that intrigued me, and to identify or establish the vantage point from which such understanding and interpretation could emerge, but also to explain why I was interested in pursuing either of these objectives. And this latter required me (at least in my thoughts) to moderate a discussion between two contending and opposing viewpoints, while I was searching diligently for a mode of discourse that would prevent either side from controlling the terms of the discussion. I found myself wanting to do all of this—being high-minded and evenhanded, but without relinquishing my deeper suspicions.

When speaking of interpretation, Thomas Merton, the late Trappist monk, frequently referred to the virtual impossibility of "seeing the eye through which one sees." One sees with the eye, Merton noted, sometimes with a trained eye, but one experiences extreme difficulty trying to see, or know, the eye by which one sees. Thus, in Merton's view, intepretation of what one sees always involves two fundamental ingredients: what one is seeing, and how one sees. These two factors are always interdependent and reciprocally influential.

Accordingly, what one finds appropriate to say, write or judge about the New Religious Right is also an index into how one sees and how one makes sense. What one finds to criticize about the movement lends expression—at least by apposition—to what one cherishes and prizes. What one finds worthy of praise within the movement is also indicative of where one stands. Whatever analysis is offered tells one something about the subject, perhaps, as well as something about the inquirer. For the inquirer, such analytical work is also a kind of hermeneutical self-examination. Not every subject is so analytically reflexive, at least not so directly and intensely. But the subject called the New Religious Right does indeed work this way, since it tends to force a disclosure of the interpreter's own sense of values. Thus, interpretations of the movement may or may not convey reliable information and valuable insight about the movement. But, without fail, they will reflect the attitude and perspective of the interpreter. This is a predictable equation.

Coming from where I was, I was in no confident position to make sense of the subject except through the assistance of a number of people who could help take me to where they were. I think first of William Billings, who, when I was first introduced to him in 1981, was the chief executive officer of the National

Christian Action Coalition. Billings made telephone calls on my behalf to arrange on-site interviews, invited me to sit in on planning sessions of the leadership of the movement, and helped me sift through my findings, impressions and reflections. Paul Weyrich, of the Heritage Foundation and the Committee for the Survival of a Free Congress, was helpful too, even after discerning that I was not a likely supporter of the causes he was espousing. Roy Barton of Bob Jones University and Jerry Horner of Pat Robertson's CBN University both worked diligently to make sure that I had the information that I wanted or needed. All of them were willing to give me hours of discussion time when I was trying to interpret what I had encountered and uncovered. Harald Bredesen, Pat Robertson's pastor and confidant, with whom I had a full day's conversation in his beautiful home in Escondido, California, provided valuable history (still unrecorded) concerning the rise of neo-Pentecostal Protestant Christianity over the last decade and longer. And there were numerous others with whom I spoke, either on campuses, in churches, or in conferences, whose names are not explicitly recorded here, but from whom I also learned considerably. I do not expect them to agree with everything I have written, but I do hope they recognize that I have heard them and have worked conscientiously to be fair and informative.

My largest gratitude, however, goes to those who listened to me when I returned home. I think particularly of my faculty colleagues in religious studies at the University of California, Santa Barbara, and of (then) doctoral candidates John Simmons, Keith Naylor, Michael Burdick, Sam Porter, Kathryn Alexander, and Kjell Lejon. Good friends Endel Kallas, James Quay, and King Harris played key roles, as did my undergraduate students in the "Religion and Politics" class. Some of the material has been presented in lectures at Creighton, Cal Poly, California Lutheran, and Willamette universities; as the Olive Woods Lecture at Western Illinois; as the Ransom-Butler Lectures at Wichita State; as the Meade Swing Lectures at Oberlin; and in other forms.

I thank my family, my father Holden, my wife Lois and our children, Lisa, Todd and Laura, my brothers Roger, Don and Douglas and their families, and Milton Grimsrud and Nathan Brostrom for the discussions around the dining-room table. The book is dedicated to four persons who have been part of our Santa

The New Religious Right

CHAPTER ONE
THINKING ABOUT
THE NEW RELIGIOUS
RIGHT

I didn't know what to think, back in 1978, the first time I saw Jerry Falwell on television. There he was, robust, blue-vested, taking up center stage on our television screen, surrounded by an assortment of theologians, evangelists, and some national notables. Adopting the role of a biblical prophet, and holding forth from the steps of the Capitol in Washington, he had purchased expensive air time to tell as many citizens as he could reach that he was asking God's forgiveness for our moral degradation. On that particular day few viewers would have given any serious consideration to the prospect that a New Religious Right (there was not yet an incorporated entity called the Moral Majority), or anything Jerry Falwell was sponsoring, would ever become a potent religious or political force within the country. Most would have been shocked had they been told that this television evangelist would soon have the support of the next President of the United States, and that on a number of crucial moral and legislative issues they would be making successful common cause. And who could have believed that by 1984 candidates for high national office would be competing for the support of the movement Falwell was espousing, or that by 1988 the movement would be offering a serious and viable presidential candidate of its own?

Back then there was no compelling evidence of the possibility of a conservative religious and political revival in the nation. Hence, a Falwellite movement could accurately be prejudged to be little more than a rather incidental and accidental claimant to the

1

nation's momentary attention, with no real capacity to be anything more than a sideshow. If a new conservative force showed some promise of coming into prominence, or so many would have thought, it might be able to grab some easy headlines for a short period—for such an occurrence would indeed be a novelty. It might even enjoy a round of early successes, in the short run, but it would be no more than a short run. Few suspected that American religion might be shifting significantly into a conservative mode. Few detected that Falwellite religion stood for an alternative version of American civil religion. Few anticipated that the movement would generate durable staying power.[1]

By contrast, the currents that seemed to carry deep and abiding religious significance exhibited direct attachment to the situation in the third-world regions of the globe. Here, on each of the continents, the fundamental human desire to overcome the ravages of hunger and poverty, and to establish economic justice, had become compelling and insistent.[2] Those living outside the third world were only beginning to learn some of the terms and shape the appropriate categories by which such social, political, and economic developments can be described and interpreted. But our nation's tragic experience in Vietnam served as a brilliant example of what can happen when such developments are called by mistaken names or are explained in ways that turn out to be unworthy of trust. It was this set of global dynamics, and not any prospect that American religion might be adopting a resuscitated conservative stance, that invited close watching, that is, back in 1978.

Yet, even then, if one thought further about it, it was possible to place these two items into correspondence with each other. The prolonged national suffering and collective post-traumatic stress over what had happened to the United States in the Vietnam War had indeed stimulated deep soul searching. Such soul searching could serve as a powerful nurturing environment toward the restoration of national pride. And the restoration of national pride can find powerful support and instrumentation within the conservative temper. Looked at in this way, it might have been expected that the necessary restitution and resuscitation of the threatened national ideal would provoke or rekindle a spirit of resolute or even feisty sovereignty. Furthermore, it is possible, when the specifics are added, that such a spirit would fuel a fresh blush of militant anticommunism; it might find itself doing this simply in its desire for effective self-expression. Moreover, everyone, whether liberal or conservative or somewhere in-between, seemed to be agreed that the national governmental institutions had failed the people; perhaps conditions were ripe, therefore, for a reinvigorated populist emphasis. One could perceive, this is to say, that there are compelling ways of making sense of the rise of a Falwell-like figure. At least one could approach his appearance as being plausible, regardless of how one judged its worth, viability, and effectiveness.

But to reason this way, namely, to try to tease out cogent reasons for the rise of a New Religious Right, is to indulge in hypothetics. It made some sense to proceed this way in 1978, when the movement was new, relatively untested, and certainly yet without sure interpretive classification. But the fact is that the movement has been on the national religious and political scene for some time. Though it has suffered numerous misadventures, has encountered widespread public disfavor, and has invited scorn and ridicule, the movement has indeed had an impact. Moreover, the objectives that brought the movement into being are deemed to be as challenging today as they were in the beginning. The leadership of the movement will always be dedicated toward achieving an effective working relationship between national piety and national patriotism so that the two might function as harmonizing collaborative teammates in the pursuit of the common good. The movement remains committed to synthesizing selected Christian theological judgments with specific conceptions of how a democracy ought to function. In working toward this objective, the New Right believes that it carries the authority of both the Bible and the guiding philosophical principles of the nation's Founding Fathers.

And yet, from the interpreter's perspective, it does matter how one feels about it. For how one feels about it will influence the attitude one takes toward it, and the seriousness with which one approaches an analysis and interpretation of the movement. Furthermore, one's feelings and attitudes toward the movement are prompted by the nature of the movement itself. The New Religious Right has requested responses to its propositions. It has also positioned itself, at times, as being deliberately adversarial to gain attention, and has understood that such confrontational tactics are sometimes required if the truth is to be uncovered.[3] In these respects, the way in which the movement has pursued its goals is no different from that of any other ideology that regards itself as the repository and defender of the true faith. Such absolutistic claims dictate zealous dedication, which zeal and ardor are to be found frequently in the history of religious and political movements.

All of this, then, prompts the primary question for the analyst and interpreter. Is it possible to construct an objective, illuminative and even dispassionate account of a subject that is embedded in intense emotion and passionate conviction? Is there ground from which to engage the subject not through the wish to confirm or reject, defend or denounce, but simply to understand, and then to report such understanding accurately and compellingly? Can such an interpreter successfully penetrate through the polemics to discover some reliable basis that will encourage findings that defenders, opponents, and impartial observers alike will acknowledge to be useful and fair? Is it possible to be objective about a set of religious truth claims without deciding for or against such truth claims? Can an interpreter find such interpretive high ground even while being temperamentally suspicious?[4]

Once I recognized that the subject presented special challenges to interpretation, I initiated my investigative work by proceeding in the manner that I understood to be most impartial of all. I simply gathered the most obvious information by having my name placed on the mailing lists of the principal groups and organizations. I also listened to hundreds of hours of tape-recorded addresses, attended regional and national meetings at which leaders were present, and tried to engage them in conversation. I also traveled. As the chapters in this study illustrate, I went to cities, churches, and educational institutions of special significance to the movement. Of course, I sought out the best analyses and interpretations of the movement that are available in books and monographs, but my intention was to encounter the subject in those concrete situations where it is enveloped in primary data.

In my travels from place to place, I was attentive to some guidance offered years ago by Professor Thomas F. O'Dea, an extraordinary sociologist of American religion, who concentrated on instances of religious and political conservatism.[5] O'Dea was convinced that the most effective way to approach a conservative movement is by trying to identify its primary *instinct,* that is, the social and psychological sources of its motivational power. He believed that such instinctual impulses can be isolated, and then can be named and analyzed. When properly identified such instinctual factors stand as focal points around which the perceptible features of the subject can be seen to cluster. O'Dea affirmed that the driving forces of such movements are always instinctual first, before being translated into philosophical principles and sometimes even into ideology. In most instances, the ideological translation functions primarily to undergird the prevailing instinct with authority and legitimation.

Further, O'Dea cautioned that interpreters who have learned to conduct investigations within established academic environments sometimes mistake—or misread—the significance of a conservative movement because their own attitudinal propensities and convictional sentiments get in the way. Their cherished intellectual interests, their political preferences, and/or their religious persuasions may lead them to concentrate on selected *ideational* aspects of the movement, which may turn out to be less than central or fundamental. Moreover, sometimes, confident that their own viewpoint is superior to the body of belief and thought they are analyzing, some scholars may even be prone to dismiss the validity or significance of the subject because they are approaching it with disdain. But, in O'Dea's view, such a judgment may indeed reflect an attitudinal decision that was made before the subject was fully engaged. Consequently, whatever interpretation results from such an approach merely demonstrates that the analyst's anticipations were at odds with the subject. The preconception has been misguided. And whatever conclusions are presented are only reflective of the assumptions and convictions the interpreter feels an obligation to express and protect. In the end, no real knowledge has been acquired, and the interpretation adds no enduring insight.

Following O'Dea's leads, when New Religious Right religion is encountered and represented in its own terms, there are a number of features and characteristics that simply stand out for the interpreter to seize upon. Therefore, there is no reason at least at the outset, to try for some meta-interpretation, that is, to distinguish what the movement claims to be from what, say, we suspect it *really* is. Rather, in the beginning, it is important to take the movement's own claims—and own efforts at self-definition— seriously. And, in the case of the New Religious Right, it is appropriate to start with the linkages between religious belief and democratic ideals. As we have already noted, the movement gained national attention by making provocative claims about compatibilities between individual piety and national patriotism, yes, even between the tenets of biblical religion and the professed ideals of a democratic society. The New Religious Right insisted on being specific in this regard. It was intent on understanding that the United States of America is a "Christian nation" in some literal sense. It was intrigued by the possibility that religious and political convictions could be synthesized, and that individual piety and individual patriotism could be based on one and the same creed. This, for starters, cast the New Religious Right as a conservative version of American civil religion.

It is to be expected, then, that the movement would stand in sharp judgment against other, less literal-minded posited nexuses between religious beliefs and political ideals, particularly those that have been proposed under liberal or progressive sponsorship. The movement has found such formulas to be weak and ineffective. So it has charged that these tenuous liberal harmonies, if they ever actually existed, have broken down completely. Thus the primary intellectual task, as New Religious Right advocates view the matter, is to bring religious beliefs and political ideals into mutually sustaining alignment, to stabilize the vitality of the nation's common life.

When the issue is posed this way, it can be seen to belong to the set of intellectual interests introduced by Max Weber and Emile Durkheim in the nineteenth century.[6] Both social theorists were intrigued about the ways in which the ideals and aspirations of a people are reflected in their habits, laws, customs, contracts, sanctioned protocols, and about the ways in which a given society respects, honors, fears, celebrates and commits its noblest energies. Both nineteenth-century thinkers understood religion to be pervasively implicit in societal order, both as a sanction and an expression of such order. Thus, analysts who are guided by Weberian and Durkheimian intellectual sensitivities will take note of the fact that New Religious Right theology cannot be stated, for instance, apart from a strong, unqualified reassertion of the propriety of patriarchy. It must be significant, too, that the movement gained prominence at the very time that the patriarchal ordering of society was being challenged by changes in attitudes toward the roles of men and women, and by extensive alterations in the demographics of American family life. Most of the prevailing teachings of the movement—the ones dealing with the sanctity of traditional family values, the evils of abortion, the ways in which pornography and homosexuality are understood to undermine national nobility, and anti-feminist fervor—can be fitted to the mode of analyses that Weber and Durkheim inspired.

So too can the interpreter draw upon the insights of Clifford Geertz, the distinguished Princeton anthropologist, who defines religion in terms of the multitudinous and complex ways in which motivations and aspirations function as cohesive and synthesizing forces within a society.[7] Such motivations give direction to the activities of the citizenry, and support their recognizable accomplishments. When Geertz describes this process, he understands himself to be offering a portrayal of the social functions of religion. It must be appropriate, in this regard, that the desire to "bring America back again" is a fundamental aspiration of the New Religious Right. It is also telling that when such aspirations are being expressed, there is deliberate and conscious recollection of a happier, though bygone day, when social cohesiveness is remembered, or assumed, to have been present, and when shared religious and patriotic ideals were one and the same.

It is significant, in this respect, that New Religious Right advocates have been criticized for indulging in nostalgia. They confess to a longing for a time that pertained before events occurred that led to a fracturing of some previously reliable social order, a time when religious beliefs and attitudes were compatible. Geertz's work demonstrates that when the social cohesion is resilient and self-evident, religion is defined in constructive functional terms: it is the glue, the stuff and basis of cohesion, the source from which the cohesiveness flows, and the fundamental guarantor of its perpetuation. In functional terms, religion is a constructive force, contributing to the integration of the society. But when the cohesiveness is lacking, religion can only be approached in dysfunctional terms, that is, as an element that is missing, or even as counterpoint to what prevails. Advocates of the

New Religious Right have been quick to point to such apparent disarray as the basis for a call to reestablish what used to be, that is, when days were happier, simpler and more agreeable. New Religious Right sermons frequently take the form of denunciations of what has happened to upset or destroy the unity and cohesiveness that once was, when religion too was vibrant and vital.

Mircea Eliade, the historian of religions, ventured a multilayered theory to explain how the instinctual power of religious consciousness, wherever it is found, works to resist the desacralizing tendencies of societies involved in the process of modernization.[8] Eliade reiterated that religion is an early occurrence in the history of human consciousness, and that the developments of subsequent modes (for example, science, technology, as well as analytical philosophy) work progressively to undermine its authority. Eliade believed in the perennial value of religion, of course, and attested that the world of modernity remains dependent upon its resourcefulness, even in ways that are not fully recognized by its citizenry. Each age, in his view, is obliged, to its peril, to identify and recapture its own spiritual underpinnings. But no age can perform this function for another; each must do it for itself. And the necessary and inevitable exercise always places traditional religion in conflict with progress. Within the age-old conflict, religious sensitivity will inevitably come to call some aspects and products of progress "illusion," and will work to reestablish a more reliable way of apprehending reality, one that is sustained by a sense of life that pertained before such illusions were born.

Here, too, the New Religious Right might provide an intriguing illustration or test-case for Eliade's theories. The new conservative religious movement was born through at least partial awareness that the secularizing tendency (that is, the one that tends to destabilize "traditional values") within contemporary American society was doing violence to some of the ideals that the citizenry had regarded as being sacred. Hence, advocates of the program of the New Religious Right understand themselves to be resisting some of the impulses of modernity. Their rhetoric is shaped by a living memory of what the nation was like before widescale "permissiveness" (one of the movement's most-often used words) occurred, that is, before some thought-to-be inviolable moral code was broken. They talk about it as a world, consecrated by its founders, that has become tarnished, as if some primordial sacred pledge has been broken. In such terms, a permissive society is a sacrilege. It stands in violation, ontologically speaking, of what was intended to be. Thus, in proceeding in this fashion, New Religious Right believers have tapped some of the impulses that belong to religion, that is, to the nature and function of religion universally considered. But there is more.

When Alexis de Tocqueville worked to provide a descriptive account of what might be called the American national character in his classic *Democracy in America,* he uncovered compelling evidence that religion functions paradoxically at times in a democratic society. Describing the needs of democracy, Tocqueville attested that the influence of tyrannical religion must be countered by the resources of constructive religion.[9] To identify something as a religious force in society is not necessarily to anticipate that its influence will be salutary. This insight prompts the thought that there may be some fundamental reflex action—some ongoing shift within sets of contrasts—at the core of the American national and religious experience. Indeed, such shifts may have become perceptible in the story of the rise of the phenomenon now generally referred to as the New Religious Right.

One must wonder, to be more specific, about possible relationships between the resuscitation of a conservative political and religious movement and the role of countercultures in recent American national experience. Indeed, the advent of the counterculture in the early and middle 1960s illustrates the process by which elements understood to be marginal within the society move more and more into the center. When the sixties counterculture first came to prominence, it was received, by many, as being alien, even inimical, to the dominant society. It made inroads even while being resisted, and, at times, and, in part, actively rejected. Such was to be expected of a force that operates by functioning in contrast to what is prevailing. But, along the way, in remarkable and increasing fashion, some of the resistance was overcome, and there was gradual acceptance of the new movement's influence. Signs of this transformation are to be found, for example, in the ways in which the society is being influenced by newly discovered ecological and environmental sensitivities. It is in evidence, too, in altered standards for

measuring personal success and failure. It can be seen in revised
conceptions of the meaning of personal satisfaction, and within
myriad numbers of modifications of styles and tastes. What once
was marginal has moved from periphery to formative place.
"Outsiders" have become "insiders." "Marginal people" have
assumed leadership roles, not in any simple or predictable fashion,
to be sure, but in sufficient numbers to support the view that some
dialectical transposition has occurred.[10]

This same process may perhaps describe the career of the New
Religious Right. It is conceivable that its move from marginality to
a more resilient centrality, and then back again, was empowered
by some of the same dynamics that describes what happens to
counterculture movements. Virtually all of the textbook analyses
confirm that the traditional stance of conservative or rightist
religious groups in the United States is to opt for marginality.
Characteristically, many of the evangelical and conservative
religious communities have chosen to be both anti-intellectual and
apolitical. They have also operated according to the assumption
that the dominant society would not and could not understand or
appreciate them. Thus, they have made a virtue out of not being
accepted or understood. They have elected to be marginal,
standing outside of what is usually acknowledged to be the
religious and political mainstream. From this point of analysis, it
is easy to extrapolate that deliberately marginal persons and
groups are susceptible of becoming "outsiders," who, in turn, as
Richard Hofstadter has argued, become vulnerable to various
forms of paranoia.[11] The fundamentalist propensity to believe that
they are engaged in warfare (indeed, a fight to the finish, and
within which everything that one believes in is at stake) with an
enemy both malevolent and nearly all-powerful has been well
documented in scholarship.

In this respect, the contemporary phenomenon manifests
some arresting features. Instead of striving to be anti-intellectual
(which it certainly remains in some quarters), the New Religious
Right also offers compelling evidence of wanting to be taken with
intellectual seriousness. Jerry Falwell likes to boast that Liberty
University (the college he founded) is fully accredited, and is just
as respectable as any college or university in the country. He
claims that one can get as good an education there—judged solely
in intellectual terms—as one can find anywhere. He is eager to

have his institution compete with all other schools on virtually all appropriate terms, and has predicted that it will someday have enrollments equal to or greater than those of Big Ten institutions while being mentioned, academically speaking, in the same descriptive paragraphs with the Ivy League schools. The graduate programs at Pat Robertson's CBN University, in Virginia Beach, Virginia, compare favorably with similar programs in similar institutions, and as preparation for careers in communications as well as political action they are recognized to be breaking new academic ground.

And this is just the beginning, for the movement has also created or established its own newspapers, magazines, and journals, its own radio and television stations, its own broadcast systems, its own worldwide television networks, its own editorial writers and thinkpiece essayists. It has produced its own counter philosophical treatises as well as libraries of interpretive historical documents. It has its own houses of publication, which have sometimes been swamped with orders. It offers philosopher/ theologian Francis Schaeffer as an intellectual the equal of thinkers representing the philosophical, theological, and religious stances with which the movement is competing. It has its own educational theorists too.

In every respect, the movement's intellectual products were intended to compare favorably with the most distinguished available from all sides and in all other quarters. This is a marked departure from the glee some fundamentalists used to express when citing stories like that of Brother Joe Leffew, who, speaking to an outdoors Pentecostal revival meeting in 1925, at the time of the Scopes Trial, is reported to have said: "I ain't got no learnin' and never had none. Glory be to the Lamb. Some folks work their hands off'n up'n to the elbows to give their young-uns education, and all they do is send their young-uns to hell. I've got three young-uns in the cabin and three in glory. I know they're in glory because I never learned 'em nothing." There are, no doubt, some Brother Leffews still around, and there may be some within the New Religious Right movement, but the prevailing tendency is to claim that the articles of religious faith can stand the test of rigorous intellectual scrutiny.

In addition, the New Religious Right came onto the scene being openly, calculably, and unabashedly politically minded, and this, too, distinguishes it from previous manifestations of American conservative religion. Its quick acquisition of political power, finesse and success is its chief identifying characteristic when measured against the typical ambitions and proclivities of the traditional religious right, or even when compared with groups and movements that enjoyed prominence during the time of the nation's previous and various "great awakenings." Furthermore, such conversions and transformations of typical identifying features can be directly associated with the assumption of new or revised functions within the society—that is, with a transposition from political and religious noneffectiveness or marginality to a budding centrality. It doesn't matter that, in some quarters, it seems that the New Religious Right perpetuates some of the phenomenon's stereotypes. What is certain is that the movement represents an intriguing subject for anyone who wishes to reflect critically on ways in which dedicated "outsiders" contribute to the formation of a society and the composition of a culture. Perceived in this way, our subject stands as an important chapter in analyses of how values are transmitted within a culture that is experiencing complicated fluctuations and rhythmic changes in relationships between margins and centers—changes that are reflected in our continuing preoccupation to establish (or reestablish) the society's *core.* The issue is not frequently stated this way. More often one hears questions about what it means to be *a responsible American citizen in a world like ours,* when each of the key terms in this phrase (i.e., "American," "responsible," "a world like ours") is open to interpretation. But the debate is about how a society protects and cultivates its fundamentally nurturing resources.

And when referring to the dynamisms implicit in relationships between margins and centers, one must also think carefully about the specific mechanisms by which the New Religious Right got the attention of the American people, and how it came to acquire intellectual power and influence. It is significant, in this respect, that the acknowledged leaders of the movement are experts in the arts of television communication.[12] While serving as pastor of Thomas Road Baptist Church, Jerry Falwell is also known nationally as a television evangelist, whose weekly broadcast is "The Old Time Gospel Hour." Before and after running for the presidency, Pat Robertson has been host of the "700 Club" on national television as well as being president-director-producer of a vast television network. The largest money raisers within the movement are those who appear frequently on television. Just as Ronald Reagan, whom friend and foe alike referred to as "the great communicator," utilized television and the wizardry of the teleprompter to communicate his most important messages, the New Religious Right has used television as the primary medium through which the movement's gospel—as well as its creedal and ideological formulations—is transmitted. Previous national "great awakenings" took place in camp meetings, and were characterized by altar calls and sawdust trails. The current one, in keeping with the resources of the technological revolution, has, like the Vietnam War that preceded it, moved into the nation's living rooms, where, appropriately, it has placed emphasis on family values and can be monitored by Nielsen ratings. No description of the New Religious Right is complete unless it properly accounts for this transposition.

The movement also registers as national theater. Before Ronald Reagan became actively involved in state and national politics, he was a Hollywood movie actor.[13] His identity as a film actor, which he had no hesitation acknowledging—indeed, he was proud of it—is to be seen in a host of ways. When confronting difficult situations, for example, he often resorted to quoting lines from movies and television shows. He had seen himself so frequently on film and on television that, as he was ready to acknowledge, he knew precisely how he was being perceived regardless of what he did, how he moved, how he acted. He was fully cognizant of the fact, too, that politics is theater, and that, within the context of the theater, to be perceived is to be—an important modification of George Berkeley's eighteenth-century philosophical doctrine. But when the perception is the reality, or is offered and/or intended as the reality, it is difficult to know the grounds on which one can distinguish image from that to which image refers. From this vantage point, being perceived as the President is much of what it is to be the President. Moreover, the public credibility of New Right religion was communicated this way too, with television functioning both as vehicle of transmission and as primary instrument of validation. Because the New Religious Right took on prominence on the screen, available for all to see, its rightful existence could be defended on grounds of some compelling, acknowledged evidence. For the movement too, to be recognized publicly is to be.

The interrelationships between symbology and epistemology are even more intriguing when one notices that advocates of the New Religious Right have tended to accept a specific religious worldview, communicated primarily through biblical images and stories, with absolute devotion and literal seriousness. The literal seriousness enhances the propensity, for example, to expect that the world will end precisely as biblical prophecy and apocalyptic literature foretells. This absolute devotion encourages a tendency towards intolerance of others as well as doctrinal fanaticism. The translation of symbolic references to literal identifications, which are then applied in singleminded ways, dictates that mythology too will be read as a story about facts. Behind all of it is a prescribed ideology that guides and sustains such exegetical and hermeneutical activity. The ideology is motivated by an obligation to identify threatening conspiracies, whether this be the devil (the diabolical biblical figure who perennially opposes God's truth), Marxist-Leninist ideology (the errant philosophy which, among all others, is most diametrically opposed to the Christian point of view), or those destructive, subversive elements within society that carry the capacity to undermine our cherished American way of life. Like Manichaeism of old, it is a disposition that understands the ingredients of the world to be arranged as polar opposites: something is either good or evil, represents light or darkness, embodies truth or error, for there is no middle ground. But it is also a reading on the world in which no great allowances are made for distinctions between the image and its referent, the symbol and that to which the symbol may refer, or even between empirical and imaginative portrayals.

For example, the believer is encouraged to approach the apocalyptic portions of the Bible—with their myriad references to names, places, nations, and incidents in the Ancient Near East—as if all of this is primarily an authorized commentary on identifiable contemporary events. The story of Armageddon, for instance, is taken as a literal description of what is already occurring, or is imminent in the world today. Almost everything that pertains to the people of Israel is read as if applying directly to the people of the United States. The messages of the prophets are understood to be diagnostic of situations Americans face today. The biblical covenant status is transferred from Israel to America, and the God who blesses and judges biblical Israel is the same God who blesses and judges America today, and according to the same formulas. A previous fourfold method of biblical interpretation, which was established to honor the varieties of symbolic and linguistic expression that are present within the scripture, is retained. But the literal, allegorical, tropological (referring to the moral lesson that is being taught), and anagogical (referring to the mystical sense of the passage) interpretations are all made to apply to the situation being faced by the United States today. This way of reading the Bible becomes a basis for contemporary political commentary. From this source Religious Right advocates are able to develop distinctive attitudes toward national and international events, and to offer them with spiritual authority. By employing the Bible this way, the movement was able to position itself much closer to the center of national political life.[14]

There are additional ingredients in the mix. Reference has been made to the mixing of religion and politics, and to the commingling of biblical religion with the American experience to form an Americanized version of the Christian faith. Though they claim not to be intending a theocracy, New Religious Rightist intentions invite a fresh appraisal of the discussion Robert Bellah initiated when he published his now famous article on "Civil Religion in America" in 1967.[15] Bellah claimed that "there actually exists alongside of and rather clearly differentiated from the churches an elaborate and well-institutionalized civil religion in America," and he urged scholars and interpreters to give this subject "the same care in understanding that is devoted to religion in any other manifestation." He referred to the subject as "the religion of the American way of life," noting that this religion is reflective of the convictions and attitudes of the American people.

In his seminal article, Bellah could write about civil religion and dismiss fundamentalism as being irrelevant or antithetical to the subject he was describing. But now that the New Religious Right has come to prominence, this description is no longer valid. The religion of the movement has attempted to attain the status of a civil religion. In a number of significant respects, it deserves to be understood as a graphic example of the phenomenon Bellah sought to identify and describe. The story about the New Religious Right can be interpreted as an account of how a portion of American fundamentalist Christianity found the facility to achieve acknowledged civil-religion status.

Moreover, the interpreter must also consider ramifications of the fact that the New Religious Right made its social and cultural impact in the midst of an era that was being identified as "the secular age." How should this unexpected development be understood? How does one explain the fact that, as secularization was increasing, the nation seems to have become at least partially preoccupied by questions and issues of a demonstrably religious nature? Why should it have happened that—mocking the prophecies that had been offered with such easy assurances— religious values seemed to have gained, rather than lost, in comparison with secular values during the 1970s and 1980s. Some compelling evidence about this has been offered by James Reichley of the Brookings Institution who contends in his book, *Religion in American Public Life*,[16] that religious values are indisputably and demonstrably indispensable to the vitality of our democratic way of life. In this light, the rise of the New Religious Right need not be approached as if it were some strange anomaly. Rather, it may serve as a prime example of the fact that this democracy has not lost interest in establishing and certifying its most distinguishable aspirations on religious foundations.

Beyond this, the rise of the New Religious Right in our time must be witness to the fact that ours is an age in which theological concerns—as anachronistic as this may seem—are once again prominent in our intellectual life. It is an age in which some of the chief spokespersons are those who are able to participate in theological discussion, when theology is construed as being a broad and inclusive (rather than sectarian) intellectual pursuit. Though this may strike many as being either astounding or disturbing—why should theological issues surface in an age so thoroughly characterized by science and technology?—it can also be approached as being entirely appropriate. For, if there is widespread concern regarding the threat of nuclear conflagration, and that human life as we know it may cease altogether, it is fitting that the fundamental human issues be considered with utmost seriousness and in full scope and depth. In order to preserve life, it is necessary to know what life is, how to approach and revere it, and how to choose and effect vital priorities wisely. Now that there is growing sensitivity to the fact that human life is fragile—certainly this is a primary realization in the ecological age—it is essential that human beings understand what life's sustaining bases are. And if the issue concerns the destiny of the human race, one can expect to encounter the integrated range of subjects that are addressed in every major religious tradition of the world. What is the meaning of human life? How are human beings to conduct themselves? What significance do we attach to our own mortality? What is our purpose as human beings? How do our expectations concerning the future of the human race affect how we conduct our lives day by day? To what or whom do we turn for spiritual nurture? Upon what sources can we depend for reliable insight?

The traditional religious questions are back again. Therefore, what distinguishes our age from others is not, as some would wish or say, that it has been radically secularized, or that theology has become thoroughly obsolete. Rather one of the distinguishing characteristics of this age is that traditional theological concerns have moved from marginal sectarian status, where they were frequently lost or trivialized, into the mainstream of public discourse and debate. In short, traditional theological questions have reappeared in the most prominent public issues. And, as in medieval times, the prominent political players are those who know how to take responsible positions on the religious issues.

When our subject is approached from this vantage point, it is not at all surprising that Ronald Wilson Reagan was the President, who, more than any of his predecessors, spoke most frequently, publicly and forcibly on the subject of religion. It is also understandable, from these considerations, that several of the major aspirants for the highest office of the land reflected ministerial and/or divinity school training. Among the candidates in 1988, for example, both Jesse Jackson and Pat Robertson were ordained Protestant ministers. Gary Hart graduated from Yale Divinity School. Paul Simon was the son of a minister, as was George McGovern, the Democratic presidential nominee in 1972. Thus, the rise of the New Religious Right need not be approached as some thoroughly unexpected, unanticipated, anomaly or phantom event. On the contrary, its occurrence mirrors much that has come to prominence in contemporary American society and culture.

It is probable, too, that the new conservative religious movement significantly reflects, and, perhaps, directly feeds upon the increase of pluralism in American society. There was a time, rather recently, when it was possible to draw clear distinctions between majority and minority populations, but this is becoming more and more difficult. The state of California, for example, will soon be a place where minorities constitute the majority, that is, a region of the country where no race or ethnic group can be identified as enjoying majority status. The diversification of the national population is a fact of increasing prominence, and is being felt with particular acuteness within the religious communities. There was a time when one's religious opposite—if one were Protestant, for example, the opposite was a Catholic—was clearly identifiable. There was a time too when much was made, for instance, of the differences within the several branches of Lutheranism, or within segments of the Presbyterian and Methodist churches. Such distinctions continue to be significant within the religious communities to which they pertain. But they have become less prominent differentiating factors within the religious community of the United States. Here Asian religious traditions are making a significant impact. Here, too, the Islamic community is growing rapidly. And Christians are having to face the fact that advocates of such religions do not live (as once could be assumed) in far-away lands. Rather, the global situation and the national situation are becoming more and more like each other. The internationalization and diversification of American culture are significant religious trends.

The intellectual challenge, in such a situation, is to assist in making the heterogeneity intelligible, if not altogether comprehensible. And this places demands on religious communities for which many of them are hardly prepared. There was a time, not very many years ago, when missionary activity constituted the prevailing mode of engaging or confronting religious traditions other than one's own. More recently, such missionary zeal has been tempered by a recognition that it is necessary to understand the other tradition, if one is to be in a position to engage it at all. And with the interest in understanding, rather than converting, has come a willingness, sometimes, to take what is best from the various traditions and put such elements together in symbiotic combinations. Thus, Christians are borrowing from Zen Buddhist meditation practices, Jews are learning from Protestants, while talented Catholic theologians are exploring the riches of the Hindu tradition—and these represent only a few of the more obvious examples.

Therefore, on these bases, one can observe that the rise of the New Religious Right has been encouraged by important demographic shifts. However, instead of making still another important contribution to the heterogeneity of the culture, the movement stands as a bold and unequivocal defense of *homogeneity.* Knowing that heterogeneity encourages relativism in religious belief and ethical standards, the movement argues the case for absolutes again. It emphasizes that there can be no salvation outside certain prescriptions. Instead of celebrating the varieties of religious experience that are available to human beings, the movement's leaders prefer to talk of normative faith, correct teaching, indispensable doctrine, enduring values, permanent truth, and of the absolute conditions of human salvation. Within this framework, New Religious Right religion appears to be a deliberate and calculated effort to reassert a particular way of life, yes, even a normative culture, against a variety of menacing threats. And, as the guarantor of its claim, it professes that the Christian faith and the democratic form of government (as practiced and championed within the United States) are thoroughly and absolutely compatible, both of which, in this precise combination, are intended for all people, wherever they live, throughout the world.

Anti-Falwellites perceive this attitude to be reactionary, simplistic, and woefully inadequate. But the fact is that this absolutistic stance of the New Right has become attractive because the increasing internationalization and diversification, of American society and culture has shown numerous unsettling and destabilizing sides. Many citizens find real virtue in recommending intellectual openness to social and cultural diversity—including openness to religious stances very different from the ones that are most familiar and most prominent. But an attitude of openness does not always equip the adherent effectively to come to grips with the many built-in challenges of diversity, heterogeneity, and dissimilarity. Moreover, there is also striking evidence that not everyone in the society regards openness as a virtue or diversification and heterogenization as occasions for rejoicing.

Numerous questions remain unanswered. In doctrinal terms, for example, on what authoritative basis can anyone decide to choose one tradition over another? If each of the cultures can make claim to the same status, on what basis is it appropriate to protect a preferred one? How are such protections justified? Within a national social context which finds wide varieties of traditions and ways of life existing side by side, how is it possible any longer to talk about "our culture," or "our tradition," or even a distinguishable "American way of life?" How does one move with intellectual and spiritual confidence within such circles? How does social and cultural pluralism escape religious and philosophical relativism?

In principle, at least, the New Religious Right has wanted to honor religious and cultural pluralism. Many of its advocates have declared an openness to diversity. But, it is extremely difficult to maintain this attitude while remaining resolutely committed to absolute truth. What must be avoided at all costs, according to New Right convictions, is the adoption of relativistic postures, even should such relativism be understood to be fashionable. Ronald Reagan told members of the Conservative Political Action Conference in March 1986, that the greatest triumph of modern conservatism has been "to stop allowing the left and the intelligentsia to tell average Americans that they are hopelessly out of date, utterly trite, and reactionary." The strong reassertion of the conviction that true culture, true religion, and a normative way of life are clearly discernible, and that all of this was divinely intended, stands as evidence of the new confidence. The challenge to the New Religious Right is to affirm this confidence in a pluralistic context.

When all of these considerations are put together, one cannot escape the conclusion that the rise of the New Religious Right is a significant subject because it is reflective of some comprehensive shifts within contemporary American society. And, in spite of its record of blunders, miscalculations, slanders, scandals, oversteppings, and acts of self-indulgence and self-righteousness— which debilitating factors are very well known—it deserves to be studied seriously.

In the chapters following, my intention is to let the subject unfold as it might be encountered were one to search for it, as the example of Alexis de Tocqueville would encourage, in the specific locations and under the particular auspices by which it came to prominence. To assist this endeavor, I have selected five narrative accounts—four of them involving figures whose influences within the movement have been formative and substantial, and the fifth concentrating on a celebrated court case. The first portrayal focuses on Jerry Falwell himself, under whose influence the movement was originally set in motion, and the person who has remained most closely identified with it from that point forward. The second deals with an intellectual theoretician, the prominent philosopher/theologian and educator, Francis Schaeffer, whose ideas have played a seminal role in helping conceptualize the programmatic intentions of the movement. The third essay concentrates on the court case involving Bob Jones University of Greenville, South Carolina. The Jones community saw the issue to involve a most serious challenge to the constitutional basis of religious freedom, while the United States Department of Justice understood that it had an example of racial discrimination. The fourth account directs attention to the celebrated Jim and Tammy Bakker episode. The fifth vignette deals with another television personality, Pat Robertson, who was a serious and legitimate presidential candidate in 1988. Our intention is to examine each of these five subjects in detail so as to develop a composite picture.

Readers who are approaching these chapters intent on coming to sound conclusions as quickly and confidently as possible may lose patience with the markedly anecdotal style of the several portrayals. The style has been selected and cultivated to reflect the way in which the subject is encountered on its own terms, on its own ground, and nurtured by its own climate of opinion and conviction. As has been noted, the book is a product of several journeys to the settings within which the movement was born and raised, where numerous interviews were conducted. The story about Jerry Falwell came into shape during exposure to the subject in Lynchburg, Virginia. Similarly, the chapter on Pat Robertson found its design during conversations in Virginia Beach, the home of Robertson's CBN University, and after interviews with persons who work with Robertson on a daily basis. The chapter on Bob Jones University's court case was conceived in the library of the United States Supreme Court, as well as on the BJU campus in Greenville, South Carolina. The chapter on the Bakkers was written following time spent with PTL Club members in the environs of Heritage USA, outside Charlotte, North Carolina. With Francis Schaeffer, there was no interview, but a significant personal encounter just a few weeks prior to his death. The

CHAPTER TWO

THE PROPHET, THE PREACHER

The visitor can acquire an accurate sense of the climate of Jerry Falwell's home working environment simply by passing through the corridors into the lobby of the airport in Lynchburg, Virginia. There, prominently placed on the most obvious wall, is a "Freedom Shrine," put there by the Exchange Club of Lynchburg, "to strengthen citizen appreciation of our American heritage." The club has made picture-framed copies of the Bill of Rights, Declaration of Independence, Monroe Doctrine, George Washington's "Farewell Address," Thomas Jefferson's "Inaugural Address," the Instruments of Surrender for both Germany and Japan at the close of World War II, and various letters and statements by United States presidents and officials.

Parked outside on the runway, hardly a stone's throw away, is a small, sleek, white jet, marked only by letters and numbers painted on its tail. Alongside the plane is a faded blue sedan, with a uniformed security officer inside.

"Is it Jerry Falwell's?" I ask the airport car-rental clerk.

"Yes, it's his." Then, quickly, "it costs him a million dollars a year just to have it, but it's well worth it. It helps him bring in millions more each year." The speaker pauses, then continues the commentary. "Dr. Falwell just loves his family. Sometimes he comes home for dinner, then takes the plane out again in the evening."

My informant is Randy, a tall, thin, strikingly pleasant young man, who is also, I learn, a second-semester junior at Liberty

University, the school Jerry Falwell founded and presides over. Processing car-rental agreements is his part-time job.

"What is he like?" I ask, coveting a response from someone who sees Falwell from a vantage point not available to those who only read about him or watch him on television.

"Well, he's controversial," he replies.

Randy explains that he hasn't made up his own mind about Falwell. "Sure, he's a minister and a good one," he continues. "He is there each Sunday for church services, and he is usually there on Wednesday night for prayer services. But the church has become so large that he has to do most of his work through assistant pastors. It isn't the same as it used to be."

Randy pauses. Recognizing that he has been critical of the president of his university and the pastor of his church, he wishes to alter the tone. "But I'll say one thing for him," he attests, "Dr. Falwell is a man of conviction. He stands up for what he thinks is right. He is not afraid to speak out when he feels something needs to be said. And he's done a lot of good for Lynchburg." Then, as if reciting lines from a list of adulations, Randy adds, "and sir, Dr. Falwell loves the students."

"What about the students?" I ask. "What is it like being a student at Liberty University?"

"It is strict," Randy responds, "but not as strict as Bob Jones." He explains that Bob Jones University, in Greenville, South Carolina, is where many of Liberty's faculty were trained. "We have a dress code. Everyone is required to attend chapel. There is a curfew. Nothing but double-dating until the junior year. No drinking. No drugs. No dancing. No rock music."[1] He pauses, then adds, "and if anyone sees someone breaking the rules, we have to report it."

"You mean you have to tell on each other?" I question.

"Yes," he answers. "Yes, we do."

He leans over the counter, looks at me intently, studying my reaction. "Like if I wanted to have a glass of wine with dinner some night, off campus, and someone from the college saw me, do you think it's right that I'd get reported?"

"I admit that I wouldn't like it," I responded, "but you must have known about the rules before you came."

"My parents wanted me to come here," Randy continues. "They love Dr. Falwell. They study the literature he sends out.

They usually vote what he recommends. I don't think they could stand if if I were to leave. I don't know how I would explain it to them."

"You are thinking of leaving?"

"Well, no, at least not until the end of the year. I've been thinking about it. I've been pretty happy here, I guess. I'd like to be able to stay, but I feel like I'm always being judged. In the beginning I was happy to be at a Christian school. My faith in Jesus Christ means a lot to me. I wanted to come to Liberty because it is a Christian school. But the atmosphere—so many try too hard to be holy, but on the outside. Everyone wears it on the outside."

I arrive on campus early the next morning to witness it for myself, and find my way to a front-row seat in the auditorium of the multipurpose building—a structure that serves not only as the gymnasium, but, temporarily, also as its chapel. And when Falwell first steps up to the podium, he beckons the school's star football player to come forward. For the first time in the history of the university, a member of a Liberty team has been named the "outstanding performer in the nation" for his play in an intercollegiate contest. Falwell, the school's chancellor and chief pep booster, is eager to pay tribute.[2] He quotes from Vince Lombardi, the late coach of the Green Bay Packers, who said that "Winning is not a sometime thing; it's an all-the-time thing. You don't win once in a while. You don't do things right once in a while. You do them all of the time. Winning is a habit." Falwell encourages his hearers to emulate this counsel, adding that Lombardi also said, "Yes, I believe in God and I believe in human decency. But I firmly believe that any man's finest hour—his greatest fulfillment to all he holds dear—is that moment when he has worked his heart out in a good cause and lies victorious in the field of battle."

Looking out on the crowd of students, Falwell adds his own injunction: "Not a bad creed. Not a bad statement. This is what St. Paul says in his letter to Timothy. Be strong! Be victorious! Be a winner in the grace that is in Christ Jesus." The assembly of more than 5,000 students, faculty, and visitors applaud and cheer as Falwell beams and the young athlete modestly looks down at his shoes. Falwell is wearing a "Jesus First" pin on the lapel of his vested navy blue suit. He is dressed in high-top shoes, a white shirt, and the striped blue and white tie I had seen numerous times on television and in many of the pictures that have been taken of him. He too could pass for a one-time athlete who, since the days of competition, has become a frequent after-dinner speaker. One would expect him to look sober and serious, but much more apparent, this day, is his eagerness to smile, offer humorous one-liners, and revel in his recent successes. He enjoys the feel of being a "champion for Christ."

The students about me are dressed to play their part too. All of the gentlemen wear ties (a campus requirement) and the ladies are in dresses or skirts, many in heels. The young men have short haircuts. There are campus prohibitions against men's hair styles that allow the hair to touch one's collar or extend down over one's ears.

First, in the formal proceedings, come the school announcements, most of them having to do with rules of deportment. The dean reminds the students that final examination time was approaching and that extra precautions would be enforced. Then, after a guest soloist has sung several stanzas of "What a friend we have in Jesus"—" a plum purty outfit you're wearing today, sister," the song-leader had said in introducing her—the audience settles back for Dr. Falwell's sermon.

He is as a father talking to a large family. He mentions being in Nashville the night before, and Birmingham the night before that. He had met a number of parents of some Liberty students. He recites the names of some of them. "James Clark" he calls out to one of the students in the large assembly, "don't you have a brother named Mark?" Looking about, he continues, "Where's James? Oh, there you are?" James waves back. "And June Beason, I talked with your family in Birmingham. Your aunt and uncle were there too. I shook their hands on Monday night."

Then he tells of the money he had raised at the banquets at which he had been speaking—$143,000 the night before, and "all of it for the college." The people assembled give each other that pleased, gratified look that seems to befit moments of shared success and satisfaction. He says he is going to Pennsylvania the next day. Wherever he goes, he promises, he will speak about the needs of the college and the mission it represents. He is striving to raise an additional $5 million by the end of the quarter, and he asks for the students and faculty to pray for this.

He is being serious, but more playful than somber. The banter back and forth gives evidence of Falwell's reputation for being mischievous, a practical joker. Occasionally, for example, he likes to startle callers to the "Old Time Gospel Hour" by picking up the telephone himself, and saying, "Hello, this is the Lynchburg Police Department. May I help you?" Clearly, he is having fun this morning too, enjoying his place among the people with whom he feels most at home. He enjoys having the story told about what happened when, quite by accident, he and Billy Graham found themselves residing in hell. After two weeks, the story goes, the devil telephoned St. Peter and asked for assistance. The devil said that Billy Graham had missed the point about the end of the world; he was making his way about hell trying to convert people, to save them from the wrath to come. Clearly Graham was confused. But much more serious for the devil was Jerry Falwell. He had been in hell but two weeks and had already raised $2 million for air-conditioning.

Falwell's sermon this day concerns the rigors of the Christian faith when the church was a new phenomenon in the Roman world. The apostolic period fascinates him most. This was when persecution because of one's strong convictions was overt and dramatic. Falwell welcomes the decisiveness of the choices such situations forced then. It was either Yes or No, True or False, Right or Wrong, Good or Evil, Committed or Uncommitted. Either the Bible is the Word of God, or the Bible is not the Word of God. Either Jesus Christ is the only savior of humankind, or he is not. Overt opposition forces advocates to clear-cut, resolute decisiveness. Falwell sees marked parallels between the challenges that faced the first Christians and those of the present time. His evaluation of other, succeeding historical periods is far less positive. Little truth was exhibited, for example, during the Middle Ages. But the Reformation, at least by the time of the radical Reformers, is another story. And the period around 1776, when the United States of America was founded by men (underscore *men,* as in Founding Fathers)[3] whose guiding principles were informed and supported by the authority of that same authentic Christianity he is working diligently to reinstate, this too was an era about which one can be proud.

He speaks of how the first Christians were regarded by the people of their time. And he is pleased to say that in that era, as

today, virtually everyone knew of their presence. "Not everyone
liked them, but everyone respected them. Everyone knew they
were there. Even people who hated what they stood for had to
respect them."

It seems too early in the discourse to be making the
application. But this is how he preaches. It is also how he
advertises. Over and over again, throughout the thirty minutes
that he speaks, he sounds the same alarm. He tells his hearers (the
family gathered before him) that they have become well-known in
society, well-respected too, finding favor in others' eyes, in spite of
the fact that they also have "vehement and belligerent enemies."
But it shouldn't bother them that some so-called religious leaders
oppose them. Instead of concerning them, this should be received
as a sign of their effectiveness. It shouldn't trouble them either that
there are politicians who wish to do them in. Such opposition—
coming from the liberal side—is predictable. He asks them to take
comfort in the assurance that the vast majority of people in this
country, no matter how shy, no matter how inarticulate, are on
their side. Such support may not always be overt, he declares, but
they can be certain that they are being upheld by a prevailing
national sentiment.

He recalls his own upbringing,[4] of growing up in adjacent
Campbell County, and listening to Charles E. Fuller, of the "Old
Fashioned Revival Hour," on the radio in his bedroom. He quickly
traces the historical development of evangelical preaching, from
radio to television, emphasizing that what he is doing in this
generation is a continuation of the work initiated and exemplified
by Fuller, Oliver Greene, and Billy Sunday. Because of television,
for the first time in history, it is actually possible to bring the
gospel to every corner of the world. This is the challenge that has
dictated the terms of his ministry.

Never mind that "mainstream schools, liberal theologians,
and modernist philosophers" haven't accepted the truth of the
Christian message yet. The sentiment—yes, the sentiment—of the
majority of the people is on their side. And don't even think that
secular humanism and communism might do them in. No, all they
need to do here is think about what might happen if all emigration
and immigration restrictions were suspended for thirty days. At
the end of thirty days, the United States would be teeming with
people; they'd be all over, in bus depots, on the highways, in the

streets, everywhere. And, at the end of thirty days, there'd be but two people in the Soviet Union, Mr. and Mrs. Gorbachev, and "even Mrs. Gorbachev would be thinking of packing her bags." Don't worry about liberation theology either. "Nobody believes it but the idiots who thought it up." Sure, he knows that "there are some Elmer Gantrys in the evangelical movement today." But only "a few." But why aren't the liberals on television? "Because no one out there wants to hear what they have to say."

And, to the accusation of some of his opponents that he mixes religion with politics. Well, he thought he had explained this sufficiently before. Simply put, he is pastor of Thomas Road Baptist Church, and Liberty University is one of its ministries. He is also involved in the work of the Moral Majority, but this is a political, not a religious, organization. It deals with political issues. He admits that these several agencies have overlapping interests. "But what else would you expect? One's religious convictions impact on every area of one's life. If a man is religious it's him. It's part of him. It's all of him."

He reminds his hearers of some of the principles for which the university stands. They believe that life is important and sacred, "from fertilization to conception and beyond." They oppose abortion resolutely, both as a matter of principle and a primary component of their collective identity. Planned Parenthood, by contrast, is "doing all they can to kill life." They, by contrast, are working to restore the sanctity and stability of the family and the home. He recounts his establishing of the Save-a-Baby Program (distinguished from abortionists' "kill-a-baby" program) to place children who might otherwise have been aborted in Christian foster homes, and to care for their mothers in a similar way. Much better this way, through the workings of voluntary activity than to follow the misguided advice of NOW. "What is NOW?" he asks. Then, responding to his own rhetorical question, he replies, "the national organization of witches?" After the laughter and applause, Falwell says, "Oh, excuse me, but I'm talking about the Betty Friedans, Gloria Steinams, Eleanor 'Schmeels' [not Smeal], Bella Abzugs, and all the other thugs."[5] (More laughter and applause.)

He reminds the students and faculty of the debate that occurred on their campus, when a Professor Doolittle, who has tenure at the University of California, and an avowed evolutionist, was bested by Duane Gish, a fundamentalist, representing the

Institute for Creation Research, in San Diego. (The task of the institute, led by Nell Seagraves and her son Kelly, is to require that authorized school textbooks specifically acknowledge that evolution is a theory and not a fact.) He holds up a copy of the *Washington Post*'s coverage of the debates, and with obvious satisfaction, reads the headline, "Science Loses One to Creationism." He cites a nationwide poll that indicates that the majority of people in this country believe that the biblical account of creation ought to be taught alongside the scientific theory of evolution. He looks out on the multitude, wearing a pleased smile on his face. "We are winning," he says. They cheer. "We are winning. We are winning. We are winning," he intones.

And they shouldn't think that they are out there in the arena alone. They have plenty of help. He cites an article by Daniel Yankelovich in *Psychology Today* which speaks of "the hidden appeal of the movement."[6] According to Yankelovich, as reported by Falwell, 67 million Americans are secretly hoping for their success, knowing that the outcome will be better for their children. And in the U.S. Congress, Senators Jesse Helms, Strom Thurmond, Bill Armstrong, and lots of others are lending strong support to the effort to restore voluntary prayer in the public schools and to overturn the *Roe vs. Wade* decision by the Supreme Court. He is pleased that the President of the United States approves of these restorative measures too.

Then, with a broad grin on his face, looking supremely pleased because he senses that he will soon be triumphant, he says, "we're blowin' the minds of our opponents." He knows that many in the audience are being "cussed out" by those who feel frustrated by the movement. But they should pay no heed to such momentary setbacks. "The only folks against you are the liberal clergy and the godless politicians because you are threatening the security of their little empires."

Now he is ready for the command. Charge! "We ought to move right in. We can significantly change the course of human history. Ignore the other side. The doors are wide open. Let us move right in. March through the doors, and let the whole world know that the Bible-believing churches are moving out to claim the cities for Christ." Cheers and applause greet his announcement. The woman sitting next to me, overcome with enthusiasm, leaps to her feet, exclaims "glo-ry," grabs for my hand, and, in the excitement, drops the book she has been clutching, with the title *When Mom Goes to Work.*

Dr. Falwell has spoken this way many times before. Francis Fitzgerald quotes the Lynchburg evangelist as explaining to one group of church workers that "the local church is an organized army equipped for battle, ready to charge the enemy. The Sunday School is the attacking squad. The church should be a disciplined, charging army. Christians, like slaves and soldiers, ask no questions." Then, making the military references even more explicit, Falwell said:

> It is important to bombard the territory, to move out near the coast and shell the enemy. It is important to send in the literature. It is important to send that radio broadcast and to use that dial-a-prayer telephone. It is important to have all those external forces being set loose on the enemy's stronghold.
>
> But, ultimately some Marines have to march in, encounter the enemy fact-to-face, and put the flag up. . . .
>
> I'm speaking of Marines who have been called to God to move in past the shelling, the bombing and the foxholes, and with bayonets in hand, encounter the enemy face to face and one-on-one bring them under submission to the gospel of Christ, move them into the household of God, put up the flag and call it secured. You and I are called to occupy until He comes.[7]

The tone and the fervor are the same. Military, athletic, and religious incentives are mixed together, as if they derive from the same human impulse. The collective pumping-up, the rhetorical force with which the injunctions come, the feeling of comraderie with others devoted to the same righteous cause, the energies unleashed before one is placed in a position of serious challenge— all of it belongs to the world of the most intense competition, where the troops are prepared for battle, and the issue is do or die. It's about war, yes, about war. But, for now, it's enough to recognize that one is in the enthusiastic company of a team that understands itself to be on the tournament trail. If we're not slated for the Roman arena, like the early Christians, perhaps we can at least get to the regional finals in Richmond, or perhaps even in Charlotte. Talk is animated. Expectations are high.

I had arranged beforehand to meet the preacher following the service. Falwell left the building, and made his way to the stout, four-wheel drive vehicle that is parked at the door of the gym. He is genial, open, and responsive. He gives me a heavy dose of criticism of humanists and humanist scholars.[8] "If humanists really have something to say, why, for heaven's sake, don't you say it?" He wonders if humanists and liberals will ever find a way to denounce communism. He simply cannot understand why they are so gullible. He shares some impressions about California; he had been in San Diego just days before. He wants to be sure that I'm being well cared for during my stay in Lynchburgh. He puts me under the care of Nelson Keener, one of his close associates, and, in a short time, I find myself in the administrative offices of the "Old Time Gospel Hour" on Langhorne Road, a large, unmarked building, adjacent to an A&P supermarket.

Keener rehearses the important statistical information first. Thomas Road Baptist Church started with only 35 people after Falwell graduated from a Baptist seminary in Missouri. Today it has more than 18,000 members, and the "Old Time Gospel Hour," one of its ministries, boasts a mailing list of 4.2 million names, significantly larger than many Protestant denominations. Over 1,000 persons are employed in the work of the church, with approximately 75 assistant ministers under Dr. Falwell's direction. The "Old Time Gospel Hour," Liberty Baptist College, the Academy, together with a Bible institute, a theological seminary, a ministry to the hearing-impaired, and a program of Bible study by correspondence are all regarded as belonging to the work of Thomas Road Baptist Church, a parish that has an annual budget of $60 million. I am shown how the mail is processed, the books sent out with repeated requests for financial assistance. I watch the telephone operators take calls over the 800-number that Falwell claims is the busiest in the nation. There are boxes and boxes of "Jesus First" pins and a warehouse of boxes of printed materials, including Falwell's book, *Listen America.* Falwell's picture is on the wall in nearly every room. Some of the photos show him with his family, several with Ronald Reagan (who was President at the time of the interview), and one or two with Phyllis Schlafly.

Nelson Keener announces himself ready to respond to any questions I might wish to raise with him. He appreciates the associations he has had with certain members of the religious studies faculty at the University of Virginia in nearby Charlottesville. He tells me this to assure me that he has been in these academic discussions before.

But, by now, I am eager to get past some of the surface characteristics, and find out how someone, on the inside, understands what is happening. I'd like to hear Keener talk about Falwell.

"What's it all about?" I ask.

"Falwell?"

"Yes, Falwell. What are his goals. You're close to him on a day-to-day basis. How do you read his intentions?" I ask.

Keener leans back in the chair in his paneled office. He tells me he has become accustomed to answering questions about specifics. Something like this will require a few moments' thought.

He closes his eyes, opens them, looks at the ceiling, then sits up straight, leaning forward, placing his clasped hands on the large glistening wooden desk in front of him. He is an alert man, slightly built, friendly, committed to the cause, a corporation man.

"Sure, I'll tell you. I'll tell you what it's about," he commences. "Jerry Falwell is trying to help people live by their moral beliefs and standards. This is what he is doing. He senses that society is encouraging them to live below their moral standards. He wants to assist them to live where the inside hearts tell them they should. They know they should be there, but they aren't. And Jerry is helping them find their way back." An associate, who is taking notes, says quietly that she has never heard it as concisely before. Keener laughs and asks me if I got all of it down in my notes.

"The problem is that many of the social influences we encounter each day wish us to live beneath our standards," he elaborates. Such negative incentives work upon us, from all sides, all day long. Falwell wants to counter these negative forces with some positive ones. No, he doesn't want to take programs off network television, but only, in Keener's words, "to clean them up."

He cites the program "Three's Company." The situation portrayed there—unmarried persons of both sexes living together under the same roof—is suspect from the outset. Young viewers watch it, then come to assume that it's acceptable to live that way. What Falwell says about television he believes he is saying as a professional in the communications industry. He simply believes that children today are living under too many exploitative pressures. The purveyors and marketers of sex come at them before they are capable of responding properly, yes, before they've had a chance to find out who they are. Advertisers pursue them, simulating and creating needs they didn't know they had. The avenue through which a large portion of this exploitative conduct occurs, in Falwell's view, is the media. He knows why he has incensed Norman Lear, in particular, and others within the television industry. What he says is threatening their livelihoods.

"Falwell's strength is that he can articulate what a lot of people feel, but don't know how to put into words," Keener continues. "He knows that people recognize that television has a negative effect upon home and family. What singles him out from the others who feel this way is that he has the courage to stand up and say it, and with words other people recognize to express their own fears and feelings too."

"He is a fundamentalist preacher who is also a social reformer," I observe.

Keener chuckles, "In this respect, Jerry is a renegade. Think of fundamentalist Christianity before he became involved. It had the reputation of being anti-intellectual, and it displayed hardly any political or social involvement at all. Jerry is changing this. He has founded a college which, in a very short time, has become fully accredited. He saw the need for a credible liberal arts academic program on a conservative theological base. So he did it. He built a college. In addition, he has become directly involved in social and political issues. It surprises people to learn this. They expect him to be some Bible-banging preacher, but he stands for much more."

"But the social and political issue on which he expresses himself most fervently is abortion," I comment. "Why?"

The answer comes quickly.

"Because, in Jerry's mind, the family is the first institution that God created. It is the primary institution on earth. Most of the things he speaks out against he believes are conspiring to destroy the sanctity of the family." In addition to abortion, Falwell lists the growth of feminism (which, in his view, diminishes the role of woman as homemaker), the licensing of homosexuality (which, in his view, diminishes human nature), society's permissive attitude toward pornography, sex education in the public schools (by the government's incentive at taxpayer's expense), and the easy availability of drugs. Falwell believes that when any of this is condoned or, worse yet, offered, supported, or sponsored by the government, it makes it all the easier for individuals to live beneath the standards of their own moral beliefs. The wholesale inclusion of these factors as accepted components of society helps explain why families are deteriorating and the society itself has lost its quality.

"But not all of what Falwell says is about the family," I continue. "He also speaks frequently about Israel. He is firm, too, in calling for a strong national defense." I am thinking of course about Falwell's celebrated friendship with former Prime Minister Menachem Begin of Israel, and of his frequent expression of love for that nation.[9]

"Jerry Falwell is the best friend in America that Israel ever had," Keener responds.

I counter that I've heard this said before, while also being aware of certain statements Falwell is alleged to have made, concerning whether or not the God he worships hears the prayers of Jews. "But he would prefer that Jews become Christians?" I offer. "His objective is conversion."

Nelson Keener would rather not respond directly or in detail. Instead he cites names of prominent Jews in New York City and in Los Angeles who are in Falwell's corner. He also identifies American rabbis whom Falwell knows to be on his side. The principle is a literal interpretation of Genesis 12:3—that "he who blesses Israel will be blessed, and he who cruses Israel will also be cursed." In Falwell's mind, the United States has an obligation to support and encourage Israel, that is, if the United States is to remain strong and vital. But it's the principle of the thing that counts. And Falwell stands in opposition to the Arabs, not in small measure, or so he claims, because of their susceptibility to communist influence.

"Is the United States the new Israel?" I ask this, knowing of Falwell's belief about America's special covenantal relationship with God.

Here Keener wishes to be exceedingly careful. The answer, I judge, is yes and no. Falwell doesn't wish the nation to be a theocracy.[10] He recognizes the difficulties with this concept. He is aware too of the problems involved in referring to the nation as "Christian America." At the same time, he wishes to affirm that the United States does stand in a position of special favor with the Almighty, because of the principles and convictions upon which the nation was established. For the rest of it, Keener would prefer to speak matter of factly rather than speculatively. The point he wishes to reiterate is that Jerry Falwell has perceived that the United States stands in grave danger of losing its favored status because it is abandoning the principles its forefathers secured. And with this we are back to a repetition of Falwell's perception of the changes that have occurred. As Keener is talking, I recall the statement Falwell has made on a number of occasions in which religious fervor and patriotic zeal become mixed:

> I remember the time when it was positive to be patriotic, and as far as I am concerned, it still is. I remember as a boy, when the flag was raised, everyone stood proudly, and put his hand upon his heart and pledged allegiance with gratitude. I remember when the band struck up "The Stars and Stripes Forever," we stood and goose pimples would run all over me. I remember when I was in elementary school during World War II, when every report from the other shores meant something to us. We were not out there demonstrating against our guys who were dying in Europe and Asia. We were praying for them and thanking God for them and buying war bonds to help pay for the materials and artillery they needed to fight and win and come back.[11]

And this called up another one:

> We are not a perfect nation, but we are still a free nation because we have the blessings of God upon us. We must continue to follow in a path that will ensure that blessing. We must not forget that it is God Almighty who has made and preserved us as a nation.[12]

And another:

> Americans must no longer linger in ignorance and apathy. We cannot be silent about the sins that are destroying this nation. The choice is ours. We must turn America around or prepare for inevitable destruction. I am listening to the sounds that threaten to take away our liberties in America. And I have listened to God's admonition and his direction—the only hopes of saving America.[13]

In Falwell's view, Keener explains, America is the only nation that can protect peoples and nations who cannot protect themselves. It is the last strong bastion of defense against the onslaught of communism. Falwell fears that if liberals had their way, the country would have been sold away. The liberal attitude equivocates, qualifies, and becomes so abstract that issues are complexified beyond anyone's comprehension, and whatever direction is provided fails to capture the enthusiasm and commitment of the people. Because liberals provided no clear guidance when they had the chance, the society became overly permissive and the public became too tolerant.

"Sure, *Penthouse* and *Playboy* got angry with Falwell," Keener continues, "because he rattled their foundations and threatened their growth. He did this because he doesn't believe in the liberals' goal of creating free minds." Keener explains that Falwell thinks secular schools teach facts without providing guidance. It is Falwell's conviction that children ought to be taught, really taught, not just given facts. He believes in educational guidance, and he believes in spiritual formation. When secular humanists gain control, he believes, they abandon intellectual training for free thinking. Then it's always wishy-washy, unprincipled, unstable, unsubstantial, permissive, and relativistic. Absolutes are abandoned. Authority becomes arbitrary. Falwell believes that today's society is shallow because it is suffering the effects of the influence of this permissiveness.

Keener acknowledges Falwell's appreciation of Ronald Reagan. Falwell found it particularly gratifying to hear Reagan attribute most of the failures of the nation to the prevalence of false philosophical views. The vocation of the Reagan presidency was to insert and maintain effective correctives. Falwell regarded the election of Reagan to be "the best thing to happen to America in at least twenty years." When he took office, Keener explains, "in no time at all the country started looking and feeling better again." Keener cites the incident early in the first Reagan term, when Libyan planes attacked United States planes over the Mediterranean Sea. He is animated as he retells the story. "We were fired upon, and keboom, we fired back, and we nailed those dudes right there on the spot." He laughs to great satisfaction as he praises the President for his prompt, forceful response, indicating by his words as well as by his posture that this, by God, is the way things ought to be all of the time. In his opinion, Ronald Reagan was able to reestablish a certain dependability, a "rectitude." He adds, "Nobody's going to mess with us anymore. Reagan has shown too much stamina and resolve."

As he talks, I am reminded of a similar incident, on June 7,

1981, when Israel carried out a sneak attack on a French-built nuclear reactor that Iraq was about to reactivate near Baghdad. On that occasion Falwell conveyed his congratulations to Menachem Begin, who was then Prime Minister of Israel. Begin had telephoned Falwell to explain why he had decided to do this. He had been fearful that some of his friends in the United States would interpret the action as being that of a potential warmonger. Falwell responded, "Mr. Prime Minister, I want to congratulate you for a mission that made us very proud that we manufacture those F-16s. In my opinion, you must've put it right down the smokestack."

This, of course, is just the beginning, for had Keener wanted to he could have cited the examples of Grenada, the attack on Khaddafi in Libya, and the tough stand that the Reagan administration exercised in the Persian Gulf against the threat that Iran posed with respect to the free passage of tankers carrying oil shipments.

"But look," he continued, indicating that he understood himself to be engaged in an argument, "there are international laws, and Libya violated the rules. The United States was not the aggressor. We do not start wars. We don't go around taking land from people. But we can't let them push us around forever. Falwell didn't like it when Jimmy Carter let everyone push the United States around."

Utilizing this opening, I ask Keener about Carter, wondering how he will explain the movement's dislike of the former President.

The question draws a long pause. Or perhaps we both need to rest after the excitement and animation of the simulated fight with the Libyan planes. It is a difficult question—more difficult than it would appear on the surface. After all, Jimmy Carter is a professed born-again Christian. His ascendency to the presidency helped give born-again Christianity a visibility it hadn't enjoyed in recent decades. Besides, Carter hails from the same general region of the country. He too is a Baptist. There are a multitude of strong affinities.

Clearly, Keener would rather not respond because he wishes not to have to say anything negative.[14] But, at last, he ventures. "In all candor, Jerry was disappointed with Carter. Carter was a liberal and Falwell thought him incompetent. He couldn't understand how a born-again Christian could ever become an abortionist run wild." But there is more. "Also, Falwell thought Carter made the country look bad. He was indecisive, and people took advantage of us. But this changed with Reagan." And we are again talking about U.S. fighter planes over the Mediterranean then contrasting the way Jimmy Carter handled the Iranian hostage crisis with what Ronald Reagan achieved, in swift order, on the island of Grenada.

I shift to another question. "Do you, does Falwell, really wish or intend that the entire world become Christian?" As he prepares to respond, I add some implications. "You know what this means, that Hindus, Buddhists, Muslims, everyone else, and, most significantly, Jews, would be converted to the Christian faith?"

The query troubles Keener. He wants to exemplify openness and tolerance. But convictions are convictions. And he knows where his leader stands.[15] Yes, democracy is intended for the entire world. It is the best, the most superior, form of government yet devised for humankind. And Christianity and democracy, in his view, are entirely compatible.

It has gotten quiet in the room. Even Keener's answer comes softly. "Sure, Jerry would want the whole world to become Christian, but he's realistic enough to know that this will not happen until Jesus Christ returns in glory."

I go from Keener's office to the headquarters of the Moral Majority, less than two miles away. As I listen to all that the staff members tell me, I realize that I've heard much of it already. Yes, I know that Jerry Falwell loves his family. I know about the money he raises, the dedication he exemplifies, the extraordinary energy he expends. I know too that he speaks out courageously and is an organizational wizard. More than one citizen of Lynchburg tells it this way: "Jerry just dreams something, and, before long, it happens." I know too that Thomas Road Baptist Church started in the old warehouse of the Donald Duck Bottling Company. From every indication, the folks of Lynchburg know the mythology and tell it consistently. The local consensus seems to be that Falwell has done much for Lynchburg too, although, as one would expect, there are people in the town who don't like him. A priest of one of the two Catholic churches in the city says that his parish is hardly affected by the presence of Thomas Road Baptist Church. He explains that Roman Catholics account for no more than 3 percent of the population of the state of Virginia. This, and not Jerry

Falwell, is what he has a difficult time contending with. He adds that Falwell's influence is strongly felt in the meetings of the local ministerial association.

In the Moral Majority offices I have the opportunity to talk with Cal Thomas, who was serving the agency, at the time, as vice president for communications, and who, since that time, has been writing a syndicated column for such publications as the *Washington Times* and the *Los Angeles Times*. He has also edited the *Moral Majority Report*, and is the voice that introduces Falwell on the "Old Time Gospel Hour." Thomas is tall, lanky, quick-witted, alert, sure of himself, engaging, and manifests a variety of signs that he has long and extensive experience in communication fields. Before joining Falwell's forces, Thomas was a radio announcer and television commentator for NBC News. He moved to Lynchburg, he confesses, because he believed that modern big city life was having a negative effect on the vitality of his family. He wanted to raise his children in the kind of environment Lynchburg affords.

I ask Thomas about the goals of the Moral Majority, and he responds by talking about its diversity. Instead of being some monolithic group of people with the same religious creed and the same manner of worship, it represents persons of all religious views alongside others who would call themselves atheists and agnostics. He is pleased that approximately 30 percent of the membership of the Moral Majority is made up of Roman Catholics. All of them are interested in returning the nation to the set of priorities it honored before the social, political, and economic changes of the 1960s moved things off course. Thomas says that his primary task is to offer "an alternative information choice" to citizens who, for too long, have been hearing everything from the liberals and are thus getting only one side. "The people don't have to get their news about what is happening among conservatives from the liberal press, filtered through their presuppositions. Now they can turn to us and get it in our own terms."

Thomas adds that none of this would have happened had there not been significant shifts within the conservative community. The general tendency before Falwell incited the conservatives to an active disposition was to keep one's religious views private and to conceive of one's faith primarily in spiritual terms. Under such convictions there was no opportunity to translate religious beliefs into effective public policy. But, gradually, conservatives recognized that "when we keep our beliefs to ourselves, we leave the country to be run by people who believe otherwise." Thomas is pleased that conservatives have joined the public debate, at last. And he is confident that the conservative contribution to that debate will strengthen the character of the nation. In no sense do conservatives and liberals have mutually exclusive agendas. Such a perception has been stimulated by the fact that, for as long as anyone can remember, the liberals have been the only ones talking; hence, anyone who even whimpers anything else is understood to be in opposition.

Cal Thomas's *apologia* for the objectives and practices of the Moral Majority has been tested and polished in numerous lectures and debates on college and university campuses. It is a portrayal that is calculated to exhibit intellectual authority so as to carry weight with academic audiences. But what, I ask, does he say about the so-called lunatic fringe of his own movement? After all, persons in positions of high responsibility within the Moral Majority have accused others, with whom they disagree, of being "anti-Christs." Others in authority have participated in book burnings, the removal of controversial books from library shelves, and radical censorship. Thomas understands the question, but points out that "we have to recognize that a lot of our people are still new in the political arena, and they view certain things in apocalyptic terms. For them everything is black and white; there aren't any gray areas." Thomas doesn't want to defend this. He admits that he has often been embarrassed by it. But he understands it to be "part of the educational challenge" toward which he carries a heavy assignment. "Sure, I wish that some of those statements had never been made. I certainly do not endorse them and neither does Jerry Falwell. You should see him when he hears about it. He just rolls his eyes and shakes his head."

Quickly, he shifts to the offense, and raises some questions about censorship. Censorship occurs, he proposes, when school children are not given access to traditional human values, as, for example, that "some people continue to live according to certain basic moral beliefs, and some people are virgins when they get married, as quaint as this may seem."[16] He doesn't find any of this reflected in the textbooks that are certified and prescribed for use in the public schools. He reiterates that today's youth have been hearing from only one side about what it is to be a citizen within the United States, indeed, what it is to be a significant human being.

Certainly, he admits, it is an ideological clash that is occurring, a contest between worldviews. He cites Timothy LaHaye's contentions about Enlightenment philosophy's having stimulated a secular society against which Christians (and others) of a more conservative and/or traditional bent have risen in opposition.[17] He understands that it is through a revitalized fundamentalist religious position that this alternative has been offered. He believes that it is through the work of Jerry Falwell, and others, that the stance carries political force. Similarly, it is through the reconstructive intellectual work of theologians like Francis Schaeffer that the position carries authority within academic circles. For too long, Thomas believes, it was believed that only a liberal could be a good Christian and an effective participant in the political process at the same time. So good liberals believed. Now it has become possible for conservatives to be good Christians and effective political participants at one and the same time. He adds that, in his judgment, conservatives have stronger and more reliable access to the more fundamental truths of Christianity than liberals. Then he returns to the point that what the current dialogue between liberals and conservatives does is to broaden the intellectual base, broaden the understanding of social issues, so that the issues facing the American people are not treated in any facile fashion. All of this, he affirms, will prove to be good for the country.[18]

On a Wednesday night, I find my way to Thomas Road Baptist Church for the weekly prayer service.[19] I've been told to get there early because available seats go quickly. When I arrive, thirty minutes before the service is to begin, the parking lot is already full of cars, vans, and at least twenty school buses the church uses to transport its members. Once inside the sanctuary, I am greeted by people I have met at the other Falwell institutions in the city. They recognize me by now and seem pleased that I have come.

The church has seats for about four thousand persons, and is nearly full. Folding chairs have been placed in the only available remaining space, in the aisles. It is a mixed-age group, with the majority appearing to be in the twenty- to thirty-year-old range.

But this may be due to the influx of students from Liberty University. The school library closes at 4:30 on Wednesday afternoons to give students time for dinner and the prayer service afterward.

As a joy and enthusiasm-builder for the events to come, the congregation sings boisterous gospel songs, many of them allowing the faithful to express their confidence in the salvation they have come to experience. When they sing "What a Friend We Have in Jesus," a man behind me, kneeling in prayer, implores, "Keep reminding Dr. Falwell, Lord, that he is only a man." And, in the next moment, the "man" appears, surrounded by several assistant pastors and coworkers. The only woman seen prominently is the church organist, who is also Falwell's wife.

Falwell looks pleased as he scans the audience. He knows many of the people personally. He nods here and there, waving discreetly, demonstrating his recognition and affection.

Nearly always, when he steps into the pulpit on Wednesday nights, he talks of family matters first.[20] This night, he begins by announcing the engagement of two members of the singing group. Turning the attention to them, as they blush, he teases, "If you two didn't want me to announce this, just yet, we can ask everyone here to keep it quiet for a while. They're good people. They'll do what we ask them."

The congregation enjoys the banter. The preacher is having a good time too. He talks about the joys of the Christian home, where individuals are properly related to each other because they are properly related to God. One of the privileges of being pastor of Thomas Road Baptist Church for twenty-five years, he says, is that he now announces engagements of persons whose parents' engagements he announced years ago. He thinks this pattern will continue, perhaps for several generations, until Christ returns or until he and his associate, Brother Wemp, "will come hobblin' up here trying to remember just what it is we're supposed to be saying."

He continues with geneology. He cites names of mothers, fathers, and children, recalling stories about each one, taking time to get the relationships specified correctly, asking the congregation for help when he isn't sure. "Is the Tait I know your daddy or your uncle? Your uncle? But I know your daddy too. That's T-a-i-t and not T-a-t-e, isn't it?" Nothing gives him greater satisfaction, he recounts, than watching "good clean Christian boys and girls growing up to be giants for Christ." He reminds the people assembled that this is why they have their ministry at Liberty University. Through all of it, he speaks as a father addressing his children. One can see him as the progenitor, the advocate of patriarchal order, Father Abraham, who is called to lead his people forth, through an environment that is usually hostile.

The sermon, like many of his sermons, is based on a chapter of the New Testament which tells of the last days.[21] Falwell says that he firmly believes we are living in the last days, yes "in the last of the last days." All of the signs point in this direction. Hedonism is rampant. Everyone is looking out for himself. People are claiming individual rights, asking "What can the country do for me?" There are vast outbreaks of moral perversion, greater now than ever before in the history of the nation. And Christians, living in this situation, are called upon to "swim against the tide, to walk against the wind, to move upstream."

He enumerates the menacing national sins. Abortion. Disintegration of the family. Breakup of the home. Divorce. Drugs. Pornography. Sex education in the schools. Homosexuality . . . homosexuality.

He pauses to tell about a gay bar that has just opened in downtown Lynchburg, not far from the city hall. He asks the song leader if he knows the address. Startled, his "no" response brings laughter to the congregation. Falwell tells about the night he and his wife sat in their car across the street from the bar and watched "all of the strange people going in and out of there." He tells of the two male associates he had directed to go into a gay bar in Washington, not long ago, not far from the White House, just to find out what was going on. "We dressed them up real sweet," he says, "got 'em smelling good, had them wear these tight britches, got them sashaying back and forth, and gave them a small camera. Trouble is they got so fascinated with what they saw that they forgot to get any pictures. [Laughter.] Brother Wemp? You know what I should have done that night? I should have telephoned the bar, and said 'Hello, this is Jerry Falwell. Is my photographer there?' That's what I should have done."

He reminds the parishioners of the *Penthouse* magazine episode, a wearisome subject, he acknowledges. The good news is that a woman who had worked on the *Penthouse* story—"she must have been a woman, because she couldn't have been a lady"—had been to Lynchburg recently, and "got saved, and gave her life to Christ." The ministers on the dias behind the pulpit smile, and nod to one another knowingly and approvingly. The man sitting next to me slaps his knee exclaiming "praise the Lord!"

Falwell takes up the subject of United States military might. He attests that he is frequently asked if he is frightened by the fact that the nation has so many MX missiles and that there is increasing talk about the possibility of war. "Heck no," Falwell responds. "I'm going to meet the Lord in the air." Then turning the point to the preacher's advantage, he adds, "but some of you out there are getting ready for the soft landing. You've got your landing wheels down, and you're coming in for the soft landing." As he speaks about the need for a strong military defense posture, one recalls the references Falwell has made to the time, March 22, 1983, when he was briefed on this subject by Reagan administration staff members in the White House. The information he gathered on that occasion, he explains, has made him very nervous about the possibility of a nuclear freeze. He believes this would destroy the United States deterrence capacity. He calls it "phony arms control, a fraud," while restating his support of President Reagan's position on the subject. He concludes:

> We must never allow ourselves to be permanently locked into a position of inferiority with the Soviet Union . . . but a nuclear freeze would do just that.
>   Our children, our precious heritage, are depending on us to protect them from both slavery and nuclear destruction at the hands of the Soviet butchers. We can only do this if America remains strong.

As he finishes this peroration, applause mounts from all quarters of the church sanctuary. Clearly the congregation likes what it has been hearing.

The preacher lists some successes. He talks about the support Congressional leaders need to help return voluntary "non-animated" prayer in the public schools. (More applause.) He is gratified that the entire population is beginning to recognize that the public schools "have gone to pot and academic standards have nose-dived." People have been aware of this for a long time, but were afraid to mention it. But this is the role of the prophet; to rebuke evil, to preach against sin, to name particular sins, "to cry out against Nazis, communists, feminists, homosexuals, and moral perverts." The trouble is that "parents don't tell their children what *bad* is." And the permissive churches (which is most of them) say that "what is wrong is right." But the "raw culture out there has to be shown that there is another way to live. We have to show them. Kids today—we know it—are victimized by a society those of our generation never had to deal with."

Falwell reminds his hearers that when evangelists like Dwight L. Moody and Billy Sunday would come to town, the meetings might continue for two weeks, "and sometimes for as long as thirteen weeks, maybe even for six months. And before the evangelist left town," he adds, "the saloons and houses of prostitution would be shut down, not because anybody had passed a law, but because they ran out of customers." Contrasting this situation with the one that prevails today, he comments that "it's more fun being the light of the world than being the salt of the earth."

> Salt causes burning. It causes a stinging effect when it reaches open sores. It produces thirst. It kills weeds. Salt is a preservative that prevents spoilage. What's happened to America? Why are we spoiling morally? Why is America in a state of decadence today?

Falwell answers his own questions:

> It is not because of the Democrats or the Republicans or the secular humanists or the liberal theologians—they're already out of it. It is not because of the politicians and the bureaucrats. It is because, in my opinion, Bible-believing Christians and Bible-believing churches have not, in this generation, been the salt of the earth.

He lets this sink in, then closes with some words of comfort about the family of God. He knows of nothing on earth that can provide greater satisfaction. And, besides, "wherever Christ is present, you can recognize all of the other members of the family."

Then, as if to demonstrate that fundamentalism, voluntarism, and beneficence go together, he announces a special offering for a boy in the congregation who needs to be taken to Boston for treatment of a severe case of diabetes. Falwell's associates have arranged for someone to take him there by private jet.

Arrangements have been made to keep the boy's mother on regular salary during whatever time she needs to be away from Lynchburg. A family in Boston has been secured to provide her with meals and lodging. But large additional costs are involved. And Falwell wishes the congregation to be generous in their support. As he requests this, he reaches down over the pulpit to make the first contributions as the offering plates are passed.

As this is happening, another man comes quietly up alongside me, clasps my arm, and asks me if I am prepared to go to heaven. I thank him for his interest, and try to explain, without attracting other hearers, that I had been expecting to attend a meeting in Washington in the morning. At least this had been my immediate plan. But I recognize that this is not the subject he envisioned. He leaves me alone, as the service ends.

I contemplate what I have just witnessed as I return to the place at which this chronicle began—the "Freedom Shrine" in the Lynchburg airport, erected there by the city fathers to strengthen citizen appreciation of our national heritage. From a position in the center of the airport, the viewer can place both shrine and plane in a single image. From this vantage point it becomes easy to envision Falwell as the messenger—the patriot—who flies from place to place to teach the message of the shrine. The postscript reads that he probably will not be away very long, for this is the setting from which he draws his nourishment.

When I return the car-rental agreement to Randy's desk, I learn of his decision about leaving school. Next year, he believes, he will probably transfer to another college. He prefers to study in a place that is less intense religiously and more flexible morally. The dilemma now involves breaking this news to his parents.

"Do you think that I have made the right decision?" he asks, as he processes the agreement forms. "Well, I think you have to do what you have to do," I respond, in the non-directive way I recognize Falwell would criticize.

Randy and I stand there facing each other, each sharing a desire to be in another locale, another set of circumstances, a place where the interplay of formative human energies is guided by some other agenda. I can flee, or I think I can, because I am a visitor, the possessor of a ticket out of Lynchburg. But Randy is stationed there, and is troubled about securing an effective instrument of release, or, if he did so, of being able to defend such actions to his friends and family, and justifying it to his conscience. To be a committed Christian is not simply to believe the teachings, and to allow them to guide one's life. It is also to keep faith with and remain loyal to the institutions through which such spiritual nurture has come. As a Christian Randy also wishes to affirm that "where the spirit of the Lord is, there is freedom," which, significantly, is the motto Jerry Falwell selected for Liberty University. But the slogan doesn't always work for Randy. He suspects that there is greater freedom elsewhere. Yet he cannot be certain that he can relinquish this commitment to complete compliance with the Falwell tradition without also losing the core of his faith. Freedom must also have content.

As I approach the gate to board the plane that will take me away from Lynchburg, I walk past Falwell's sleek white jet—his way of exiting from time to time. I recall his comment about "soft landings" and about "meeting the Lord in the air." As soon as the plane is in the air, I leaf through some of the literature I have acquired. Falwell's picture and statements are omnipresent. In one booklet, behind the smiling face, he is pictured promoting his talk show. Prospective viewers are invited to "tune in, phone in," for "Jerry will be waiting to hear from you," for "Everything you've always wanted to ask him but never had the chance." The show Falwell is hosting is being televised on Sunday evenings from Atlanta.

In another of the leaflets I have acquired, Falwell is offering his personal views on the most urgent needs of our time—all of them, apparently, or at least those that are most prominent. He is concerned about the adequacy of the nation's defense. He is afraid that the Marxist-Leninists will take over all of Central America, including Mexico, and that there will be a large influx of "feet people" from the troubled region, across the border with Mexico, into the United States. He chastises the Marxist government of Ethiopia for policies that created the drought that is responsible for the hunger epidemic. And while he is critical of apartheid policy in South Africa, he urges the United States to temper its reaction so that the progress being made by the government of South Africa—"our strongest ally against communist expansionism on the African continent"—will not be undermined.

On this latter issue, Falwell got himself in trouble, when, after returning from a five-day fact-finding mission to South Africa, he called Bishop Desmond Tutu "a phony." At the time he was trying to launch another of his campaigns, this one to encourage continued investments in South Africa, and he criticized Bishop Tutu for not speaking for the majority of the people there. The contentious statement was: "I think he is a phony as far as representing the black people." He explained that he also denounced the system of apartheid, adding that "no sensible person, certainly no Christian can support it."

Falwell's statement about Tutu was inflammatory, and he was soundly criticized for it. On ABC's "Good Morning America," on August 21, 1985, Jesse Jackson charged: "Falwell, you supported apartheid in Southern America until it was over. Now you're supporting apartheid in Southern Africa while it's still alive." Falwell responded, "I'm sorry that Reverend Jackson still thinks whites are bad people."

But within days he was on the trail again, and had gotten himself involved in other issues. On September 4, 1985, Falwell led a Dallas rally of 5,000 persons against pornography. The particular focus was the policy of the 7-Eleven Stores to sell adult magazines. His comment: "We find it difficult to 'Thank Heaven for 7-Eleven' when they are defiling our women and children." He added, "It's time for Catholics, Baptists, Methodists, Jews, Mormons, and Evangelicals to stand up and say, 'No, we don't thank heaven for 7-Eleven.' " But, as Falwell spoke, he was protested against by 350 anti-apartheid demonstrators. Then he was off again, this time to the Philippines, to show his support for Ferdinand and Imelda Marcos.

Falwell faced even larger challenges in 1986 and 1987. During the very months when financial support for his own ministry was decreasing, he was called upon to help bring some stability to the PTL, Jim and Tammy Bakker's organization in Ft. Mill, South Carolina, after the Bakkers found it necessary to flee to Palm Springs, California, because Tammy Bakker had needed drug-dependence therapy at the Betty Ford Center and Jim Bakker's sexual liaison with Jessica Hahn, in 1981, could be kept secret no longer. When news of the scandal broke, there was Jerry Falwell, standing before the rank of television cameras, trying to explain the situation, hoping to calm the anxieties of those who had been supporting the PTL ministry. "The cause of Christ has received a real broadside," he admitted that day. But he extolled the deep moral character and firm Christian conviction of those he had gathered to help put matters right again. Within a few days, he was declaring a "May Emergency," telling all supporters of PTL that the ministry would come to an end if the dollars didn't flow. And then, after he decided that Jim and Tammy Bakker could not return to the ministry, which decision put him in position to be accused by Bakker of "stealing our ministry," he denounced the former head of PTL as forcefully, though without sarcasm, as he had been shaming liberals and socialists and feminists and others outside the boundaries of what he understands to be authentic and genuine Christianity. He did all of this on television too, though this time, he wasn't standing in a pulpit, or on the steps of some capitol. He was responding to questions in a press conference, which, in spite of the circumstances, must have pleased him.

While he was experiencing this turmoil, he was also being accused of diverting funds from his political organization for use in his religious ministry. When the charge was first made, he responded with disclaimers, assuring his followers that he would be cleared of all such accusations as soon as the true facts were brought to light. But after his auditors prepared their report, the charges were upheld. In 1983, Falwell's I Love Liberty political action committee had sold Bibles to the "Old Time Gospel Hour" by a price that was inflated by $28,000, so that funds could be transferred from the one organization to the other. Each group was fined $6,000 on grounds that the transaction involved an illegal mixture of finances, according to the Federal Election Commission. The criticisms and judgments against Falwell resulted in loss of revenue to Thomas Road Baptist Church. Moreover, there were many within the Baptist community— Baptist preachers who had been Falwell's friends and coworkers— who strenuously disapproved of his new alliance with PTL, as there were Bakker loyalists who worked to undermine whatever tenuous authority he tried to claim.

Meanwhile, while the "May Emergency" had saved PTL from certain immediate disaster, the possibility of swift and total bankruptcy remained. As a fund-raising incentive, Falwell promised in July to plunge down the 65-foot water slide at Heritage USA, fully clothed, if 1,000 contributors would send $1,000 each to PTL.

When the goal was reached, on September 10, 1987—and on

the very day that Pope John Paul arrived in Miami to begin his visit to the United States and Canada—Falwell took the plunge. But before leaping, he closed his eyes, pressed his hands firmly to his chest, and prayed, "Now I lay me down to sleep. I pray the Lord my soul to keep." He also recited the words of Psalm 23, "The Lord is my shepherd, I shall not want," then eased himself into the water slide. And, at the bottom, coming out of the water, wringing wet in his blue suit and red tie, he anticipated the network television coverage of the event. "Can you image the fun? Split screen, the distinguished pope stepping off the plane from Rome in Miami, and this nut, this Baptist preacher, coming down the water slide for $22 million."

The more serious challenge was yet to come. On October 7, 1987, Judge Rufus Reynolds of the Federal Bankruptcy Court in Greenville, ruled that a reorganization plan submitted by Falwell and Harry Hargrave, PTL's chief operating officer, was unacceptable. Judge Reynolds ordered the creditors of the ministry to submit their own plan for PTL to pay off more than $60 million in debts. The next day, at Heritage USA, Falwell called a press conference to announce that he and his entire board of directors were resigning from PTL. Two reasons were given. First, the lenders Falwell had assembled to provide interim financing for the ministry would not proceed on the judge's terms. These lenders, whom Falwell did not identify, wanted veto power over who controlled the ministry. Second, the judge's ruling made it technically possible for Jim and Tammy Bakker to return to the ministry. Calling Bakker's leadership "the greatest scab and cancer on the face of Christianity in two thousand years," Falwell explained that "the ten members of our board could not remain if there was even a chance that the travesty of Jim Bakker's leadership at PTL could happen again." Under questioning Falwell repeated, "the problem is, barring a miracle of God, Mr. Bakker will be sitting here in six months running this ministry, and I cannot think of a greater ill that could befall this ministry." Appealing to the dictates of his own conscience, Falwell added that Bakker had not yet won the right to return, but, in his judgment, "the Christian family has lost the war." Before departing, Falwell's board enacted a clause that would transfer authority for the ministry to the Assemblies of God, subject to the approval of Judge Reynolds. While conceding that his group had lost, Falwell protested that "we were just this close [holding up his thumb and index finger], so close, to the goal," before they were thrown off course by the judge's ruling.

Noting that his wife had opposed his involvement at PTL from the first, and that he had lost friends and financial support for doing it, never, in his months of service to PTL, had he "taken one dime for himself or for his personal expenses." But it was time now, as he put it, to tend to his ministry at Thomas Road Baptist Church and at Liberty University. "The Lord is saying to me, 'Come home now, Jerry, it's time to come home,' " he explained as he took leave of his associates at PTL. He returned to Lynchburg as disappointed and as despondent as a born-again Christian can allow himself to be. But he carried the confidence that he had followed the right path, that is, in the Lord's eyes, which path would one day be powerfully vindicated.

Within days, he had withdrawn even further: he resigned as president of Moral Majority and the Liberty Foundation. Explaining this action, on November 3, 1987, he admitted that he was tired of "being the lightning rod" for opponents of the Religious Right. Borrowing an image from the vocabulary of warfare, he added, "there is no need now for Jerry Falwell to walk point." His desire, he attested, was to be a full-time pastor and television minister. "My first love is back to the pulpit, back to preaching, back to winning souls, back to meeting spiritual needs," he asserted. And he said that while he would continue to speak out on issues, he would "not be stumping for candidates again. . . . I'm rededicating my life to preaching the Gospel. My real platform of influence is my spiritual ministry. . . . I will never work for a candidate as I did for Ronald Reagan. I will not lobby for legislation personally." And while there was some sadness in this decision, the Lynchburg evangelist believed that his accomplishments had been considerable. What he had done, he suspected, was to "break the psychological barrier that religion and politics don't mix." He had convinced evangelical and fundamentalist Christians that "it is no sin to vote." But his heavy political involvement had not enabled him to expand his ministries, and he needed to do this, especially since such ministries were suffering attrition. But he was torn. And even after relinquishing his political role, he admitted that it would be difficult for him simply to stand aside.

After only the briefest respite from intense political involvement, he found a new cause, and made his offices available to Oliver North, who on the first day of his retirement from the U.S. Marine Corps, May 2, 1988, journeyed to Lynchburg, to deliver the commencement address at Liberty University. When introducing North to the 900 graduating seniors, their families, and friends of the institution, Falwell called North "a true American hero," and suggested that the former White House assistant was not the first person to be falsely accused. "We serve a savior who was indicted and convicted and crucified," Falwell reminded his followers.

North's appearance in Lynchburg was part of Falwell's effort to wage "the largest petition drive in Moral Majority history" to get 2 million signatures to support a pardon for North. Falwell attested that he had talked with North "heart to heart," following which his "belief in that man has been multiplied." He called North a Marine who had "won medal after medal for gallantry, for dedicated service, for his abilities and his dedication." He observed that North "has been recognized by his peers, by everybody who knows him and loves him, as a leader among leaders," adding that this principal figure in the Iran/Contra affair "deserves the support of every American."

In his commencement address, North said that he had been caught in "the middle of a political dispute between the White House and the Congress." He had been "vilified," he commented, for "trying to help the young men of Nicaragua, trying to rescue American hostages and prevent terrorism." Generalizing on his situation, North added that the lesson of the Reagan years is that "even a strong, right-minded, God-fearing president cannot alone" accomplish his goals, since these can easily be frustrated and rejected by the power of Congress.

Falwell used the occasion to present North with an honorary doctorate of humanities, and announced to the commencement audience that his petition drive had secured 600,000 supporters, nearly one-third of what was necessary. Repeating that Oliver North deserved to be regarded as a national hero, Falwell reiterated that "if I must go into battle with anybody, I want it to be Oliver North." Pleased with the success of the effort he was making, and smiling broadly, he reiterated that he personally would present the petitions to President Reagan. It was a cause that he enjoyed leading, for, once again, he had gotten there first, and was confident that he could draw upon his influence with the President to advance the objectives of the Christian gospel in face of the secularizing tendencies of an increasingly decadent society.

But, in spite of the boasts and the promises, not everything went well, neither for North nor for Falwell. On June 11, 1988, Falwell announced the closing of the doors of the Moral Majority. He praised the organization for encouraging religious conservatives to become involved in the political process—"ten years ago," he said, "we sat in our citadels and fired out cannonballs instead of sitting down and reasonably debating things." But he acknowledged that the primary issues—abortion, school prayer, divorce, drug abuse, teen pregnancy, pornography—are "still unresolved." Assessing the Moral Majority's successes and failures, Cal Thomas observed the next day that the organization "never lived up to its supporters' highest expectations or its detractors' worst fears," but he too wished to affirm that Falwell's effort changed the minds of many who previously had believed that "politics was dirty and secondary to Christianity's primary goal of equipping people for heaven."

It is a difficult balance to maintain. Falwell wishes to exercise responsibility in the world, but he recognizes that the world invites uncompromising choices within radical and indissoluble contrasts. There are no shadings, no sustainable mixtures. The forces of good and evil are unalterably and forever juxtaposed: human beings are compelled to identify with one side or the other. In this world of ever-whirling atoms, darkness challenges light at every moment, and evil is always on the prowl to diminish or eliminate good. It is imperative that whatever life there is be shielded from death. Falwell's gospel professes that God loves his own and sends his son to rescue them from reprobates and death dealers. Accordingly, as God watches faithfully over his own, so too can he be relied upon to protect the people of his chosen nation, that is, so long as the leaders and citizenry honor God's laws, obey his commands, and remain obedient to his will. The ideal is that the entire world should live and conduct its affairs according to these life-sustaining principles. Therefore, it is essential now that the United States live this way, that is, if it is to continue to receive the blessing of God. This is the vocation of Falwell's "champions for Christ," even those who have also experienced how much satisfaction lies in sipping tea (and sometimes sherry) with other national notables in the Rose Garden of the White House.

Falwell's gospel of sharp and radical contrasts leaves him vulnerable when he is given mediational tasks to perform, a role to which he is remarkably suited by temperament. He has needed to bring the fundamentalist and evangelical communities into the national political process. He achieved great success in this, yet, predictably, drew the ire of critics on both sides who were convinced that the two entities did not go well together. He has needed to mediate between Christians and Jews, particularly if he was to make good on his professed attitude toward the state of Israel. But this was not easy to achieve either, for an absolutistic "born-again" Christianity is not an accommodating basis for a working partnership. And when he assumed administrative responsibilities at PTL, he was obliged to mediate between fundamentalists and Pentecostalists within conservative Protestant Christianity. But, no matter how much he talked about the need for forgiveness and cooperation, he was not successful in convincing the Pentecostals that he could be trusted while being severely criticized within the fundamentalist community. In this circumstance, as in all of the others, he found himself in a marginal position, unable to dictate the terms of the desired mediation.

This, however, seems to be his destiny. He is programmed to assume responsibility for numerous gigantic tasks, to cultivate both his mediational talents and entrepreneurial instincts to the maximum, and yet remain a fundamentalist Christian, in superlative standing. One can understand and appreciate how such constructive, enterprising work might be undertaken on behalf of Thomas Road Baptist Church. One can understand and appreciate how such constructive, enterprising work might be directed toward making Liberty University the envy of both Notre Dame and Brigham Young. In these instances, though the challenges are formidable, the leader knows precisely how to channel his efforts. It is much more difficult, however, to draw upon the same ambitions, say, on behalf of fundamentalist Christianity within the United States, for here Falwell is challenging forces and energies that he cannot expect to control or even tame.

If the mediational work within the religious community is difficult, think what a challenge the Lynchburg evangelist has undertaken when wanting to influence the legislative agenda of the nation. Here, predictably, Falwell has encountered indefatigable resistance. This is why he sought effective partnerships, not only with other fundamentalists and Pentecostalists who were willing to work with him, but also, within the circle of larger political influence, with key members of Congress in Washington, and with no less than the President of the United States. As he envisioned the situation, all of them together could achieve what none of them could effect individually. But even when it happened, it was a very fragile coalition, a source of personal pleasure and satisfaction at times to Falwell, but, on numerous other occasions, an arrangement that failed to live up to its promise.

Judged in light of the roles he had assumed and acquired in the national corridors of power, Falwell is a study in vulnerability. In many instances, he has been tempted, but he has not succumbed. He has been close to the seat of power, but he has made no long-term requests for himself. He knows what would be required of him were he to take the next steps, and, satisfied that he possesses such knowledge, he has backed off, leaving the field open to others, the majority of whom are less disciplined, more vulnerable, less capable, but certainly no more ambitious. Though he has enormous capacity for entrepreneurial ventures, he has only been moderately successful in enacting the political and religious alliances he has striven for, and has never attained the national political influence to which, by instinct and temperament (though not by sanctioned resolve) he aspires. Unlike his fellow Virginian, Pat Robertson, he could never bring himself to relinquish his ordination for political purposes, even temporarily, for this would be a violation of his primary vocation. At heart he sees himself not as a political operative, or even as a religious broadcaster, but as a parish pastor—the leader of a local church that is motivated by a global ministry. When the chips are down, when the terms of the choice are clear, at least so far, he has been willing to subject his personal ambitions to a higher will and a loftier set of priorities. And yet, as when he left the PTL operation to "return home" to the place from which he started out, he continues to be attracted to entrepreneurial political ventures, one after another after another.

Perhaps he carries some resentment toward colleagues in the ministry whose daring is not countered by intrinsic vocational restraints. Perhaps there are times when it bothers him deeply that few others within the movement can begin to understand what "walking point" really means, for he has been placed in this risky position ever since he decided openly to oppose prevailing government opinion. And yet the stance he has adopted can sustain his self-assurance that the sensational stories and scandals will probably be about someone else. His soul has been subjected to sustained and intense warfare; still he has found stability and comfort in knowing that he has devoted his life and work to the principle: "One thing have I desired of the Lord, and this will I seek after." However, as he kept faith with this vow, if he hadn't also been seeking after some other objectives his single-minded ministry would not have attained such expansive dimensions, and if he hadn't also learned how to be vocationally multifaceted, as both friend and foe will attest, Christian fundamentalism would certainly not have acquired acknowledged and recognizable collective political acumen in the United States in the 1980s.

CHAPTER THREE

THE THEOLOGIAN, THE TEACHER

As breaker of innovative theological ground, his role among many conservative Protestants is similar to the one attributed to Hans Küng by progressive Roman Catholics, or to Paul Tillich, nearly three decades ago, within liberal Protestant circles. For nearly fifty years Francis Schaeffer was teacher, intellectual provocateur, and spiritual guide to thousands upon thousands. He wrote the books that the people within the movement cherished, and which gained a status of respectability attained by no one since the time of the Oxford scholar, C. S. Lewis. Within the movement, he is the intellectual authority most often quoted, the one most trusted. He is the one who has been judged to have reflected most creatively, intelligently, and profoundly on the contemporary situation in light of conservatively sanctioned theological principles, always fortified by an abundance of scriptural references. For the followers within the movement, he was the one on whom they relied—and continue to rely—to be able to compete with rival theological stances on equal terms.

I once witnessed the respect they accorded him. As it turned out, it was Francis Schaeffer's final public address before his death. The performance was unforgettable. He would speak, making assertions about the downward drift of decadent modern secularized society, and, even before the sentences of condemnation were finished, the "Amens" would resound. "He's right, you know," said a man next to me. Others nodded in assent. When he directed his prophetic fervor against contemporary moral ills, a woman leaped to her feet, got the attention of the audience, and chided, "shame, shame, shame." The wisdom he displayed—"biblically principled," the same man assured me—gave his hearers confidence. It may have stirred them to thinking in ways to which they were not accustomed, perhaps. But they trusted the thoughts and their new ideas because they trusted him. They liked the feel of the intellectual pathways on which he took them. For them, they were safe passageways, perhaps because he demonstrated eloquently that he had already become familiar with the places to which they needed to travel. They can move where he did and be certain, from the very outset, that they will come back home again, richer and stronger, and surer of the ground on which they stand. This was their confidence.

In his lifetime he wrote nearly thirty books, the majority of which appeared in his last years. But none will be remembered as long as *A Christian Manifesto*,[1] which was written to serve the evangelical Christian community as the *Communist Manifesto* served the movement it informed and as the *Humanist Manifesto* summarized the convictions of the community it represented. Francis Schaeffer intended his *Christian Manifesto* to offer a new and compelling restatement of the major tenets of the Christian faith—phrased in twentieth-century terms and highlighted according to his perception of contemporary needs—as well as providing a challenging call to radical Christian discipleship. It is the manual of inspiration and recommended conduct with which the contemporary warrior of faith—today's respondents to an "Onward Christian Soldier" call—must be armed and equipped if they are to carry out their responsibility confidently and vigorously.

Francis Schaeffer's religious roots were in American Presbyterianism, wherein he took his theological orientation from the conservative reaction against the liberal Auburn Affirmation of 1924. The Auburn Affirmation declared that Presbyterian ministers were to be accorded some liberty in interpreting the Westminster Confession. It also provided some flexibility on questions about the inerrancy of Scripture. But, most importantly, the theological statement rejected the famous five Presbyterian "fundamentals" (or "list of essential doctrines")—inerrancy of Scripture, the virgin birth of Christ, Christ's substitutionary atonement, his bodily resurrection, and the authenticity of biblical miracles. American religious history records that the Auburn repudiation of the famous five points became the rallying cry for a conservative Presbyterian reaction—led by J. Gresham Machen, who taught New Testament at Princeton Theological Seminary. After considerable controversy, in which a number of divines wrote sarcastic, but, in their words, "well-intended" letters to each other, Machen was defrocked—that is, his ministerial ordination rights were taken away—by the liberal wing of the Presbyterian Church in 1936.

The story of J. Gresham Machen is an important introduction to the teachings of Francis Schaeffer, because what happened to Machen made an indelible impression upon Schaeffer, who, in many respects, regarded himself as Machen's successor in the cause. Schaeffer called Machen's defrocking "the most significant U.S. news in the first half of the twentieth century."[2] Why was it so important? Because, as Schaeffer interpreted it, it represents the culmination of "the drift of the Protestant church from 1900 to 1936," and that drift helped lay the groundwork for "the cultural, sociological, moral, legal and governmental changes" that have occurred from that time to the present. As he explains it:

> It was the culmination of a long trend toward liberalism within the Presbyterian Church, and represented the same trend in most other denominations. Even if we were interested only in sociology, this change in the churches and the resulting shift to a post-Christian sociological base is important to understand if we are to grasp what is happening in the United States and other Northern European Reformation countries today.[3]

From 1924 forward, in Schaeffer's view, Protestant Christianity (specifically, American Protestantism with roots in Northern Europe, which he judged to be Christianity's most authentic form) has been off course. Being off course, it has demonstrated itself unable to cope effectively with the deepest needs of humanity. Unable to cope, it has encouraged a spiritual vacuum that has been quickly filled by false religions and surrogate faiths. Thus, in many respects, Francis Schaeffer understood his ministerial role to involve encouraging Christians to return to the theological orthodoxy and religious enthusiasm that was characteristic of the pre-1924 conservative Protestant situation. Schaeffer would have been pleased had the famous five fundamentals been reinstated.

But until they could be, he understood himself to have inherited the role that J. Gresham Machen was destined to play. This prompted him, virtually every time he spoke, to concentrate on the tragic nature of American Christianity, and upon the most urgent need to bring the true followers of Christ back to their fundamental religious senses.

The tone of Schaeffer's complaints is similar to Machen's. In 1923, for example, in his book *Christianity and Liberalism,* Machen wrote:

> . . . the present time is a time of conflict: the great redemptive religion which has always been known as Christianity is battling against a totally diverse type of religious belief, which is only the more destructive because it makes use of traditional Christian terminology. . . . But manifold as are the forms in which the movement appears, the root of the movement is one; the many varieties of modern liberal religion are rooted in naturalism—that is, in the denial of any entrance of the creative power of God.[4]

Schaeffer's version of the same set of problems is expressed this way:

> The world spirit of our age rolls on and on claiming to be autonomous and crushing all that we cherish in its path. Sixty years ago could we have imagined that unborn children would be killed by the millions here in our own country? Or that we would have no freedom of speech when it comes to speaking of God and biblical truth in our public schools? Or that every form of sexual perversion would be promoted by the entertainment media? Or that marriage, raising children, and family life would be objects of attack? Sadly we must say that very few Christians have understood the battle that we are in. Very few have taken a strong and courageous stand against the world spirit of this age as it destroys our culture and the Christian ethos that once shaped our country.
>
> But the Scriptures make clear that we as Bible-believing Christians are locked in a battle of cosmic proportions. It is a life and death struggle over the minds and souls of men for all eternity, but it is equally a life and death struggle over life on this earth.[5]

Schaeffer could say it in other ways too:

> . . . we must not forget that the world is on fire. We are not only losing the church, but our entire culture as well. We live in the post-Christian world which is under the judgment of God. . . . Some

people think that just because the United States of America is the
United States of America, because Britain is Britain, they will not
come under the judgment of God. This is not so.[6]

Indeed, when one places the following passages side by side, it is
as if they were written by the same person, representing a single
voice:

> The modern world represents in some respects an enormous
> improvement over the world in which our ancestors lived, but in
> other respects it exhibits a lamentable decline. . . . The loss is
> clearest, perhaps, in the realm of art. . . . No great poet is now
> living. . . . Gone, too, are the great painters and the great musicians
> and the great sculptors. The art that still exists is largely imitative,
> and where it is not imitative it is usually bizarre. Even the
> appreciation of the glories of the past is gradually being lost, under
> the influence of a utilitarian education that concerns itself only with
> the production of physical well-being.
>
> This unprecedented decline in literature and art is . . . only one
> instance of that narrowing of the range of personality which has
> been going on in the modern world. The whole development of
> modern society has tended mightily toward the limitation of the
> realm of freedom for the individual man. The tendency is most
> clearly seen in socialism: a socialistic state would mean the
> reduction to a minimum of the freedom of choice.[7]

This was J. Gresham Machen writing in 1922 and 1923. Francis
Schaeffer expressed the same sentiments almost sixty years later.
Consequences of the events he deplored are to be found in all of
humankind's contemporary cultural endeavors. The underlying
problem is that the true basis of human life has eroded:

> Christianity is no longer providing the consensus for our society.
> And Christianity is no longer providing the consensus upon which
> our law is based. . . . Until recent decades something did exist
> which can rightly be called a Christian consensus or ethos which
> gave a distinctive shape to Western society and to the United States
> in a definitive way. Now that consensus is all but gone, and the
> freedoms that it brought are being destroyed before our eyes. We
> are at a time when humanism is coming to its natural conclusion
> in morals, in value, and in law. All that society has today are
> relativistic values based upon statistical averages, or the arbitrary
> decisions of those who hold legal and political power.[8]

Their understanding of the tasks that Christians should be performing at the present time is similar too. Schaeffer's books and sermons cited the need for a new Jeremiah, to stir the people to action. But, more than anything else, he believed in educating Christian people—thus, the establishment of his Christian communities, his frequent lectures to Christian study groups, his published study guides, educational films, and television series. Machen felt this way too. The "most important thing of all," he said in 1923, is "the renewal of Christian education." He explained that "the rejection of Christianity is due to various causes, but a very potent cause is simple ignorance." Machen's expanded commentary on the same subject reads as follows:

> In countless cases, Christianity is rejected simply because men have not the slightest notion of what Christianity is. An outstanding fact of recent church history is the appalling growth of ignorance in the church. . . . The development is due partly to the general decline of education. . . . The schools of the present day are being ruined by the absurd notion that education should follow the line of least resistance, and that something can be "drawn out" of the mind before anything is put in. They are also being ruined by an exaggerated emphasis on methodology at the expense of content, and on what is materially useful at the expense of the high spiritual heritage of mankind. . . . But something more than the general decline in education is needed to account for the special growth of ignorance in the Church.[9]

Analyzing the situation in this way, Machen believed this ignorance of Christian people to be "the logical and inevitable result of the false notion that Christianity is a life and not also a doctrine." He reasoned that "if Christianity is not a doctrine, then, of course, teaching is not necessary." And yet, it wasn't enough to identify causes or offer diagnoses. The remedy was to be found in education:

> Christian education is the chief business of the hour for every earnest Christian man. Christianity cannot subsist unless men know what Christianity is; and the fair and logical thing is to learn what Christianity is, not from its opponents, but from those who themselves are Christians.[10]

Certainly, in his career, Francis Schaeffer expressed the same sentiments, using some of the same words, on numerous occasions.

The large difference between Machen and Schaeffer is that the latter sought to fit the authoritative conservative philosophy to a global context while Machen's reflections concentrated very specifically upon the causes of fundamentalist Christianity within the United States. Though American born, Schaeffer made Switzerland his headquarters, and his books reflect an international scope that is not present in Machen. Furthermore, Schaeffer understood himself to be a student of the entire history of Western philosophical and theological reflection. When he spoke about the shifts and transformations that had occurred, he could do so with explicit reference to the ongoing history of the Christian Church and its theological confessions and statements. He has no books on American Christianity *per se.* Rather, he considered church life in the United States within an international religious context.

The primary literary carrier of this aspect of Schaeffer's work is his book, *How Should We Then Live?*, published in 1976.[11] The book, more aptly named in subtitle (*The Rise and Decline of Western Thought and Culture*) than title, is an extended review, with author's commentary, of Western intellectual and cultural history, from the Greco-Roman period to the present. Schaeffer's intention was "to present the flow and developments of thought that have led to twentieth-century thinking." He explained his motivation this way: "This book is . . . an analysis of the key moments in history which have formed our present culture, and thinking of the people who brought those moments to pass."[12]

All histories of culture are selective in scope and object of interest. Schaeffer's rendition is unusually selective. Histories of culture are written under the influence of some specific themes and hypotheses. Schaeffer's is exemplary in this respect too. In fact, it is an identification of such presuppositions and an examination of the commanding principles that form the core of the book. From this side, the purpose of the study is to identify the prevailing attitudes and viewpoints of previous periods of human history so as better "to understand where we are in today's world" (20). Clearly, however, Francis Schaeffer is not willing to assign comparable worth to each set of attitudes and viewpoints. Instead, his purpose is to measure all other prevailing attitudes against the absolute truth of the Christian faith. Consequently, his approach to Greco-Roman philosophy is to contrast its "weaknesses" against the "strengths" of Christianity. The contrast is drawn (and used) this way:

> It is important to realize what a difference a people's world view makes in their strength as they are exposed to the pressure of life. That it was the Christians who were able to resist religious mixtures, syncretism, and the effects of the weaknesses of Roman culture speaks of the strength of the Christian world view. This strength rested on God's being an infinite-personal God and his speaking in the Old Testament, in the life and teaching of Jesus Christ, and in the gradually growing New Testament (22).

Put another way: "Rome did not fall because of external forces such as the invasion by the barbarians" (29). On the contrary, Rome fell because it had "no sufficient inward base." The barbarians merely "completed the breakdown, and Rome gradually became a ruin." Ultimately, the error of Roman ways became self-destructive.

Error describes the prevailing worldviews, as Schaeffer interprets it, even through most of early Christianity, until the Protestant Reformation in the sixteenth century. Throughout the medieval period, the Gospel witness was infected (and thus diminished) by a strongly humanistic element inherited from the Greeks, and this uneasy synthesis encouraged the progressive deterioration of the vitality of Jesus' message. At one end of this cycle, the Renaissance symbolizes the triumph of humanism—the philosophical point of view most sharply contrary to that of authentic Christian teaching. At the other end of the cycle, the Reformation symbolizes the concerted attempt to restore the faith to its original purity and vitality. In short, the Reformation is represented by an effort to remove "the humanistic distortions which had entered the church." It also represented a reform movement that took its energies from the cultural situation in northern (as opposed to southern) Europe:

> One must understand that these two things were happening almost simultaneously. First, in the south, much of the High Renaissance was based on a humanistic ideal of man's being the center of all things, of man's being autonomous; second, in the north of Europe, the Reformation was giving an opposite answer. In other words, the Reformation was exploding with Luther as the High Renaissance was coming to its close (80).

From the Reformation period forward, Schaeffer's version of Western intellectual history concentrates on developments within the British Isles, with particular attention being focused on the situation in Scotland. Schaeffer is enthusiastic in his praise for the insights of Samuel Rutherford (1600-1661), and, especially, for his book, *Lex Rex*. He understands Rutherford's principle—that law is king, or law rules—to have informed the U.S. Constitution, under the encouragement of John Witherspoon (1723-1794), a Presbyterian, who became president of the College of New Jersey (now Princeton University) in 1768, and was a member of the Continental Congress from 1776-1779 and from 1780-1782. With Rutherford, the other single most influential individual in giving the nation a proper legal and spiritual foundation was John Locke, the author of the *Essay Concerning Human Understanding*, in 1690. Schaeffer praises Locke for recognizing that human rights are innate rather than being accorded through the whim or largesse of divine kingship. It was chiefly through the influence of Locke, Schaeffer attests, that Thomas Jefferson found access to an implicitly Christian principle regarding the source and basis of governmental authority. The implication of these correlations is that, philosophically speaking, the United States was conceived in accordance with principles supported by a pristine and fundamental Christianity.

But, from the beginning, in Schaeffer's view, there was conflict between the fundamental religious orientation of the new Republic and the teachings of the Enlightenment. As he put it:

> The humanistic elements which had risen during the Renaissance came to flood tide in the Enlightenment. Here was man starting from himself absolutely. And if the humanistic elements of the Renaissance stand in sharp contrast to the Reformation, the Enlightenment was in total contrast to it. The two stand for and were based upon absolutely different things in an absolute way, and they produced absolutely different results (121).

At this point, Schaeffer works to demonstrate that Enlightenment philosophy is representative of pre-Christian values. He also looks for parallels between the intentions of the French Revolution (inspired as they were by Enlightenment philosophy) and those of the Russian Revolution, as conceived by Lenin. Thoughts of this kind encourage Schaeffer to expound on the meaning of the current geographical boundaries and national alignments within contemporary Europe:

> Mention of the later Russian Revolution evokes the observation that a quite different dynamic was involved in the political fortunes of those parts of Europe structurally influenced by the restoration of biblical Christianity in the sixteenth century as compared to those not so influenced. In crude geopolitical terms, there is a contrast between the north of Europe and the south and east. Allowing for local influences, it would seem that the inspiration for most revolutionary changes in the south of Europe was a copy, but often in contorted form, of the freedoms gained from the Reformation in the north (124).

Some of Schaeffer's readers will find principles here that help explain the alliances of nations that, some fundamentalist prophecy foretells, will persist until the impending battle of Armageddon (the potentiality for which is explored at considerable length in books like Hal Lindsey's *The Late Great Planet Earth*).[13] But if such considerations seem too futuristic and speculative, there are other lessons to be drawn from Schaeffer's more sober utterances, such as "no place within a communistic base has produced freedom of the kind brought forth under the Reformation in northern Europe" (127). Schaeffer perceived that the differences in worldviews are clear and sharp. Communists expect their objectives to be achieved by force and repression. Humanistic societies, having lost firm hold on absolute values, retain no convincing way of distinguishing truth from error, right from wrong, or good from evil. Biblical religion, on the other hand, teaches absolutes, repudiates all relativisms whether in ideology or moral code, and upholds inviolable criteria to distinguish between the conflicting enticements of right and wrong.

The primary implication from this analysis is that no subsequent historical era has been able to advance upon the truth of the worldview of those who, during the time of the Reformation, labored strenuously and fought valiantly for the reinstatement of the convictions of original Christianity. The Reformation period attains this high place, in Schaeffer's analysis, because it is the only historical period that was committed to honoring the cardinal teachings of the Bible as theological and moral absolutes. Absolutes are necessary, Schaeffer explains: "But it is not only that we need absolutes in morals and values; we need absolutes if our existence is to have meaning—my existence, your existence, man's existence. Even more profoundly, we must have absolutes if we are to have a solid epistemology" (145).

Following the Reformation period in which absolute truth was given highest place, the Western world returned to error and decadence. The scientific revolution of the eighteenth and nineteenth centuries was attached to a naturalistic and materialistic version of reality, which, in turn, supported the attitude that the cosmos is a closed system and machinelike in its operations. Much of modern philosophy, according to Schaeffer, takes its cues from this imagery. If man is nothing more than a part of the machinery, then, he attests, the nihilists (Feuerbach, Marx, Nietzsche, and the others) are correct: life is devoid of meaning. Similarly, the Darwinian idea of "the survival of the fittest" belongs to the "world in chaos" attitude that materialistic philosophy reflects. The historical consequence of these enormous errors is the Nazi movement, which makes survival-of-the-fittest convictions the norm while proclaiming the existence of a master race.

> Hitler stated numerous times that Christianity and its notion of charity should be "replaced by the ethic of strength over weakness." Surely many factors were involved in the rise of National Socialism in Germany. For example, the Christian consensus had largely been lost by the undermining from a rationalistic philosophy and a romantic pantheism on the secular side, and a liberal theology (which was an adoption of rationalism in theological terminology) in the universities and many of the churches. Thus biblical Christianity was no longer giving the consensus for German society. After World War I came political and economic chaos and a flood of moral permissiveness in Germany. Thus, many factors created the situation. But in that setting the theory of the survival of the fittest sanctioned what occurred (151).

The result, Schaeffer believed, were the gas chambers. And the current deterministic and behavioristic philosophies are influenced by the same false convictions. All of the mischief derived from a supplanting of original Christian convictions by the humanists' sense that "man instead of God is the measure of all things." This, in sum, is what happened:

Now having travelled from the pride of man in the High Renaissance and the Enlightenment down to the present despair, we can understand where modern people are. They have no place for a personal God. But equally they have no place for man as man, or for love, or for freedom, or for significance. This brings a crucial problem. Beginning only from man himself, people affirm that man is only a machine (169).

Or, put in another way, "humanistic man tried to make himself self-sufficient and demanded that one start from himself and . . . build his own universals." This, in Schaeffer's depiction, is the philosophical basis for the dreaded current worldview he calls "secular humanism."

From this swift portrayal of Western intellectual history, it is easy to draw implications regarding the philosophical confusions and theological errors of the present time. Following the turn to "unreason," as Schaeffer views it, modern humanity has fallen victim to hallucinogenic drugs; surrealistic art (as exemplified by the works of Salvador Dali); "nonrational religion" in the form of Buddhism, Hinduism, and the other Asian religions; existentialism; liberalism (in political theory); form criticism (in biblical interpretation); and assorted fusions of Eastern and Western religious attitudes that only breed, encourage and sustain "pessimistic attitudes." Furthermore, these influences are powerful, and they carry large destructive force:

All of this gives us today . . . an almost unified voice shouting at us a fragmented concept of the universe and of life. And as it comes at us from every side and with many voices, it is difficult not to be infiltrated by it. We and our children now get this message from every side—from art, music, general culture, modern theology, the mass media, and even comic books (198).

Schaeffer's arresting conclusion:

Modern people are in trouble indeed. These things are not shut up within the art museums, the concert halls and rock festivals, the stage and movies, or the theological seminaries. People function on the basis of their worldviews. Therefore, society has changed radically. This is the reason—and not a less basic one—that it is unsafe to walk at night through the streets of many of today's cities. As a man thinketh, so is he (204).

In the face of such thorough and comprehensive

condemnation, what can human beings do? How are they to respond? What recourse do they have? In other words, to ask Schaeffer's question: *how then shall we live?*

Schaeffer's reply is that it is exceedingly difficult to go back home again, to find one's way back to some place of previous but now abandoned haven of safety and stability. The work of the enemy has been so successful that the forces that militate against a deeper spiritual humanity are now authorized and prescribed by the prevailing culture. How ironic, Schaeffer observes, that the advent of the drug culture was hailed, in the media, as "the beginning of a new and wonderful age." No less curious is the astounding fact that the Marxist-Leninist hold on America's social and cultural mainstream is supported by the media and even, at times, by governmentally funded programs. Why, he wondered, have both "promiscuous sex" and "bisexuality" been accepted and condoned by the dominant society, but communism, which is advancing throughout the world, does not generate the disgust and repulsion it deserves? Why this inconsistency? Has the society gone soft? Has it lost its moral sanity? Is there no collective conscience any more? And why is there such willing acquiescence, such uncritical, knee-jerk condoning of abortion rights? This, in Schaeffer's view, is the surest sign of a decadent society. It is a society that has lost all sensitivity to the presence of moral absolutes.

> Humanism has led to its natural conclusion. It has ground down to the point Leonardo da Vinci visualized so long ago when he realized that, starting only from man, mathematics leads us only to particulars—and particulars lead only to mechanics. Humanism had no way to find the universal in the areas of meaning and values (226).

Schaeffer has concluded that humanism is not only philosophically wrong and spiritually bankrupt, but it is also motivated by a death wish, that is, by "an impulse to beat to death that which made our freedoms and our culture possible" (226). And, given the enormity of the problem, not even the established church can be of much redemptive assistance, since most of what passes as institutional Christianity has been thoroughly co-opted by secular humanism.

The only possible satisfactory recourse, in Schaeffer's view, is to return to the authenticity of the original Christian worldview, and this will only be accomplished through a reestablishing of "fundamental Christian values." Christians must learn how to live their lives in ways that make the alternatives they offer clear and compelling. They must learn to speak out effectively against all forms of authoritarian rule. They must do all within their powers—counting on God to assist them—to change the course of history so that human life might be directed away from the pathway of destruction.

The cultural critic made his recommendations even more explicit in *A Christian Manifesto.* Here Schaeffer called for a reawakened and restrengthened evangelical Christian leadership to assist in halting the advance of the debilitating and dehumanizing secular-humanist movement. And when providing examples of the forms such resistance might take, Schaeffer cited the work of the Moral Majority. Jerry Falwell's efforts are of the kind and quality that deserve the support of Bible-believing, deeply committed evangelical Christians.

> . . . we must realize that regardless of whether we think the Moral Majority has always said the right things or whether we do not, or whether we think they have made some mistakes or whether we do not, they have certainly done one thing right: they have used the freedom we still have in the political arena to stand against the other total entity. They have carried the fact that law is king, law is above the lawmakers, and God is above the law into the area of life where it always should have been. And this is a part of true spirituality.[14]

Continuing, Schaeffer explains:

> The Moral Majority has drawn a line between the one total view of reality and the other total view of reality and the results this brings forth in government and law. And if you personally do not like some of the details of what they have done, do it better. But you must understand that all Christians have got to do the same kind of thing or you are simply not showing the Lordship of Christ in the totality of life (61–62).

Given the enormity of the challenge, Schaeffer believed that contemporary evangelical Christians should be specific about what they can and cannot do, or, more importantly, what they should and should not do. In the first place, there is no reason why they should not engage in acts of civil disobedience, that is, if the situation warrants this.

> When discussing [the use of] force it is important to keep an axiom in mind: always before protest or force is used, we must work for reconstruction. In other words, we should attempt to correct and rebuild society before we advocate tearing it down or disrupting it. If there is a legitimate reason for the use of force, and if there is a vigilant precaution against its over-reaction in practice, then at a certain point a use of force is justifiable. We should recognize however, that overreaction can too easily become the ugly horror of sheer violence. Therefore, the distinction between force and violence is crucial (106).

Schaeffer also called upon true Christians to protest the use of tax monies for abortion. The intrusion of government into areas of human life over which private jurisdictional rights should prevail is incontrovertible evidence of the power of secular rule. As always, Schaeffer urged that restraint be exercised. But he was willing to let his point of view be drawn to its logical conclusion: "Simply put, the Declaration of Independence states that the people, if they find that their basic rights are being systematically attacked by the state, have a duty to try to change that government, and if they cannot do so, to abolish it" (128).

In essence, as Francis Schaeffer saw it, the United States is imperiled because the powers of government are utilized to enforce a false and distorted view of reality. Christians have no recourse but to oppose this government-sanctioned and assisted importation of unreality in whatever ways are most skillful and effective:

> What is now needed is to stand against that other total world view. We must see and make clear that it is not the truth of final reality; and we must understand and show that it is producing its own natural results which are opposite to those upon which the United States was founded. It is opposite to the great freedoms produced which everyone now enjoys. What is needed at this time is to take the steps necessary to break the authoritarian hold which the material-energy, chance concept of final reality has on government and Law.
>
> The result would be freedom for all and especially freedom for all religion. That was the original purpose of the First Amendment (136).

Schaeffer's work is highly regarded by proponents of the New Religious Right because of its theological range and sophistication. But it is even more significant, perhaps, because of the intellectual sanctions it gives to causes about which the movement feels deeply and intensely. For example, Schaeffer's judgments against the increasing power of humanistic philosophy offer vigorous intellectual (and symbolic) support for the campaign to abolish secular humanism. Before the errant philosophy can be abolished, however, it has to be recognized for what it is. And more than any other writer or preacher, Francis Schaeffer was the one who has identified this evil and compellingly called it to the attention of conservative Christian believers.

The treatise that gets cited most often on this subject, Timothy LaHaye's *The Battle for the Mind,* is hardly anything more than a simplified and condensed highly charged paraphrase of Schaeffer's most potent observation. In LaHaye's restatement, however, some of Schaeffer's contentions are so thoroughly oversimplified as to be distorted. Indeed, LaHaye reads *A Christian Manifesto* to attest that "there is yet time for us to defeat the humanists and reverse the moral decline in our country that has us on a collision course with Sodom and Gomorrah."[15] Put in another way, there is only one way that this tide can be arrested, and this is through the resistance that can be offered by committed Christians: "Only one organization in America can stop the complete 'humanization' of our nation—the church of Jesus Christ."[16] And it is evident from everything that is occurring that this decisive battle for the spiritual soul of the nation is already underway.

> If America is going to be saved from the humanist onslaught . . . , it will take the combined efforts of the pro-moral majority, particularly the Christian community. . . .
>
> We are in a battle—and it takes armies to win wars. We need an army of moral activities, led by their Bible-believing ministers, who will provide America with the moral leadership for which this country hungers. . . .
>
> Remember, we are in a war that the enemy has been planning for over seventy years. Only dedication, hard work, sacrifice, and cooperation with other moral activists will insure victory. After our triumph over humanism and its dreadful effects on our culture and children, there will be ample time to voice our theological and other differences. But for the next few years, we are obliged to fight

a common enemy, and it will take the combined efforts of every morally concerned and informed American.[17]

Onalee McGraw, a Washington, D.C., educator, feels similarly and has made LaHaye-like charges in her treatise, *Secular Humanism and the Schools,* published in 1976. McGraw too believes that the public schools have been advancing an erroneous, human-centered, anti-God, personally self-indulgent philosophy, from which basis the public schools have been conspiring to form human beings whose aspirations are compatible with the objectives of the socialist state. For McGraw, the dangers the public schools pose lie both in the philosophical content that is being promulgated as well as in the ways in which educational priorities are established and certified. The public schools, she believes, are more interested in process than substance. Their intent is to help students adapt to the social and cultural status quo rather than to become thoroughly immersed in a reliable body of knowledge that can give them access to fundamental human truths. She calls humanism (the prevailing viewpoint of the public schools) a "progressive life-adjustment philosophy" in contrast to an educational program that stresses basic reading, writing, thinking, and communication. In her words:

> Humanistic education places all emphasis on the child's social and psychological growth, instead of on the learning of basic reading. . . .
> The learning of basic life skills and factual subject matter have been relegated to second place by humanistic curricula that focus on the child's social and psychological development by emphasizing the thoughts, beliefs, values, opinions, feelings, and the peer group and family adjustment of the student.[18]

Based on its intentions and performances, McGraw understands humanism to be a religion. Therefore, the issues she addressed are both educational and religious. She contended that humanistic philosophy undermined the fundamental values taught and upheld by the Judeo-Christian tradition. These are the same values "being taught by most families at home," but which, under auspices of public education, are modified "to suit the wishes and convenience of the majority or society as a whole." Within the prevailing educational system such traditional values are forced to compete with the theories of John Dewey, Jean Piaget, Carl

Rogers, Lawrence Kohlberg, Abraham Maslow, William Glasser, Jerome Brunner, and others. And they lose because they have no skilled and committed advocates within the institution. There, their boisterous but polished and practiced enemies promote philosophical and ethical relativisms, usually, without forceful, worrisome, or challenging opposition. And, in the process, a largely unsuspecting public is indoctrinated into the teachings of a materialistic philosophy. McGraw recognized that it would be extremely difficult to transform this situation overnight. But she was heartened by the accelerated development of the Christian School system as an alternative to what was being taught—or, in her view, not being taught—in public education:

> Inasmuch as humanistic curriculum programs and "values-clarification" and "moral-education" teaching strategies are based upon materialistic values found only in man's nature itself, they reject the spiritual and moral tradition of theistic faith and religion. Thus, many parents who subscribe to Judaeo-Christian belief oppose humanistic education in the tax-supported schools on grounds that such programs promote and advocate the religion of secular humanism in violation of the First Amendment to the U.S. Constitution.[19]

The final clause in the last sentence represents Onalee McGraw's primary point. She affirmed that the humanism that is being taught and disseminated in the schools is indeed a religion, but, of course, a very false and dangerous religion. Further, she charged that this religion deliberately intends to undermine the traditional faith of many Christians and Jews. In other words, the public schools are involved in an ideological crusade. Their philosophy of humanism, she argued, ascribes powers to human beings and rights to the state that belong properly only to God. Further, humanistic philosophy discounts the possibility that God is the source of life, and, thus, the author and sustainer of justice and happiness. Humanism is also responsible for the *Roe vs. Wade* decision of the U.S. Supreme Court to legalize abortion. Furthermore, humanism is implicit in the accelerating permissiveness of American society. It is the attitude that functions to undermine mentorship, propriety, and authority. Instead of upholding moral absolutes, and understanding the human being to be a creature of God, made in the image of God, humanism approaches men and women as being products of circumstance, environment, or whatever additional background factors should be included in the collective entity called society. In addition, rather than approaching time-tested educational objectives by teaching the truth about facts—and the facts about truths—humanism utilizes such diversionary tacts as group counseling, group therapy, sensitivity training, survival games, various forms of values clarification techniques, and other modes of "sharing." It bothered Onalee McGraw that the schools are encouraged to do all of this. It incensed her that tax money is being used for this purpose. But the larger concern is that because humanism is a religion, prevailing educational practices are in direct conflict with citizen's First-Amendment constitutional rights. Succinctly, prevailing public-school practices violate the principles of the Constitution. This is the crux of the charge.

Faced with this nearly overwhelming situation, advocates of traditional values do indeed have some recourse. McGraw, like Schaeffer, counseled them to take matters into their own hands, as it were. They should make their wishes known to school boards and school officials. They should even work diligently to establish alternative schools: Christian schools, Jewish day schools, Catholic parochial schools. All of these are intended to reestablish a climate of mutual respect and order. McGraw also wanted concerned parents to develop effectiveness in lobbying to enforce rules that prospective teachers not be allowed to major in education in college. Instead, they should be required to be certified as being knowledgeable in substantive subject areas. History courses should not degenerate into "a mish-mash of current social studies fads." Textbooks should include and portray attitudes other than those condoned by the liberal press and by advocates of humanistic philosophy. Parents are encouraged to do all within their power to help supplant the prevailing educational philosophy with one that accords a larger place to the view that life is a gift from God and human beings have been created in the divine image.

In California, another public-spirited citizen, Betty Arras, has regularly published several mimeographed pages monthly under the title *California Monitor of Education* to call attention to the number of state-mandated "psychosocial programs in the schools" that, in Arras's words, "intrude upon the family."[20] These pages reiterate that the public schools are being looked to as "the

principal change agent" to effect "the socialist-utopian agenda."
In Arras's opinion, such a program creates psychological harm
for the nation's young people, weakens academic skills, and
carries totalitarian implications in the form of "governmental
involvement in the personality development of children." Her
publication charges that sex education has "spread like bubonic
plague largely because of propaganda from organizations like
Planned Parenthood, Zero Population Growth, and the Sex
Information and Education Council of the United States." Public
education has also been influenced, the documents contend, by the
requirement in federal grants that the recipient demonstrate that it
is fulfilling a need within the community. Education provides one
of the instruments through which such demonstrations can be
offered. That is, the recipients of federal monies offer classes of
instruction on the subjects of their interest. And this, in Arras's
view, is what happens next:

> Once the need is proven (and often times by manipulating various
> data to prove their case) school board members, school officials, and
> parents are easily enticed into accepting an infinite variety of
> placeboes.
>
> Those who resist these programs are made to appear as the
> "bad guys," made to feel guilty, and often lack articulate rebuttals
> to the arguments of the social engineers. Because of current school
> district policies allowing greater autonomy in curriculum at the local
> school site, these programs are not always subjected to school board
> scrutiny and approval.[21]

Arras has objections to such social-engineering projects in
principle. But she also believes the results, so far, to have been
disastrous.

> Past experience has demonstrated that the life-adjustment
> programs have not solved the social problems they were intended
> to and in some cases have even contributed to their aggravation.
> For example, sex education introduced into the schools nearly 30
> years ago was intended to reduce teen pregnancies. Teen
> pregnancies are higher than ever. Drug and alcohol abuse
> programs were introduced into the schools at least 25 years ago.
> A recent Gallup poll found that only 23% of teenagers stated
> they abstain from the use of alcoholic beverages. . . . Although
> the schools cannot be blamed for these problems their
> involvement has not solved them, and there is every reason to

believe that teaching these subjects on the basis of "making responsible decisions" which means "there are no wrong or right answers; it's all up to YOU!" contributes to self-gratification rather than self-responsibilty.[22]

The conclusion is that such "brainwashing by the social engineers" has not created better citizens, but, on the contrary, has only contributed to a worsening of conditions.

Thus, as the injunctions within the *California Monitor of Education* (and numerous other publications) make clear, the heartfelt desire of Christians for a biblically principled education of the nation's young people is not restricted to the creation of effective alternatives to what is being offered in the public schools. Christians are to exercise their efforts and influence to shape the public-school situation according to their ideals. We have already noted that this intention is implicit in the desire to legislate the possibility of voluntary school prayer, whether the form such prayer assumes be spoken or silent. The same intention informs the careful scrutinizing of state-authorized school textbooks—an effort that has been championed by a Texas-based husband and wife team of Mel and Norma Gabler.[23] The Gablers have appeared before numerous state departments of education to criticize specific textbooks on the grounds that these communicate an alien philosophy, subvert Christian truths (for example, by promoting evolutionist views of the origins of the race), and leave today's students with little more than relativist moral and ethical sensibilities. They have also appeared before hundreds of gatherings of conservative Christian groups to teach others how to discern and identify the marks of anti-Christian teachings in textbooks. Such signs become most self-evident when textbook writers express their views on the American national character. Because of the prevalence of an antipatriotic tone within textbooks, the Gablers believe that their efforts will not only lead to a rejuvenated sense of what it means to be a Christian, but they will also assist in revitalizing an awareness of what it is to be an American citizen. They understand themselves to be pro-Christian and pro-American at the same time.

This attitude has been graphically expressed by Phyllis Schlafly who, in recommending that "parents should study textbooks," has put the issue this way:

> If you wonder why young people today are often alienated from
> God, family and country, if you wonder why they choose socialist
> experiments and reject proven free-enterprise solutions, the reason
> just might be their school textbooks. Some parents today are starting
> to read their children's textbooks, and they are often in a state of
> shock at what they find.[24]

After providing some vivid examples of what she and these parents
have uncovered, Schlafly concludes that any student who is
subjected to such books will receive "a warped picture of America,
history, morality, and private enterprise." For Schlafly, whose
views are typical of the majority of New Right advocates, the
problem is so enormous that it cannot be satisfactorily met by local
individual and collective measures. The only effective way to deal
with the issue is to abolish both the federal Department of
Education and the National Institute of Education:

> The American people don't want federal agencies developing new
> textbooks, curriculums, and methods of instruction for local school
> districts. That kind of governmental thought control is simply not
> the kind of society we want in the United States. We are much better
> off if private publishing houses offer their wares and local school
> boards make their selections of textbooks and curricula.[25]

The fundamental objective in all of these measures is to do
effective battle against the alien philosophy. More and more, New
Religious Right supporters have come to agree that the public
school system is the most influential and dangerous disseminator
and sustainer of the godless, profoundly anti-American, secular-
humanist viewpoint.

   The responses chronicled so far in this chapter are ones
that encourage voluntary individual and collective action. But
something additional is involved in the intentions of a watchdog
group, Accuracy in Media (AIM), which was established in
Washington, D.C., for the expressed purpose of exposing the
"liberal bias" of the press. AIM received considerable national
attention in 1985 when, with the backing of a grant from the
National Endowment for the Humanities, it offered its own
documentary, "Television's Vietnam: The Real Story," narrated
by Charlton Heston, to counter alleged misinformation that was
disseminated through PBS's first presentation on the subject. Reed
Irvine, the founder of the group, is a Washington syndicated

columnist, who also prepares an *AIM Report* and writes regularly for publications sponsored by Sun Myung Moon's Unification Church. Irvine has encouraged his supporters to buy stock in publicly owned media, like the Washington Post Company and ABC Television. He himself has done this, and utilizes his legal position as the basis for appearing at the annual meetings of shareholders to confront managers with unsettling questions. For example, after ABC Television News sponsored a program called "The Fire Unleashed," on June 25, 1985, dealing with the Reagan Administration's recommendations regarding the Strategic Defense Initiative research, Irvine presented a resolution to the meeting of ABC shareholders calling for the establishment of a committee of science advisors.

In August 1985, Irvine announced a new program for his organization, to be called "Accuracy in Academia." The intention is to utilize the presence of selected students on college and university campuses—and other citizens who might volunteer to perform such services—to sit in on classes to take notes on the lectures of teachers and professors who may be preaching a communist or Marxist-Leninist line. The new program was prompted by information Irvine received that an English professor at a large state university had told his students that there is more injustice in America than there was in Nazi Germany. Irvine and his associates suspect that the nation is full of colleges and universities within which statements or allegations of this kind go unchallenged. Thus, by offering incentives to selected students and auditors (the majority of whom may be senior citizens who have time to sit in on classes) to expose such practices, AIM believes that it can do for the campuses what it has been trying to effect within the media. Specifically, those chosen as auditors are asked "to supply us with tape recordings or notes of statements made by the teachers of such courses." After the professors are given an opportunity to make corrections, if they prove unwilling, AIM will "publicize the error in existing campus publications, in an Accuracy in Academia newsletter," and, presumably, in whatever additional papers or periodicals will attract the widest circulation. The volunteers are also being called upon to enlist other students to support this investigative work on their campuses. Irvine believes that students in such academic situations are "entitled to some outside help when confronted with teachers who insist on inflicting inaccurate information on them." His intention is to provide such assistance when, in the judgment of AIM, students have legitimate grievances.[26]

So far, we have provided examples of action that involve the efforts of individual citizens and private organizations. But the effort took a giant leap forward, on March 4, 1987, when Judge W. Brevard Hand, of the United States District court of the Southern District of Alabama, in Mobile, banned 31 textbooks from all public school classrooms in the state of Alabama, on grounds that they illegally promote the "religion of secular humanism." Judge Hand rendered this decision in a class-action suit initiated by over five hundred parents, assisted by the National Legal Foundation, who objected to the books on grounds that they give expression to particular *religious teachings,* namely, those of the secular-humanist faith. The ruling of Judge Hand goes far beyond the removal of certain textbooks on grounds that they use objectionable language or treat subjects that are not deemed to be edifying. Judge Hand's decision affirms that the attitude commonly referred to as "secular humanism" does indeed carry the status of a religion in certain segments of our national life. Therefore, any official teaching of the tenets of this religion, as occurs when the viewpoint is being recommended in officially state-sponsored secondary-school textbooks, is a violation of the principle of separation of church and state. As the Judge put it: "The Supreme Court has declared that teaching religious tenets in such a way as to promote or encourage a religion violates the religion clauses [of the constitution]. . . . The facts showed that the State of Alabama has on its textbook list certain volumes that are being used by school systems in this state, which engage in such promotions." Eventually, Judge Hand's decision was overturned by a higher court, but not until he had been hailed repeatedly as a champion of true religion.

Francis Schaeffer probably did not have most of these specific strategies in mind when he implored Christians to become active politically. But it was apparent to him that the battle lines had been drawn, and that the rival errant worldview carried the official sponsorship of the public schools, and, even worse, was being promulgated there at taxpayers' expense. Because this subversive attitude was anti-God, anti-religion, and even anti-American, if not effectively challenged and repulsed it would eventually destroy the nation.

As he sounded this litany, Francis Schaeffer frequently paused, looking up from his notes, and asked his audience: "Are you following? Do you understand what you are listening to? Do you understand what I am telling you?" Then, characteristically, he would answer his own questions: "What we face today is no different from Hitler's, Stalin's and Mao's killing of human life because they thought they were killing for the benefit of society." The implication: "once the door is opened, everything is susceptible to arbitrary tyrannical choice."

Schaeffer's picture of the world is one that finds the alien forces marshaled everywhere, poised to destroy whatever good abides. The positive social and cultural supports that Christians were able to take for granted in previous periods of the church, have been undermined. The sense of the sanctity of human life has been eroded. The recognition that this is God's world, and that its human inhabitants can enjoy life lived under God's care and blessed with his beneficence—this too has been laid to ruin by the destructive attitudes that have come to prominence in what Schaeffer referred to as "modern pseudo-civilization." The modern world, in contrast to the biblical ideal, has been shaped by the passions of pride, greed, self-satisfaction, wholesale and grand-scale permissiveness (encouraged and condoned by television programs watched by "parentless" children in their homes), self-indulgence, and all other forms and manifestations of collective adultery. In Schaeffer's view, contemporary civilization evinces clear signs of instantiating the biblical Sodom and Gomorrah. It is the city that has been constructed to glorify human perversity. The world has become so thoroughly corrupted that its inhabitants commend and praise sin rather than denouncing it. Moreover, under the transforming powers of license and permissiveness, an illusion is created that evil is actually good. Watching the transformation take place right before his eyes—in music, literature, the arts, politics, education, sexual mores, and, even in theology and worship in the church—Schaeffer felt the responsibility to take up the vocation of the latter-day prophet who warns his people that perdition is imminent. "This is not time to be sleeping," he cautioned. "Christ, not Caesar, must be the final lord." Only the possibility that "young radicals for Christian truth" will rise up, and that the Messiah will come, can save the world from oblivion and destruction. But with each passing day the light of hope becomes dimmer. Its presence now is no brighter than the light of a candle flickering in strong wind. The world is nearly dark.

Much of the work that Francis and Edith Schaeffer started is being continued by their son Franky, who had been carefully groomed for such responsibilities. It is significant in this respect that Francis Schaeffer's last book, *The Great Evangelical Disaster,* and Franky Schaeffer's book, *Bad News for Modern Man: An Agenda for Christian Activism,* [27] were published at the same time, by the same publisher. Though the supporting illustrative materials are not the same, the respective arguments are. Francis Schaeffer concentrated on the plight of the church. Franky Schaeffer directed attention to the lack of spiritual vitality throughout the world. Each, it suffices to say, assessed the conditions they portrayed with dismay and alarm.

And yet the tone of Franky's injunctions is more intense, even strident. He calls Planned Parenthood "a highly lucrative murder industry," for example. He denounces television, saying he would sooner have Charles Manson educate his children than have them subjected to the influences of "the likes of Norman Lear." He refers to the permissive society as the one that licenses the mass production of babies, and then the mass murder of the same babies. Latchkey children are evidence that the society has collapsed. Biblical form-criticism has "bankrupted the churches." Both the National Council of Churches and the World Council of Churches have strong Marxist connections. The United Nations is no better. Wheaton College, traditionally a bastion of evangelical teaching, is criticized for being dominated by "pro-choice" professors. Former fundamentalists, who have subsequently written books that espouse a progressivist philosophy, are identified as leaning toward Marxism. The American Civil Liberties Union, the National Organization for Women, the National Educational Association, and Equal Rights Amendment initiatives gain ground only within a society that is moving increasingly toward "statism," which, as in the Soviet Union, is totalitarianism.

The only recourse, for Franky Schaeffer, as for his father, is for Christian radicals to respond effectively. Christian colleges will have to become "think tanks of Christian resistance." Theological orthodoxy will have to become strengthened through its confrontation with secularism. Planned Parenthood's activities must be picketed; so too the network television stations. Biblical Christians will need to develop their own media expertise with greater efficiency, effectiveness, and power. Christian television programs must rival those of their opponents both in sophistication and in magnetic drawing power. National newspapers must be produced to contend against the alien, establishment press of the eastern seaboard (most of whose reporters and essayists hardly ever go to church). All of this involves taking one's stand "with the saints who have stood before." The alternative is to give "the field to the devil and his emissaries." Franky Schaeffer reminds his readers and hearers that the first Christians were thrown to the lions because they refused to worship Caesar. Then he poses the question: "Will you follow Peter who declared that Christ is Lord, or will you follow Judas? This is the crucial choice."[28]

I watched both of them in action together—father and son— in an emotion-filled rally. It was Francis Schaeffer's final appearance before his death. He entered the auditorium supported on each side by a strong assistant. Because of his weakened condition, he had to utter his final prophetic pronouncements while sitting in a chair, with the microphone attached to one of its arms. His audience knew that he was suffering a terminal illness. Seeing him in this condition, one recalled the story of the Apostle John, who, legend has it, when too weak to stand was carried into the Christian assemblies to remind the people of the message he had been bringing. In terms of the larger drama in which he had been playing a crucial part, Schaeffer's presence was as significant as whatever words he might be able to speak. To see him this way, the embattled Christian warrior now on the edge of death itself, was to sense the message even had he offered no more than a few words of greeting and encouragement.

It is difficult to be critical of the performance in a drama of such proportions. Yet, one cannot help but recall that the Apostle John is reported to have faced a similar situation with the admonition, "Little children, love one another." It is helpful to observe too, that the evidence a prophet amasses is always selective. The situations on which the prophet chooses to focus are always taken from a larger range of possibilities. Yes, the events chosen for commentary are selected because they can be fitted together to compose a compelling, even shocking scenario. Francis Schaeffer picked out certain items for emphasis because they enabled him to tell the story he wanted to tell. It is a story whose last chapter (or, perhaps, the one next to last) is designed to sound the alarm. Its plot line emphasizes that whatever hope there is transcends confidence in nations, civilizations, indeed, all of the ways of humankind in this world. Legitimate leaders are bound to have fallen victim to corruption. Schools of thought, one can be assured, have already encountered grave error. People of most religious persuasions have departed from the truth. Most of those people who deign to call themselves Christians are probably of a lukewarm or pretend variety. Almost all of the churches that are identified this way are flying under misleading or false banners. Most of the information on which misguided critical judgments are made is badly distorted. The media is also part of the conspiracy to confuse and lead astray. In Schaeffer's view, virtually everything one encounters is unreality—including the present version of the United States. Thus, the prophet can warn that unless something drastic and dramatic happens fast—and how could any but a transcendent remedy be sufficient?—civilization will be finished. Christians can anticipate no real winning in a world like this. But they are to live in the way that the prophets (Jeremiah of old, J. Gresham Machen of post-World War II America, and the Schaeffers themselves) recommend. The primary role of the prophet, the Schaeffers attest, is to call the people to repentance, the passageway from false to true reality.

One can find biblical warrants for the Schaeffer position, if one searches selectively enough, and reads the Scripture from this theological vantage point. But there are other perspectives on the subject, and there are biblical supports for additional and alternative views. In this regard, there is nothing in the religion that forces the reader of the Bible to place emphasis upon Jesus' words, "I have come to bring a sword," to the virtual exclusion of any personal attention to the need to create a society in which justice and righteousness prevail. There is nothing in the religion that requires the believer to fix attention on biblical and/or dogmatic statements that speak of the exclusivity of Jesus Christ without regard for the statements attesting that the God Christians worship is the God of all peoples, who desires the well-being of all the earth.

Interpretations of the Bible are both drawn from and brought to the Bible. The Schaeffers have found the Bible to be enormously fertile illustrative ground by which to enunciate a theism that certifies world-denial. But the viewpoint is instinctual and temperamental before it is exegetical and interpretive. Its most compelling instinctual appeal is to the conviction that truth—deep and abiding truth—can only be identified by a small minority of the people, and then can only be uttered with a lonely voice. The Schaeffers believe that those who steadfastly desire to live the life that the gospel of Christ enjoins should simply expect it to be this way. They will never be in the majority. The hostility toward them will not cease until their deaths. For, if it did, they would fear that they have not been living resolutely enough.

Nicolai F. S. Grundtvig, the great nineteenth-century Danish theologian, poet and bishop, saw it another way. Grundtvig was fond of employing the principle "human first, then Christian"[29] to clarify for believers how they were to relate to others, and understand their own status in a world that is understood to be the creation of a living God. According to Grundtvig's view, any diminishment or foreshortening of any natural human capacity, even in support of the cause of religion, constitutes a direct violation of this divinely ordered formula.

Francis Schaeffer would take Grundtvig's dictum, and reverse the sequence: Christian first, then human. He believed it to be an essential article of faith that the genuinely human is that which is born-again. This, then, is to limit the genuinely human to that which is specifically Christian. It is to require a person to become a born-again Christian if human life is to possess substantial and enduring worth. And the world itself must be reborn too if it is to become the occasion for any genuine satisfaction or pleasure.

Certainly the rules of a democracy must be elastic enough to protect the Francis Schaeffers of the world—that is, those critics, protestors, and reformers of the society who often offer compelling evidence of wanting to be somewhere else. But a democracy ceases being a democracy when it becomes subject to some law or program requiring it to be thoroughly transformed before it can be validated. Schaeffer has every right, of course, to work for improvements within American life, to encourage greater dedication to the ongoing and necessary pursuit of the common good, and to make certain that the freedoms of the Republic are resilient and accessible. But his intentions are much bolder. Approaching every form of faith in humanity with deepest suspicion, and manifesting a kind of "world-weariness" of his own, his only recourse is to advocate some idealized alternative that can only be portrayed in the very sharpest contrast to the order of life that prevails.

As it turns out, J. Gresham Machen does not stand as the only parallel to Francis Schaeffer in the annals of the history of the Church. As far back as the second and third centuries C.E.—very close to the time period Schaeffer regards as being normative—the Christians often had difficulty distinguishing biblical faith from a prominent variant called Gnosticism. Though Gnostic theology sounded very much like normative Christian theology, and was communicated through some of the same words and concepts, while drawing upon a similar mythology, its basic intent was world-denial rather than world-affirmation. In denouncing it, some of the Apostolic Fathers affirmed the reality of God in this world, and went to considerable length to safeguard the status of the creation. In fact, one such teacher, St. Irenaeus, Bishop of Lyons, talked of the gospel in terms of the vision of "Christ extended lengthwise throughout the entire created world." The force of the imagery was to affirm that if this world is merely a shadow, or a dim reflection of that transcendent, idealized world, then God is not truly God. Irenaeus was insistent that the world that human beings experience enjoys real status, which status is undermined when the present world is too sharply distinguished and too thoroughly separated from some idealized society. Furthermore, when declaring that "the glory of God is a human being fully alive," Irenaeus also attested that "the creation is suited to man, for man was not made for creation's sake, but creation was made for the sake of man." Irenaeus's affirmations apply to this world, and to his own society, as decadent as it may or may not have been, and not to some idealized alternative thereto. Because of its insistence on the real status of this world—which status is confirmed by the fact that Jesus Christ partook of real flesh—the Christianity Irenaeus espoused is sharply divergent from the Gnostic viewpoint. This, too, is why the Church Fathers judged Gnosticism to be the most potent and dangerous rival to orthodox

Christian faith. Though it was dressed out as an authentic version, it proved, on closer examination, to be a thoroughly misleading facsimile.

It is a serious charge to make, but it is apparent that Schaeffer has fashioned a version of the Gnostic attitude, has offered it as authentic Christian teaching, and has employed the force of its intrinsic dualism to bring judgment against contemporary American society as well as Western culture. One can find compelling evidence, in contemporary American life, that judgment and criticism are appropriate. But the effective prophets within the biblical tradition did more than cast judgment: they also offered a redemptive proposal, to assist those who lay under judgment to find some compelling way out. In the Schaeffer version, redemption is to be found in some idealized and supernatural alternative to the human situation as human beings know and experience it.

Once again, what Irenaeus attested against the Gnostics centuries ago must be attested to again: That which deserves to be improved, and perhaps needs to be transformed, must first be acknowledged, and must always be affirmed. When Irenaeus made this profession, he understood that he was offering a testament of authentic Christian faith. When the nation's Founding Fathers described the workings of democracy, they knew themselves to be declaring that this world too is of God.

CHAPTER FOUR

A PROMINENT
COURT CASE

Bob Jones University, in Greenville, South Carolina, is a bastion of fundamentalist Christian teaching. It is the school from which many of the leaders of the New Religious Right received their undergraduate education as well as much of their training for the Christian ministry. Through the years the school has attracted some public attention because of the provocative and sometimes inflammatory pronouncements of one or another of the three Bob Joneses who have served as its leaders. But nothing that has happened there could begin to match the attention Bob Jones University received after the Internal Revenue Service declared that the institution's restricted admissions policy was in violation of the Civil Rights Act, and thus the university could not qualify for tax-exempt status.

I visited the campus once, during the height of the controversy, because I was curious—curious about the school, and intrigued by the case that had been heard by several courts, and was soon to be tested before the U.S. Supreme Court. It was an easy visit to arrange. I simply telephoned the school, asked to speak to Bob Jones's secretary, with whom I requested an interview. I explained that I teach courses on contemporary developments in American religion, and coveted the opportunity to talk with someone who could interpret the attitude and position of the school from the inside.

After I arrived at Mr. Jones's office, I was introduced to Roy A. Barton, Jr., the business manager of the school, who also carried major responsibility for dealing with the officials of the Internal Revenue Service. Since 1976 they had been journeying to the campus to examine official records to determine the extent of the alleged violations. Barton is the one who had the assignment to explain the university's position both to the federal agents and to people, like myself, who were drawn to the institution because of the case.

"Bob Jones University began more than fifty years ago," he began. "In those days we could have established a school exclusively for bow-legged boys under twelve years of age, and no one would have thought we were violating anything. But the climate was different then."[1]

Barton explained that this is the problem. In the years since 1927, when the Reverend Bob Jones, Sr., established the school, national public opinion has adopted a left-of-center orientation while the sponsors of the school have simply tried to remain obedient to the principles upon which the institution was founded. It isn't that they feel obligated to buck the trends, whatever they are. Nor is it that they would prefer to be somewhere else, and in some other time period, rather than here, in the southeastern section of the United States, dealing with the challenges of the last quarter of the twentieth century. The point is that the founders of Bob Jones University firmly intended to base the purpose and life of the institution solidly on the teachings of the Bible. They understood biblical principles to be permanent, inviolable, and unaffected by the whimsy of collective human opinion.

"The school's philosophy is that whatever the Bible says is so," Barton continued. "The truths of the Bible do not change. Scripture is inerrant." He has reasoned that if there was a divine revelation— he has confidence about this—that revelation was meant to be understood, and the one responsible for issuing it intended that the rules be kept. Human life is marked by challenges and uncertainties, but human beings have been given reliable guidance. Disorientation, confusion and prolonged personal disequilibrium were not intended to be facts of life. In Barton's view, the criticisms and hostility that have been directed toward the school are signs of the world's persistent resistance to the only truth that really matters. "The world is changing rapidly. Religion is changing too. But Bob Jones University continues to hold to the same position. No wonder the world is ill at ease with us."

Roy Barton took his viewpoint to be both thoroughly Christian and appropriately American. He knew himself to be a patriotic citizen, fully committed to the ideals of the nation. For years he has been active in local politics, and has always understood this involvement to be an important ingredient in his Christian vocation, thoroughly compatible too with the responsibilities he carries at the university. The stimulation of the same combination of involvements is one of the prime objectives of the school. "The country needs the type of person we graduate," he stated. Included in this is a proven ability to succeed in a rigorous academic setting. Everyone on campus is committed to making the institution thoroughly competitive, in academic terms, with the very best colleges and universities in the region. The mode of citizenship the school enjoins also includes the cultivation of individual independence. Students are motivated to become self-sufficient, always dependent upon the grace of God, but never looking to the government or some other agency for assistance.

Barton's brief description of some of the formative characteristics of Christian citizenship provide an opening to talk more specifically about the administrative principles of the university. He is pleased that the institution is debt free, in spite of the fact that it has been forced to spend well over a million dollars in recent years in court expenses related to the Internal Revenue Service challenge. The school carries no mortgages. And it has steadfastly refused to be tainted by accepting government money. How could Bob Jones University ever become subservient to external control?

Roy Barton found it gratifying too that the institution has been able to attract a dedicated faculty of Christian scholars and teachers who are willing to labor sacrificially at relatively low salaries. The salary schedule is not competitive, but the ones who dedicate their lives to the cause are not out to make a lot of money. "Look around the campus," Barton urged, "and you will see ten-year-old Fords and Plymouths. Few among our faculty drive new cars."

The inside story is that students are drawn to BJU because they know of its reputation and choose what it stands for. Roy Barton is pleased that there has been very little trouble on campus. When other institutions were experiencing significant upheaval,

Bob Jones University remained calm and industrious. The school's administration likes to contrast what did not happen here with what was happening elsewhere during the riotous 1960s. The following contrast appears in the commemorative booklet celebrating the silver anniversary of the university in 1977.

> In 1964 campus unrest erupted at the Berkeley campus of the University of California, and set off a chain-reaction of radicalism and disruption that has affected almost every school. In many American universities, goals have become obscure. Confusion reigns. Every vestige of discipline has toppled, the victim of protestors and demonstrators. The sick-sweet smell of marijuana wafts into the corridors of the average American college. Coed dormitories dominate an increasing number of campuses.
>
> During the 1960s, while many campuses were being physically destroyed by their students, BJU was building to accommodate hers—a science building with a planetarium, two new dormitories, a new dining common, a ninety-bed hospital, a million-dollar apartment building for faculty and staff, new faculty homes, a new administration office wing, and an expanded art gallery.[2]

There was little on-campus trouble in the turbulent 1960s. Apparently there has been little trouble since. But the rules are strictly enforced. Everyone is made to understand, in the language of the *Bulletin* of the school, that "attendance at Bob Jones University is a privilege and not a right."

The inside viewpoint also has it that everything was going well at the institution until government-blessed "outside agitators" moved in. "There wasn't any trouble here at all," Barton attested, "until 1964 with the passing of the Civil Rights Act. When that Act was passed we began seeing the warning signals." But the real "trouble" did not occur until 1970 when the administration of the school was asked to sign the Civil Rights Compliance Act, and refused to on religious grounds. When it refused, the IRS informed the university that the tax exemption it had enjoyed would be withdrawn. In 1971 the university requested a court injunction against the Internal Revenue Service to prevent it from doing this. After a series of decisions and appeals at the lower courts, the case reached the United States Supreme Court where, in 1974, the Court ruled that the IRS could not be stopped from doing something it hadn't yet done. But in January 1976, the school's tax-exempt status was revoked. And on December 26, 1978, a federal district court ruled that the university was entitled to a tax-exempt status as a religious organization.

The Internal Revenue Service appealed the decision of the federal court, and, in 1980, the Fourth Circuit Court of Appeals of South Carolina reversed the district court's decision. Bob Jones University appealed the decision of the court of appeals, and asked that the case be heard by the Supreme Court. While campaigning for presidential office, at a rally in Greenville, Ronald Reagan deplored the situation, and promised to rectify it if he were elected.

On January 8, 1982, the Reagan administration announced that it was abandoning the IRS policy, and that it would move to dismiss the Bob Jones case on the ground of mootness. The announcement provoked an outcry from civil rights groups. A few days later the Reagan administration retreated, declaring that it would initiate legislation to give the IRS the authority to deny tax-exempt status to discriminatory private schools. The legislative initiative languished in Congress; it could find no champions anywhere. And the Treasury Department was prepared to grant tax-exempt status to the university. But, on February 18, 1982, the Court of Appeals for the District of Columbia Circuit issued an order temporarily barring the Treasury and the IRS from granting tax exemptions to racially discriminatory private schools. With the Treasury's hands tied by the order, the case ceased to be moot. The government then went back to the Supreme Court, and asked the Justices to decide the case after all. The case was heard on October 12, 1982, and, on May 24, 1983, the Court ruled against Bob Jones University and the Goldsboro Christian Schools by an 8–1 margin.[3]

The decisions that have come have been rendered in legal terms, for the issue has been approached within the context of U.S. constitutional law. But the Bob Jones community views the matter as a religious drama. In the Joneses' view, the university is involved in a contest, as St. Paul puts it in the Bible, between the "powers and principalities"—the forces, many of which are diabolical, against which Christians must always contend. Jones himself has said on more than one occasion:

> It is most significant that there is not a question of cutting off the tax exemption of institutions that are training militant blacks, revolutionaries, communists, and arsonists. No attempt has been

made to take away tax exemptions from institutions which have communists and revolutionaries on their faculty—men and women who are seeking to overthrow America and train young people for that purpose—but the government is trying to discriminate against a Christian institution that is peaceful, patriotic, and seeking to train spiritual young men and women who will go out and make a real contribution to America.[4]

On that day, Jones added: "We feel that the whole cause of Christ is at stake in this matter." He vowed that Bob Jones University would "fight for fairness and freedom for all Christian educational institutions and churches in America." I have given emphasis to this quotation because it also helps explain why the New Religious Right came into being. When the freedom of their educational institutions were threatened by governmental decisions, upholders of the tradition understood that authentic Christianity was also under siege. It is significant, in this respect, that Robert Billings, the founder of the National Christian Action Coalition, and the first president of the Moral Majority, is a graduate of Bob Jones University.

Roy Barton stressed this point too when he enjoined: "Read the Constitution and the Bill of Rights, and you'll find that what is happening in this country just ain't America anymore." And as he spoke, he looked like a man in mourning, who, though he has told the same story many times, experiences the shock and hurt no less each time.

The fact is that Bob Jones University did indeed change its admission policies in 1975 to admit all persons regardless of race. The statement in its current *Bulletin* reads as follows: "Along with all other educational institutions, Bob Jones University is now required by law to admit students of any race to all rights, privileges, programs and activities generally accorded or made available to students at the University." This principle is made even more explicit in the following: "The University does not discriminate on the basis of race in the administration of its educational policies, admission policies, scholarship and loan programs, and athletic and other-administered programs." But, while the admissions policy was modified, the school insisted on a firm and published prohibition against interracial dating. Since 1975, this is the policy that is being challenged as being racially discriminatory.

"Is this discrimination?" Barton asked. "Discrimination against whom?" Without waiting for a reply, he continued: "We treat all exactly alike. All are given the same opportunities. Each has access to the same privileges. In fact, I'll bet we have less prejudice here than almost anywhere. But one of the reasons is that everyone who attends Bob Jones University knows that it is a privilege and not a right."

"They come here to learn how to live. They desire a strict dress code. They want to live within the rules we set out for dating. But the details are not as important as the principles. Kids are happier when they have rules laid out for them."

If I had insisted, Roy Barton would have provided me with an event-by-event account of the school's ongoing battle against the United States government. But we both thought it preferable to take a tour of the campus—a walk with conversation, that brought us to the dining commons and lunch with Dr. Bob Jones III and his wife, Beneth.

After all he had been through, I expected Jones to be a bit wary of another interview with still another person who had come onto the campus from the outside, and this one from a "secular university" in another section of the country. But I found him courteous, amiable, and eager to be of assistance. Jones is the grandson of the founder of the university, Bob Jones, Sr., who died in 1979 and is buried in the center of a mote near the entrance to the campus. Jones's father, Bob Jones, Jr., is chancellor of the university and chairman of its board of directors. There is a Bob Jones IV, living under the expectation that he will succeed his father as his father has succeeded his own father and grandfather. But, currently, Bob Jones III is the Bob Jones who is most visibly in charge.

"Look all around here," he encouraged. "You'll see that this is a remarkably wholesome place. The people are happy. They love and trust one another. Their families are strong and industrious." Then, shifting his demeanor, Jones made the application. "Our people are not out there killing babies," he entreated. "You don't find our women reacting and rebelling, while leaving the care of their children to other people. We're not out to stir up trouble." (Pause) "Now, please tell me, sir, if you can, why is the United States government harrassing us?"

The question went unanswered. Acknowledging that neither

of us would elect to pursue the matter further, Jones described his grandfather who insisted that BJU be established on scriptural principles. He believed he had a call from God to do so. Even in 1927, Jones's motivation was that "the old American values seem to be slipping away, replaced in many eyes by the spectacle of gin-guzzling college boys and joyriding coeds; of bootlegger heroes who could produce a case of good Scotch; of crooked politicians who cracked jokes with fancy-Dan hoodlums." When taking the initiative to found his institution, Jones explained, "There ought to be a school that isn't afraid of the devil, founded by a man who doesn't mind being kicked around, who's used to being cuffed about." As he told more stories about his grandfather, Bob Jones III reiterated that this was the spirit that guided the institution from its founding. But this only brought us back to the controversial matter again. "For decades we were left alone, to do what we wanted to do. Then the liberals came to power in the sixties, and everything changed." He added that the institution is certain that it has been victimized by the federal government's campaign to utilize its own agencies to enforce questionable policies of detrimental social change. "We believe these policies are contrary to the changeless Word of God," Jones explained, "so we feel we must resist. We have tried to be cooperative. But we've gone as far as we can go."

"Look," the grandson Jones remonstrated, as if I had been offering some opposition, "I don't want to go to jail. I don't want war. We prefer peace. I tell my people, 'We don't want war, and we don't want to go to jail.' But it may end up that way. We may have to go to jail."

He spoke softly, pleadingly And in the quiet I observed the same combination of sadness, confusion, and fatigue in his eyes that I had witnessed earlier in the day while talking with Roy Barton.

"You are really talking about war, and you are saying that the war has already begun," I commented.

"Yes, the war has started," Jones replied.

I asked if this helps explain the emotionally charged comments he had offered on television against Alexander Haig, who, at the time, was serving as Secretary of State. Jones seemed a bit startled by the reference, but he knew what I was talking about. On that day, speaking from his pulpit to an overflow crowd in the campus auditorium as well as to the television audience that is reached by the stations which carry his program, Jones had said: "I hope you'll pray that the Lord will smite him [Haig] hip and thigh, bone and marrow, heart and lungs and all there is to him, that he shall destroy him quickly and utterly." A few minutes earlier he had called Haig "a monster in human flesh and a demon-possessed instrument to destroy America."[5]

I proposed to him that this is unusually strong language—accusatory, vitriolic, highly inflammatory—and observed that he had gotten bad press wherever the incident was reported. I asked him if he had really meant to say this, or if he had succumbed to the heat of the moment.

"I truly intended it," he responded. But he wanted to explain the context. The remarks were made to a pastoral conference which had been organized in Greenville and to which the Reverend Ian Paisley of Northern Ireland had also been invited as principal speaker. On the very day of his expected journey to the United States, Paisley was informed by the U.S. State Department that he was not being granted a visa. Jones was infuriated by this, and attributed the decision to Secretary Haig himself. He also interpreted the event according to the available categories in the narrative he draws upon to explain why such things happen to followers of the Lord, and he saw it as "Catholic bigotry." Haig, surrounded by Catholic colleagues, was showing favoritism. Nothing like this happened when Pope John Paul II was invited into the country. All of this prompted Jones to tell his audience, "I am going to pray that God will get rid of that man."

This is belligerent language which, understandably, raised questions and criticisms even among Jones's followers and supporters. Consequently, Bob Jones, Jr., issued a statement to explain why his son had spoken this way, admitting that "even some good friends have seemed to find these remarks shocking and alarming." Jones wanted to put things in context and perspective. "How long has it been since you heard a sermon on one of the imprecatory Psalms of David?" he asked. "How long since a preacher took as his text the cry of the souls under the altar who pray for God to avenge their blood upon their persecutors?" Then Jones observed, "sometimes some of us must take positions that from a human standpoint will be thought unwise and harsh in order to stir God's people to proper concern for the loss of our religious freedoms, the bitter attacks upon those who preach the Book, and the attempts to stifle the strong voice of a prophetic preacher like Ian Paisley." He added that "it would be nice . . . if our text could be, 'For God so loved the world. . . . ' It gives us great joy to deal with these subjects; but there is a Biblical command to reprove, rebuke, and exhort."

But the strong, combative, vitriolic language is not confined to isolated, momentary outbursts in sermons. The periodical, *Faith for the Family,* that Jones edits is replete with the same kind of materials conveyed in the same tone of voice. Jones has utilized the publication to denounce the United Nations and The World Council of Churches because each is "determined to produce discord, trouble and strife all around the world." He has accused John Paul II of "preaching the Communist line" in all of his visits around the world.[6] When the Pope was shot by a would-be assassin in Rome on May 13, 1981, Jones wrote:

> However much one may regret assassination attempts and violence, no matter against whom it is directed, it could be that the injuries received by the pope in the assassination attempt . . . may curtail his world travels. If so, this could be God's way of answering the prayers of His people.[7]

Jones's comment on Bishop Raymond Hunthausen of Seattle—the one who counseled his people not to pay the portion of their taxes spent on military armaments—was that "he stands for the Communist line" that "will deliver us into the hands of those who would take over this nation, destroy our liberties, and enslave both mind and body." Jones made it clear that his negative opinion of Bishop Hunthausen reaches beyond to the church (or, rather, antichurch) he represents: "The very fact that a Catholic Bishop can preach [against paying taxes] . . . and go unrebuked by the ecclesiastical authority he represents is further indication that the Roman church is, like apostate protestantism, the church of Antichrist."[8] But Jones hasn't been any more pleased with either Billy Graham or Jerry Falwell, two evangelists whom many would regard as being much closer to him on doctrinal and attitudinal grounds.

The quarrel with Graham goes back to the time Jones's father refused to support the evangelistic crusade Graham sponsored in Greenville. Jones threatened to expel any Bob Jones University student who became involved in the crusade in any way. The problem with Falwell, in Jones's eyes, is that he appears to be growing more and more into the likeness of Billy Graham. He has taken soft stands that are too liberal on a wide variety of issues. He has become soft on Catholics. He has fraternized with persons who do not uphold the strict fundamentalist point of view. He has exploited his evangelistic office for personal gain. Jones has gone to great lengths to illustrate that the rigorous fundamentalist Christianity he stands for should never be identified with whatever precepts—he is not sure what they are—the Moral Majority is advocating. Indeed, Bob Jones, Jr., has been adamant about the evils of the Moral Majority. He sees its influence as being far more damaging to the sanctity of religious truth than even that of Billy Graham. Indeed, the twin influences of Graham and Falwell belong to the same phenomenon:

> First, the devil attacked us with cooperative evangelism as exemplified by Dr. Graham. That Dr. Graham has become an apostate is beyond question in view of his praise of the Pope, the World Council of Churches, and almost everything else that is rotten in our world ecclesiastically. Then the devil came along with the so-called charismatic movement, trying to bring together weak, untaught, and disobedient Christians on the basis of an emotional deception. Now he comes along with a moral crusade that incorporates an appeal to patriotism as well.[9]

Then, noting that he has spent a lifetime watching evangelists destroy authentic biblical faith, he confessed that he has never been as concerned as he is right now. Simply put, he continued, "I consider Jerry Falwell the most dangerous man in America today as far as Biblical Christianity is concerned." Jones admitted that Falwell is likable and exudes charm. "But he is a man who is either completely lacking in spiritual discernment, or has, like Ahab, sold himself to do evil."[10]

The clash between Bob Jones, Jr., and Jerry Falwell became dramatic in June 1980 when each used the official publication of his organization to denounce the other. Jones initiated the encounter when, in the June 10, 1980, edition of his *Faith for the Family,* he branded the Moral Majority "one of Satan's devices to build the world church of Antichrist." In his newest guise, Jones explained, the devil "comes along with a moral crusade that incorporates an appeal to patriotism." Jones also objected to

Falwell's practice of introducing persons of questionable Christian standing on his television programs. He didn't like it at all that Falwell didn't mention to his audience that Phyllis Schlafly is "a devout Roman Catholic" when praising the antifeminist leader. But even more reprehensible was Falwell's Sunday-morning use of "the much-married Elizabeth Taylor," a practice which, according to Jones, "raises doubts about how genuinely concerned he is about moral standards" since "Elizabeth Taylor is a perfect example of the thing that he is supposed to be crusading against." Jones contended that Falwell has already sold himself to the causes of evil, and has used moral deception to encourage Christians "into alliance with apostasy." Strong words.

Falwell responded on June 26, 1980, in his *Fundamentalist Journal,* that he had no intention of running for the presidency, and that the Moral Majority was not striving to unite persons of differing religious faiths but, instead, "to maintain religious freedoms in this nation so that we can maintain our religious practices regardless of how different they may be." He added that without such an effort "America could well lose her freedom." And on questions concerning Elizabeth Taylor and Phyllis Schlafly, Falwell noted that Jones had once called Betty Ford a "slut," and that President Ford "wisely made no comment." The Lynchburg evangelist wanted it recorded that he was following the same policy. He reiterated that God has blessed America for two hundred years because of the nation's moral stance and that he believed it important, for the sake of the welfare of the nation, that there be a return to such fundamental principles.

Jones wasn't satisfied. In the September 1980 issue of *Faith for the Family* he stressed that he liked Jerry Falwell as a person but found his movement to lack scriptural warrants. Christians are to be thoroughly engaged. The Moral Majority is not dedicated to regeneration, Jones charged, but to modest reformation, a kind of cleaning-up activity: "It is folly to think that when America's moral problems are solved, we can be a strong nation again. The lack of morality in America is a direct result of her lacking fear of God and her lacking obedience to the Word of God." Instead of endorsing and assisting the Moral Majority, Jones urged *true Christians* to find "the soul-satisfying contentment of being a scriptural minority."

Bob Jones III has taken the same line. He has denounced

Falwell's efforts because he sees it as being an ecumenical movement in which real religious differences are minimized. But he is particularly opposed to Falwell's programmatic use of morality. As Jones sees it, Falwell's intentions, if accomplished, would run counter to the fundamental goals of the gospel. "We do not need the moral rearmament of the Moral Majority," he explains. "We need moral disarmament. We need the foundation of morality and self-righteousness stripped from those who claim it so that they might see themselves the sinners they are." In Jones's view, the irony is that if the Moral Majority is successful, it will be more difficult to evangelize the nation. To pray, as Falwell enjoins, that America might be restored to the greatness that once insured the blessing of God, is to work against the deeper purposes of God, not on behalf of them.

As he told me of his concern, and why he is opposed to Falwell and all of the others with whom he has felt compelled to do battle, it was as if he was pleading for understanding and empathy. He wished so much that others would see it his way. He needs to be vitriolic at times, he explained, and to sound mean, because the truth is at stake, and the stakes are high. He very much wanted me to be able to see it this way as well. He was able to offer very inflammatory judgments about other people with a strong smile on his face. All of it came with a "don't you see?" attitude, with no other visible signs of being upset, as if he was still very far from reaching an emotional boiling point. There was anger in the words, and, no doubt, deep anger in the man. But in the visage—in the eyes, and on the face—there was a strong attempt to be ruled by a calm demeanor.

I can only explain such disjunctures by citing what I know to be Jones's understanding of the biblical injunction, "Judge not that you not be judged." To him this does not mean that Christians are not to judge other people, but, instead, that they are not to judge hypocritically, as though they themselves—rather than God, the only true judge—are rendering evaluative, even condemnatory decisions. Jones quoted his grandfather's dictum: "Never judge things by what you see; judge what you see by what God's Word says about what you see." In his view, Christians are called upon to make spiritual judgments throughout the day because they possess "the mind of the Lord." He had explained this in a sermon: "God's Word is the mind of the Lord, and when you make a judgment according to God's word, you judge not on the basis of the way things look, but on the basis of God's description of the way those things look in His eyes." This policy supports the naming of names from the pulpit. "Faithful preachers should name religious deceivers and expose them . . . so that hearers may avoid them." This principle applies to Alexander Haig, Popes Paul VI and John Paul II, hippies, communists, womens' liberation advocates, arsonists, agitators, Billy Graham, Jerry Falwell, Moral Majority supporters, idolaters of rock music, yes, virtually anyone who opposed sacred truth. And Jones covered his own motives by expressing his denunciations in the words of scripture. Thus it is the word of God that speaks and not just somebody being hypocritical.

The supporters of the contentions of Bob Jones University, in the case that was heard by the Supreme Court, wish to contend that the world should understand that they are upholding a cardinal principle of religious liberty rather than taking a side in a dispute over racial issues. Jones explained it this way in an editorial that appeared in the *Washington Post* on January 24, 1982: "The fundamental point at issue is freedom—freedom to exercise a sincere religious faith without taxation because an agency disagrees with your beliefs."[11] But this is the way Bob Jones has learned to describe it after years of experience jousting with courts, judges, official representatives of the Internal Revenue Service, as well as critics who have come at him from all sides. And it is an opinion that befits the situation after 1975 when the university altered its admissions policy to allow blacks to enter. Prior to 1975 Bob Jones University did not admit blacks. Even after it was urged to comply with the Civil Rights Act of 1964—as requested in letters of 1970—it maintained a closed-admissions policy. Even after the change in admission in 1975, though no one will say this openly, the administration of Bob Jones University would prefer not to admit blacks. What they will say is that they vehemently oppose the mixing of races. To anyone who inquires about the basis of this conviction, the university provides a summary statement which reads, in part, as follows:

We believe . . . that the Bible in its entirety clearly indicates that God has separated people for His own good purpose. He has erected barriers between the nations—not only land and sea barriers but also ethnic, cultural and language barriers. God has made people different one from another and intends for those differences to remain. . . .

Any violation of God's original purpose manifests insubordination to Him, and no Christian has any business being involved in any such practice.[12]

Perceptions of the present drama in the world are reflected in the next paragraph in the same statement:

The world, during the great tribulation as described in the Book of Revelation, will be ruled over by the Antichrist, ruler of the one-world system. The current agitation to bring races together, to obliterate differences and distinctions between them, is a Satanic effort; and no Christian has any right contributing to that which is going to build the world of Antichrist. He can't do that and love Christ too.[13]

The final paragraph in the statement reiterates the reasons the university is maintaining the stand it has taken:

Bob Jones University is opposed to intermarriage of the races because it breaks down the barriers God has established. It mixes that which God separated and intends to keep separate. Every effort in world history to get the world together has demonstrated man's arrogance against God and his unwillingness to remain as God ordains. The attempts at one-worldism have been to devise a system without God and have fostered the promotion of a unity designed to give the world strength so that God is not needed and can be overthrown. We want no part of that. We cannot be true to the Lord and true to one-worldism; and it is for that reason we stand as we do.[14]

The point: no problem occurs as long as a people remains within the territory that God has fixed as the bounds of their habitation. Indeed, it is even inappropriate to talk about the superiority and/or inferiority of the races with respect to each other:

You talk about a superior race and an inferior race and all that kind of situation. Wait a minute. No race is inferior in the will of God. Get that clear. If a race is in the will of God, it is not inferior. It is a superior race. You cannot be superior to another race if your race is in the will of God and the other race is in the will of God.[15]

Then, then, is what Jones perceived to have happened to upset the racial equilibrium God established:

> What happened? Well, away back yonder our forefathers went over to Africa and brought the colored people back and sold them into slavery. That was wrong. But God overruled. When they came over here, many of them did not know the Bible and did not know about Jesus Christ; but they got converted. . . .
> God Almighty allowed these colored people to be turned here into the South and overruled what happened, and then He turned the colored people in the South into wonderful Christian people. For many years we have lived together. Occasionally there will be a flare-up. But the white people have helped the colored people build their churches, and we have gotten along together harmoniously and peacefully; and everything has come along fine. Sometimes we have a little trouble, but then we adjust everything sensibly and get back to the established order. . . . No two races ever lived as close together as the white people and the colored people here in the South and got along so well.[16]

The university's spokespersons have tried to be consistent when testifying. For example, when asked by the U.S. District Court in Greenville, on May 10, 1978, to clarify his position on the subject—in response to the question "does the university have any religious belief concerning the mixing of the races or the racial issue?"—Jones replied: "Yes, sir, we always have. And if the Court would like, I could turn to a few passages of scripture and discuss those matters."[17] Jones admitted that it was the desire of "rendering to Caesar what is Caesar's" that motivated the school to change its admissions policies in 1975. But he explained that it was still necessary to maintain strict rules against interracial dating and marriage. On this there could be no change of policy. Jones explained:

> We are a law-abiding people. The Lord says, "Render to Caesar what is Caesar's." Caesar has said in this case, "You have to open your doors. You can't any longer do without tax-exemption or do without whatever you have to do without in order to abide by your convictions in this regard." So, we said, "All right, we will not sacrifice our convictions against interracial dating and marriage. We will still enforce it as it's always been enforced." We think it may be more difficult to enforce it now, but our conviction was not against the admission of blacks. Our conviction was against interracial

dating and marriage. And our admission policy previous to 1975 was the easiest way we knew, the safest way, to protect that conviction.[18]

Jones also admitted that the change of policy in May 1975 went against his better judgment. The court reminded him of the statement he had made in 1971 when the pressure from the government first began to be felt:

> I . . . believe that if Bob Jones University were to admit members of the Negro race, that the university would be promoting such intermarriage and would be providing conditions under which such intermarriage is more likely to occur contrary to religious beliefs and practices upon which the university was founded and has been continuously operated.[19]

But he explained that since the Court no longer "afforded the luxury" of allowing the school to maintain the policy that provides the surest safeguards against interracial dating and marriage, Bob Jones University is "protecting the conviction the best way we know how."

To get some sense of the struggle that was taking place within the mind of Bob Jones, one must compare his more current attitude with one that was rather prominent in such circles even in those years prior to the time the Civil Rights Act was enacted. On July 17, 1960, Bob Jones, Sr., delivered a sermon on the theme "Is Segregation Scriptural" over Radio Station WMUU, and addressed himself particularly to the increase in racial trouble that could be found throughout the world. On that occasion, Jones said:

> . . . we are living in the midst of race turmoil all over the world today. Look at what they are facing in Africa, and look at what we are facing in this country. It is all contrary to Scripture. It is all contrary to the Word of God. I am going to show you that the Bible is perfectly clear on races—just as clear as it can be.[20]

To the supposition that "God is the Father of everybody," Jones responded emphatically: "No, He is not. God is the Father of born-again people." He explained what he meant this way:

> There is no trouble between a born-again white man and a born-again colored man or a born-again Chinese or a born-again Japanese. Born-again, Bible-believing Christians do not have

trouble. They may not understand some things, but when we give them the Word of God for it, they see it and understand it.

Jones further attested that he was providing the biblical position on the controversial subject. He based his claim on an interpretation of the sermon of St. Paul on Mars Hill in Athens, as reflected in chapter 17 of *The Acts of the Apostles.* It was in this famous sermon that Paul talked about the God who does "not dwell in buildings made with hands." What Jones liked most about the sermon is the line recorded in verse 26, wherein Paul says, "And he hath made of one blood all nations of men to dwell on the face of the earth, and hath fixed the boundaries of their habitations." Jones commented:

> It is no accident that most Chinese are in China. There has been an overflow in the world, but most Chinese live in China. There are millions and millions of them there, and there are no greater people in the world. I have never known lovelier and more wonderful people than the Chinese.

But the moral of the story is clear: "When nations break out of their boundaries and begin to do things contrary to the purpose of God and the directive will of God, they have trouble." More specifically:

> The Chinese people are wonderful people. The Japanese people are ingenious—they are wonderful people. The Koreans are wonderful people. The Africans are wonderful people. In many ways, there are no people in the world finer than the colored people who were brought over here in slavery in days gone by.

He is talking about the past, to be sure. And he feels the need to bring the chronicle up to date:

> Now, what is the matter? There is an effort today to disturb the established order. Wait a minute. Listen, I am talking straight to you. White folks and colored folks, you listen to me. You cannot run over God's plan and God's established order without having trouble. God never meant to have one race. It was not His purpose at all. God has a purpose for each race. God Almighty may have overruled and permitted the slaves to come over to America so that the colored people could be the great missionaries to the Africans. They could have been. The white people in America would have helped pay their way over there. By the hundreds and hundreds they

could have gone back to Africa and got the Africans converted after the slavery days were over.

Another try:

All right, now what is happening? Down in Africa there is trouble and turmoil. There is racial disturbance all over the world, and it is not of God. The Bible is clear on this. When people come along and say, "Well, God is the Father of everybody," they are wrong. He is not the Father of everybody. That is not in the Bible. That is a Satanic Lie.

Perhaps sensing that some within the sound of his voice will raise questions about the ways whites have treated blacks, Jones continued:

"Well," you say, "The colored folks have not been treated right." I agree with you. Neither have the poor white people been right. . . . But things are not going to be made right by trying to overthrow God's established order. . . . The colored people in the South today are better off than they are anywhere else in the world. The situation is not a perfect situation for the white folks or the colored folks or for anybody else, but we have never had a perfect situation in this world since Adam and Eve disobeyed God in the Garden of Eden.

Then it was time to repeat the fundamental insight:

All men, to whatever race they may belong, have immortal souls; but all men have mortal bodies, and God fixed the boundaries of the races of the world. Let me repeat that it is no accident that most of the Chinese live in China. It is not an accident that most Japanese live in Japan. And the Africans should have been left in Africa. And the gospel should have been taken to them as God commanded his people to do.

Providing some examples, Jones continued: "Whenever we have the races mixed up in large numbers, we have trouble. They have trouble in New York. They have trouble in San Francisco. They have trouble all over California."

But by now he has said the same lines over and over again, so many times, that it is as if he has been drawn into mortal combat with an unrelenting enemy, who, no matter how hard he struggles, continues to be formidable. What is worse: the churches are preaching a heresy.

For a man to stand up and preach sermons in this country, and talk
about rubbing out the line between the races—I say it makes me
sick. . . . The trouble today is that a Satanic agitation is striking
back at God's established order. That is what is making trouble for
us.

Significantly, while talking about the Chinese and Japanese,
Jones provided some insight into his attitude toward the Jews.

God gave every race something. He gave the Africans something. He
gave the Chinese something that he did not give the Japanese. He
gave races certain things. And he chose the Jews. They are the most
wonderful people who ever lived in the world. God chose them, and
God segregated them, not because they were inferior but because He
had a purpose for that race.

This is the basis for the separation (which Jones sometimes calls
"segregation") of the Jews. But, recently, Jones was pleased to
add, the Jews have been brought back to their homeland. His
interpretation:

The Jews are back in Palestine with a government today.
God scattered them, but he brought them back to their homeland.
I am for them, and I am for their homeland and for their
government. . . .
    Yes, God chose the Jews. If you are against segregation and
against racial separation, then you are against God Almighty
because He made racial separation in order to preserve the race
through whom He could send the Messiah and through whom He
could send the Bible.

To make it even more explicit: "God is the author of segregation.
God is the author of Jewish separation and Gentile separation and
Japanese separation. God made of one blood all nations, but He
also drew boundary lines between races."
    The next step in Jones's disquisition involves utilizing the
example of what was happened to the Jews to illuminate the
situation pertaining to blacks in the South.

The Jews have lived a separated race. They have been separated
from the other races of the world. They have been miraculously
preserved. Now they have a homeland. They are back there today,
and what a wonderful thing is happening.
    Now, you colored people listen to me. If you had not been

brought over here and if your grandparents in slavery days had not heard that great preaching, you might not even be a Christian. You might be over there in the jungles of Africa today, unsaved. But you are here in America where you have your own schools and your own liberties and your own rights, with certain restrictions that God almighty put about you—restrictions that are in line with the Word of God.

Dr. Jones had some lessons for his white listeners too:

You, white folks, listen to me. Just remember the good, old colored friends you had in the days gone by. I remember mine. I remember that old, colored woman who was with my wife's grandmother when she died. She used to be a nurse in the home way back in slavery days. I remember how my wife's grandmother said the happiest day she ever saw was when the slaves were freed. She owned hundreds of them, and she said, "I was so happy. I was afraid some of them would be lost; and I felt that God might hold me accountable." That spirit represented the Old South.

You say slavery was not right. Well, I say it was not right. I say the colored people should have been left over in Africa, and we should have sent missionaries over there and got them converted. That is what we should have done. But we could not have converted them as fast that way and God makes the wrath of men to praise Him. They were brought over here, and look what they have. They have their churches. They have a freedom here they do not have anywhere else in the world. They have an understanding here. Let's not wipe out the line of understanding.

Drawing upon the phrase "line of understanding" to make an additional point, Jones continued:

Whenever you get a situation that rubs out the line that God has drawn between races, whenever that happens, you are going to have trouble. That is what is happening today in this country. All this agitation is a Communistic agitation to overthrow the established order of God in this world. The Communistic influence is at work all about us. Certain people are disturbing this situation. They talk about the fact that we are going to have one world. We will never really have one world until this world heads up in God. We are not going to have one world by man's rubbing out the line that God has established. He is marking the lines, and you cannot rub them out and get away with it.

At the present time, according to this attitude, there are three classes of humanity: Jew (a segregated race), Gentile (including everyone else), and Christians. Among Christians "there are no Jews, no Gentiles, no white folks, no black folks," but all are "one in Christ." Within this framework, as Jones explained, "there is no trouble between a colored Christian and a white Christian," who operate "as individuals and deal with each other as Christians who have their citizenship in Heaven." There is a day coming when the situation will change: "Up in Heaven there will be no boundaries. We will be one forever with Christ. But we are not one down here, as far as race is concerned and as far as nations are concerned."

He concluded his sermon that day with the following prayer:

> Our heavenly Father, bless our country. We thank Thee for our ancestors. We thank Thee for the good Christian people—white and black. We thank Thee for the ties that have bound these Christian white people and Christian colored people together through the years, and we thank Thee that white people who had a little more money helped them build their churches and stood by them and when they got sick, they helped them. No nation has ever prospered or been blessed like the colored people in the South. Help us to see this thing and to understand God's established order and to be one in Christ and to understand that God has fixed the boundaries of the nations so we would not have trouble and misunderstanding. Keep us by Thy power and use us for Thy glory, for Jesus' sake. Amen.

It would be misleading to cite statements from sermons delivered in 1960, before the Civil Rights Act was passed, before the 1965 civil rights march on Selma occurred, even before the work of the Reverend Martin Luther King, Jr., came to prominence, as if they reflect current Bob Jones University attitudes or policy. I have included them here to help place the episodes I am tracing within a more extensive and wider perspective.

On July 14, 1975, the director of admissions of the Goldsboro School was asked by the District Court for the Eastern District of North Carolina to explain the prevailing policy, and the respondents began by citing the following biblical geneology:

> According to the Bible all men are descended from Noah. Race is determined by descendance from one of Noah's three sons—Ham, Shem and Japheth. God has endowed the descendants of each son

with unique characteristics and functions. The three major races are further subdivided into descendants of the sons of each of Noah's sons. These divisions are provided in the ninth chapter of the Book of Genesis in the Bible, and in the chapters that follow. Races are subdivided into nationalities. Under the three main races, the following present-day groups might be classified by way of example:

(1) Hamitic peoples:
    Orientals, Egyptians, Indians, Negroes
(2) Shemitic (Semitic) peoples:
    Hebrews
(3) Japhethetic peoples (Japhethites): Caucasian, German, Scandinavian, Greek, Roman, Russian[21]

The representative went on to explain that "the races are separate because God made them so." The Tower of Babel story illustrates what happens when the races are intermixed. God's intention, according to this reading of scripture, is that "each race should be concerned with its own cultural characteristics and should seek to preserve the best of its heritage under God." More specifically and emphatically:

God has ordained that there shall be separated races having separate functions, and He has commanded that they shall not mix—culturally or biologically. Dealings may not be had between the races that would violate His command and lead to a dilution of the culture or characteristics that are special to each race.

The representative applied these principles to the way in which he believed the Goldsboro Christian Schools ought to be administered:

God's intention is that a people of one culture and religious heritage shall not absorb the ways of another. This has obvious implications regarding dealings between races for the field of education and for the cultural activities of persons of all ages in general (apart, of course, from certain religious activities, such as worship). In such areas the races should be kept separate.

He added that the Bible provides a record of what happens when these principles are violated:

In the book of Genesis alone, for example, twice racial intermarriage or the threat of it caused God to intervene directly in human affairs; and another time it caused untold human misery. The three distances alluded to are, first, the great flood sent by God that destroyed all humanity save Noah and his family. That flood was a response to the arrogance and wickedness that developed in the world when the lines of Seth intermarried with the lines of Cain. Later, God intervened again . . . when the children of Noah's sons, who were and are separate races, undertook together to build the Tower of Babel. Again, it appeared that the produce of race-mixing, whether biologically or culturally, was arrogance and wickedness in the hearts of men. The third instance referred to . . . is told in Genesis 16. There Abraham, a Semite, took a Hamitic handmaiden and caused her to conceive. She bore a son, Ismael, who was, as a result of the interracial union, a wild man and whose descendants to this day are embroiled in warfare and unrest.

The representative concedes that "nowhere in the Bible does it say 'Thou shalt not educate little children of different races in the same school.' But to do so would clearly contravene God's will as it is revealed in the Bible because it would heighten the threat of intermarriage." When this occurs distinctiveness is diluted and "performance of separate functions" is impaired. The conclusion is that Goldsboro Christian Schools "has accepted only Japhethites," though with some exceptions. Children haven been accepted of Hamitic or Semitic parentage if one of the parents is a Japhethite.

When the director of admissions of the school was asked to amplify on the intentions of the policy, he cited many of the same scriptural passages that Bob Jones had used in his sermon of 1960. He spoke of Cain and Seth, and the intermingling of races that brought about the flood. He spoke of Paul's message on Mars Hill, certifying that the early Christians believed that "the bounds of their habitation" had been established for all races. And he found the same principle operating in the early church's desire to come to effective terms with the relations of Christians and Jews. He explained:

Now, in the New Testament, there seemed to be an idea in the early church—Paul deals with it in Acts—where primarily Caucasians—Japhetites—who are coming into the church—that the earliest church folks who were Jews, of course, first, did not want to accept these people unless they became Jews—unless they adopted the ceremonial customs, practices, and the ways of Jews. And there was quite a church deception about it, and the upshot of it was, with the leadership of the Apostle Paul that the Apostle Peter took it that it was agreed that a Jew should remain as a Jew, and the others should remain in their customs and practices, as they had remained. . . . They were not to cross these lines or force the crossing of them.

At this point in the discussion, the court wished to know how the director of admissions goes about making distinctions in specific cases:

Q. So in your mind there's no question that the Negro . . . is a Hamite, rather than a Japhethite?

A. Right.

Q. By the same token, there's no question in your mind that a Greek is a Japhethite?

A. Right. Right.

Q. Is an Italian a Japhethite?

A. Yes, yes.

Q. All Caucasians are Japhethites?

Q. Right, most of these same men [the scholars] who would deal with this have also taught the principle of racial separation as maintained in the Bible. It should be practiced by God's people.

Q. Okay, are Orientals from Ham, is that correct?

A. Right.

Q. And the Negroes also?

A. Right.

Q. American Indians, what are they?

A. You might find a little more question about it, but I think generally they're accepted as Hamitics.

Q. How about Pakistanis?

A. They're related to Indian peoples and most of the natives of that area of the world are generally accepted as having been Hamitic peoples who migrated there.

Q. How about Lebanese?

A. I think the Lebanese are predominantly Semitic.

Q. They're Hebrew?

A. They are related to Hebrews, but they have, I think, some intermarriage with Hamitic in a large grouping, but I may be wrong—I may be wrong. Maybe I'm answering too quickly there, but I think I'm right in that.

Q. I believe in your sermon you said that the Arabs are the sons— descendants of Ishmael, is that correct?

A. Right.

Q. Now, was that an interracial marriage?.

A. Yes, Ishmael was the son of Abraham, who on the advice of his wife when she had given him no children married an Egyptian who was Hamitic, and God told him that the child of that marriage would not be the son through whom the promises— heirs—or the promises that God gave would come.

Q. And the Bible tells you that the Arabs—the present day Arabs—are the product of that marriage?

A. Right, you can trace it down in the Old Testament and bring it right on up to the present time.

The high drama in the BJU case occurred on October 12, 1982, when the case was heard by the United States Supreme Court. The lines of people standing outside the Court, waiting for an opportunity to witness the proceedings, were the longest in years. The case was perceived as being diagnostic of the Reagan administration's policy on civil rights. Linda Greenhouse of the *New York Times* reported that "not only the general public, but also members of the Supreme Court bar crowded into the courtroom for the high legal psychodrama."

Appearing on behalf of Bob Jones University (as well as the Goldsboro Christian Schools), attorney William Ball argued that the primary issue is the survival of religious freedom, both for the schools involved in this case and for all other independent institutions within the country. Ball offered that it was not because of any real violations of the law that the case was being heard, but because Bob Jones's practices "run counter to a national consensus of some kind." And, in this instance, he believed the government was acting contrary to the honored conviction that "government may not penalize or discriminate against individuals or groups because they hold religious views abhorrent to the authorities." Ball summarized his position on the matter by reminding the

Court that "if there is any fixed star in our constitutional constellation, it is that no official, high or petty, can prescribe what shall be orthodox in religion, politics, nationalism or other matters of opinion."[22]

After Ball finished, William McNairy was called upon to represent the Goldsboro Christian Schools. McNairy argued that the Constitution guarantees that even a racially discriminatory admissions policy should not remove a religious institution from tax-exempt status. While explaining the basis for this, McNairy was interrupted by Justice Stevens who wondered if the Internal Revenue Service should have the power to deny tax-exempt status to a school whose primary purpose was to train pickpockets. In his reply McNairy distinguished private schools, organized for educational purposes, from any that might be organized for criminal purposes. Drawing the laughter of the group assembled, Justice Stevens replied quickly, "but it's still teaching them how to do it."

Following this exchange, Chief Justice Burger called upon William Bradford Reynolds to represent the government's position. Reynolds began by citing a principle:

> The United States government has no tolerance for racial discrimination in the field of education, both public and private. And we who are charged with the responsibility of enforcing the law . . . are unflaggingly committed to the elimination from school systems through the country of all vestiges of discriminatory treatment on account of race.

From here on the discussion was dominated by attempts to understand and/or define the word "charitable" in the Internal Revenue Code. Section 501(c)(3) of the code lays out provisions for the tax-exempt status of "charitable" institutions. William Ball argued that the word "charitable" should be construed in its narrow sense, having specific reference to "the relief of the poor." The broader, more inclusive "common-law connotation," namely, that the activities of such groups be in conformity with fundamental public policies, would seem to make the other items enumerated in 501(c)(3) redundant, he added. Reynolds and William T. Coleman (a prominent civil-rights figure who had been Secretary of Transportation in the Ford administration, and who, in this situation, was speaking on behalf of the Justice

Department) contended that an institution qualifies for tax-exempt status only if it is "charitable" in the common-law sense of the word. Coleman's argument was couched in the following observation:

> . . . these petitioners are private schools who provide state-certified education in secular subjects for children from kindergarten through high school. By doing that and going to that school, a child satisfies the compulsory attendance law of each of the states. Bob Jones also provides certain university training, most of which is secular.

Ball countered that Bob Jones University is "a pervasively religious ministry which in purpose and character and discipline is a zealous faith community which would not exist except for its religious goals." He added that the erosion of support for Bob Jones University's tax-exempt status forces the institution to "abandon a religious practice, its marriage policy, which in conscience and fidelity it cannot abandon." Then he offered this comment: "Bob Jones University's theology may not be yours; it certainly is not mine. But its theology, nevertheless, is rooted, as the record very well shows . . . in policies that are obligatory . . . as dictated by the Scripture." Ball continued: "I'm sure the Court has noted a policy with respect to male-female relationships in the university which is certainly an unusual policy, probably unique in this country. But it is followed . . . and carried out zealously because it is believed to be dictated in Scripture."

In the course of the debate, Justice Sandra Day O'Connor asked if 501(c)(3) would be applied to a church that practices racial discrimination. Coleman replied that there is presently no law or public policy condemning discrimination practiced by a church. Justice Powell voiced concern that the IRS might be assuming too much authority. "Where should the lines be drawn? Is the policy against sex discrimination any less fundamental than the policy against racial discrimination?" he asked.

Coleman replied that "we didn't fight a civil war over sex discrimination and pass an amendment to the Constitution against it." Further, "no one can say that sex discrimination is as fundamental in our history." Summarizing, he added, "you just can't compare racial discrimination with any other activity: the policy against racial discrimination is the one policy that is crystal clear." And so the discussion continued, and the participants and audience in the crowded courtroom grew to realize that the dominant issue was not one on which there could be a compromise.

The decision of the Supreme Court, announced on May 24, 1983, was decisive. By an 8–1 margin the justices voted to uphold the action of the Internal Revenue Service, with only Justice William Rehnquist dissenting.

In delivering the opinion of the Court, Chief Justice Warren E. Burger reviewed the succession of previous decisions that had persuaded the IRS to conclude that it could "no longer legally justify allowing tax-exempt status to private schools which practice racial discrimination." Citing the "national policy to discourage discrimination in education," the Internal Revenue Service had ruled that a racially discriminatory private school is not "charitable" within the common-law concepts reflected in Sections 170 and 501(c)(3) of the Internal Revenue Code. Burger added that the meaning of the key word "must be analyzed and construed within the framework of the Internal Revenue Code and against the background of the Congressional purposes." He explained:

> Such an examination reveals unmistakable evidence that underlying all relevent parts of the code is the intent that entitlement to tax exemption depends on meeting certain common law standards of charity, namely, that an institution seeking tax-exempt status must serve a public purpose and not be contrary to established public policy.

Then, after providing explicit elucidation of the code, Burger enunciated the most compelling principle: "The governmental interest at stake here is compelling," he said. "The government has a fundamental, overriding interest in eradicating racial discrimination in education, discrimination that prevailed, with official approval, for the first 165 years of this nation's history." The Court had concluded that "the interests asserted by petitioners cannot be accommodated within that compelling governmental interest." Burger added that "no less restrictive means are available to achieve the governmental interest."

The next question for the chief justice was whether the Internal Revenue Service had acted properly toward Bob Jones University as well as toward the Goldsboro Christian Schools. He acknowledged that Bob Jones University allows all races to enroll and that all are treated alike with respect to the rules of conduct that are prescribed. But those rules are racially discriminatory. In the chief justice's words: "Although the ban on intermarriage or interracial dating applies to all races, decisions of this Court firmly establish that discrimination on the basis of racial affiliation and association is a form of racial discrimination." The next sentence came almost as a matter of course: "We therefore find that the I.R.S. properly applied Revenue Ruling 71–447 to Bob Jones University."

Before the Court's ruling was known, Bob Jones III had been optimistic, telling his well-wishers and supporters that he was asking only that God's will would be done. And on May 24, shortly after the decision was handed down, Jones sounded a conciliatory note in his chapel address to the student body: "We have said again and again that the will of God is all we wanted," Jones said, "and we mean that with all our heart." He expressed surprise that only one of the justices had dissented; he had expected it to be a close decision. But the more he talked about the situation, the more difficulty he had sustaining his intended conciliatory tone. All at once Jones dramatically unleashed his real feelings. "The ruling is an attack upon religious freedom," he began. "What that decision really says is that churches and Christian schools will be tolerated only if they serve the purpose of government." Then Jones restated his own fundamental conviction in the matter: "God did not establish his church to serve the purpose of government, but to serve his divine purpose, to represent him in a heathen, dark, lost, sinful world, not to serve the purposes of the heathen." And, as he reflected further on the case as well as on the decision of the Court, he discovered that he also had strong convictions about what Chief Justice Burger had referred to as "established public policy." Jones declared:

> The decision reads further that a religious institution could not be at odds with the public conscience and enjoy tax exemption. I think the Supreme Court is totally out of touch with the public conscience. All of the public I have talked to in the last year said that it would be a terrible travesty of justice if we lost this case. I am speaking now of the unsaved as well as the saved people.[23]

Jones concluded: "The public conscience loves and desires its religious freedom. It does not want to live in a totalitarian state."

And, as he proceeded, the corollaries within his creed came tumbling out too. His reference to "totalitarian state" invoked a comparison of the United States with the Soviet Union: "Our nation has today declared itself to be the enemy of the God of heaven and the enemy of his people. Our nation from this day forward is no better than Russia insofar as being able to expect the blessings of God is concerned."[24] Looking out on his audience of several thousand, students, professors, supporters, well-wishers, Jones said, "You do not any longer live in nation that is religiously free." He confessed that he was trembling because of the gravity of the words he had just uttered. But he knew them to be true. "This is not the nation our forefathers sacrificed and hazarded their lives to provide," he continued. "This is the very thing they left Europe to avoid." Then with reference to the Soviet Union again, Jones added, "We have prayed for the Russian Christians. . . . We prayed for them that God would . . . spare them the oppression and the totalitarianism that comes to believers in such lands. Now we have that to face in America." Against this background Jones offered the following summary of the meaning of the day's ruling by the Supreme Court:

> The ruling of the Supreme Court is a totalitarian ruling, a shaking of the fist in the face of the God of heaven in saying that we have another god more important than He is in America—a god called "the State." . . . when those who worship God find their Bible convictions in conflict with the decrees of the State, they must either give way to the State or incur the wrath of the State.[25]

The only item remaining was the need to encourage the faithful. Jones admitted that the policies of Bob Jones University had incurred the wrath of the state. But he pledged that he would never yield to these dictates "where they contravene the dictates of the Word of God as we understand them." Then, in his closing prayer, he confessed "a great heaviness of heart for this nation and great pity for the heathens who sit on the Supreme Court—pity for their damned souls and their blighted minds. . . . " He added that if the justices had "come to know the Lord Jesus, then they would deal justly." At this, because the spring semester of the university was coming to a close, Jones bid the students farewell: "We did not worry about the outcome of this. We are confident today that the Lord's perfect will has been done. Now, you be confident in that.

You go home, to give praise to God this summer. You go home to magnify his wonderful name."[26]

When he made these statements, on May 24, just minutes after the decision of the Court had been rendered, Jones was responding to bits and pieces of information he had assembled through sketchy telephone conversations and abbreviated news reports. But after chapel, he went into consultation with his father and their advisors. His father, it is apparent, tends to be far less conciliatory than his son. When they emerged from their full-scale assessment meeting, they had formulated their response. And the language they selected was bold and specific: "We're in a bad fix in America when eight evil old men and one vain and foolish woman can speak a verdict on American liberties," Bob Jones III said.

But his less vitriolic response called attention to the irony of the situation. That is, instead of safeguarding the separation of church and state, the Court's ruling, in Jones's judgment, wrongly places the government in the position of supporting church schools, because it tends to treat tax exemptions as institutional subsidies. Furthermore, the fundamental issue is no longer religious freedom or even questions about the separation of church and state. In Jones's mind, the larger issue concerns the status given by the Court to "some nebulous and intangible official public policy." Thus, those who are perceived to be at variance with established policy are punished, penalized, and even ridiculed, and those who are perceived to be in agreement with the same policy are supported by the laws of the land. This, of course, is what Christians have always had to contend with: living at the margins, they have always invited the hostility of non-Christians and heathens. But this time, in the Joneses' view, the hostility is premeditated and blatant. The onslaught is direct and unmasked. As Bob Jones, Jr., put it: "The Supreme Court has violated the laws against the establishment of a State religion in America, and has, in effect, declared all who will not embrace the humanistic religion to be second-class citizens"[27] The implicit recognition of humanism—as in "secular humanism"—as the prevailing and authoritative religion of the land, in the Joneses' view, is simply the culmination of a process that was initiated long ago and that, now, has become official public policy: "The court has taken the Bible out of the public school. Now they would destroy Christian institutions where the Bible is honored. Now they would murder religious freedom."[28]

William Ball, the attorney representing Bob Jones University, also had some thoughts about the decision handed down by the Court. He was not happy either, and worried aloud about the larger implications of the decision, suggesting that "effects are visited upon our nation as a whole." Ball explained: "The first (and worst) features of the decision is the principle which is now established in our law: that religious bodies, if they are to avoid being taxed, must lockstep themselves to a thing called 'federal public policy.' "[29] Ball charged that this policy had, in effect, become "the supreme law of the land." He called it a "sort of super Constitution explaining the Constitution which has served us well for more than two centuries." Ball also criticized the Court for making a decision that really belonged to Congress. In this respect, Ball was in agreement with Justice Rehnquist, the only one to dissent in the opinion, who stated that the Court was only acting because the Congress, so far, had failed to act. Rehnquist explained:

I have no disagreement with the Court's finding that there is a strong national policy in this country opposed to racial discrimination. I agree with the Court that Congress has the power to further this policy by denying Section 501(c)(3) status to organizations that practice racial discrimination. But as of yet Congress has failed to do so. Whatever the reasons for the failure, this Court should not legislate for Congress.[30]

Clearly the petitioners in the case—both before the courts of the land and before some higher, "cosmic" jurisdictional authority—can never be happy with the outcome, perceiving it as the clearest possible evidence of increasing governmental opposition to the will of the God they worship. But, religiously speaking, the outcome has been received as a confirmation of what they have been taught to expect at the hands of civil authorities in a world that is perceived to be fundamentally alien. With this attitude, it was easy to take the next step, namely, to view the opposing force as being diabolical and the false assurances it offers as being totalitarian. Next in the sequence of interpretation came a recitation of parallels to the prevailing situation within the Soviet Union, and this was followed by a plea for religious freedom as well as a call for renewed dedication to the compelling vision. Yes, this is precisely the situation that calls for a savior: it needs someone from outside who will rescue believers from impending destruction. Believers were called upon to be faithful "until the Lord comes," for when he comes—regardless of the seeming might of government, the courts, and the prevailing alien philosophy—he will set all things right again. Then the entire world will acknowledge that this is the way the plot was meant to be resolved. There is comfort in this expectation, of course, as well as multiple reassurances that what will eventually happen is also working its way toward achieving this objective. As Bob Jones III said in his sermon on May 26, 1983:

> We need to pray one for another and ask God to manifest himself through this to the nation in a way that only this decision could have made possible. God is doing something for his glory through this. We need to be sure that we go his direction and that we are in no way an impediment to him, and we should pray that this situation be a tool for him to use in speaking to America.[31]

But the fidelity this invokes, given the collective perception of the lines along which the battle is being waged, leaves little room for any openness to the validity of the position of the other side. Despite his expressed desire to resign himself to the prevailing will of God, Bob Jones—together with his father and supporters—could not help but throw verbal stones at his enemies. Whatever will of God is implicit in the decision of the Supreme Court, in his view, is not to be found in the decision itself. Rather, God's will is to be discerned in the evidences the entire episode provides regarding the truth and authority of Jones's reading of the larger cosmic plot. In short, the decision of the Court confirms that the Joneses had been accurate when they have faithfully and repeatedly offered their version of the meaning of human events. They understand this reading to be correct and to carry divine authority, for it taught them to expect the treatment they received from the world.

In the course of wrestling with his own personal reaction to the situation, Bob Jones III sent a letter to President Reagan, expressing his disappointment that the President hadn't used his office to assist this "righteous cause." As noted, when seeking election and campaigning in South Carolina, Ronald Reagan had pledged his help and support. Apparently, Jones expected the President to make good on his campaign promise. When Jones received no help as well as no response to his letter, he sent a more strongly worded letter to the Republican National Committee, explaining that Mr. Reagan was now very much in danger of losing the enthusiastic support of conservative Christian people. He offered that the Christian coalition that had boosted Reagan's hopes in 1980 would probably not go so far as to back a Democratic candidate, but that he was also sure that any warm and vigorous support for Reagan was diminishing rapidly and deteriorating badly. Jones was invited to meet with the Republican National Committee. The meeting occurred in Washington in January, 1984, too late to be of any strategic political utility. Bob Jones was able to lodge his complaint, and to express some threats. But the conversation left him far from satisfied.

Yet, he must have found some reassurance in the inevitability—the predestinarian quality—of everything that happened. Indeed, advocates of Bob Jones's position, in spite of words and hopes to the contrary, had been preparing themselves for the bad news they expected. The hymns they sing, the creed they profess, even the prayers they offer provide evidence that they do not expect to win all battles, at least not "here below," that is, before the Messiah returns to reign. Their expressions of piety seem designed to carry protections against any deep and lasting disappointment since real salvation is of an "other-worldly" variety, involving a decisive rescue from this world of sin and woe. From this perspective, disappointments, though real and acutely felt, are always only temporary since the resolution of the human drama is projected toward a time after which current time will have ceased. Temporary victory is not prohibited, but one must be careful and prudent in one's expectations. Bob Jones people might hope that the Supreme Court would decide the case in favor of the petitioners, but the purer hope is that God's will might be done, regardless of the specific decisions of the court. Clearly Bob Jones's initial composure, after learning of the decision that was rendered, is testimony to the presence and influence of this disposition.

And yet, even within the smaller picture, Bob Jones may indeed be reading the situation accurately. He suspects that it is not his school's specific policies, not even on the matter of interracial dating, that has gotten it into trouble with the authorities, but its prevailing religious outlook. And this, it seems, the ruling of the Court will corroborate.

The fact is that a religious viewpoint that condones racial discrimination, even in hint, even in the slightest, no matter how well intentioned, hard working, and spiritually devout its advocates may be or appear to be, will no longer receive sure protection under the law, when that same law has spoken otherwise. In this regard, Bob Jones's instincts are accurate. He finds himself railing against "federal public policy," believing that this policy has legitimated a religious viewpoint he opposes. He complains that the populace has changed the signals on him, that the traditional policy of his school is in full compliance with what used to be prevailing understanding of this and related subjects. He is smarting because his view is no longer sanctionable, and the conflict runs deep. Bob Jones will never be able to acknowledge the propriety of the Supreme Court's decision.

And yet, Jones has been preparing from birth to expect such treatment by the civil courts. He was taught that there is deep conflict in the world, and that Christians are surrounded by hostile forces. If God had intended that Christians should win all of the time, there would be no need for heaven and certainly no need for a savior. Because God so loved his own that he sent his son to rescue them from the world, Christians have assurance, in Jones's view, that the ultimate victory will be theirs to enjoy. In the meantime, they are to keep themselves unspotted by the world, and are exhorted to keep their courage up. The United States Supreme Court may direct some negative forces their way, in the short run. But this makes the plot interesting. In the end, in Jones's view, Christians will be victorious; that is, when divine justice no longer allows itself to be frustrated by the merely human powers of misguided and deceptive civil ordinances.

As the Jones family sees it, Jerry Falwell's religious and moral shallowness is most apparent in his expectation that, perhaps this time around, Christians can actually win, that is, here below. For the Jones family—grandfather, father, and son—that is like believing that one can have it both ways, as if one can follow the dictates of the Christian view of the world while making concessions to its rival way of life. The truth about the human condition is that reality can never elicit a durable and satisfying *both/and.* Rather, in the world of Bob Jones, the most fundamental dynamics can only be comprehended by a mindset that is absolutely committed to an inviolable *either/or.* The challenge is certified by the incontrovertible either/or since the world is structured according to a powerful dualism that frames the drama within which salvation occurs. In the Joneses' salvation, only one of the two polar realities can be validated. The other must be thoroughly rejected or condemned.

There is really no basis in this scheme for requesting a tax exemption from the government, for the ultimate aspiration is to be exempt from earthly government altogether. Nor is there any basis here for establishing an amicable working relationship with the earthly authorities, not for people who know that earth is not their home, they're "just passing through." In summary, there is no way that Bob Jones's convictions can be translated into operational governmental policy, because those same convictions are intended to shield an other-worldly orientation against this-worldly intrusions.

Ultimately, this is how the community understands and applies the biblical reference to "establishing the boundaries of their habitations." Such a statement serves as warrant for racial distinctions. When unpacked, it also explains how individual and collective identities are protected by senses of cosmic turf. Because the statement is in the Bible, it accords an authoritative sanction to instinctual tendencies.

The absolute quality of their other-worldliness makes it impossible for the Jones-people ever to feel at home in this world, or, at the same time, ever to feel absolutely or ultimately obligated to the powers and ambitions of this world. Thus, so long as accepted and recognized laws are kept, other-worldly aspirations need never be significantly conditioned by this-worldly duties or debts. In the civil-rights case before us, to tell people of such absolute convictions that earthly government has a legitimate license to determine how they are to conduct the generative process, and form genealogical alliances, is to challenge their dualistic ontology directly. And to challenge their worldview is to question their way of making meaning and sense of human existence.

This, of course, is how the Justice Department's forays were received, interpreted, and understood. This, too, is why the Bob Jones community resisted, portraying the conflict as out-and-out warfare. Since they recognized that they held no real power "here below," they recognized too that there would be no winning for them, at least not in the world's terms. Thus, they knew the outcome even before the official verdict was rendered. They chided the inevitable victors for the destructiveness of their effort. They offered their opponents forgiveness for their evil ways. But, secretly, all along, they knew who the ultimate winners would be. Never once, in the entire episode, did the community itself confess to a fault. Never once, in the entire episode, did the community agree that it had violated a binding ordinance. For, in the Bob Jones worldview, the only enduring sin is a transgression against the lines of distinction and separation that are inherent in their cherished dualistic theology.

This, from the community's perspective, is what the United States government is guilty of. It has transgressed, violating the sanctity of the underlying dualistic structure. This, too, is what the Jones community would have become guilty of had it been willing to alter the terms by which human beings enter and participate in a protected and sanctified space.

From the day the school was founded, in 1927, the Bob Jones family had confidence that it knew who the gatekeepers are, and by which formula the gates to that sanctified space are opened. For the civil government to challenge that knowledge and usurp that function is to demonstrate that it intends to challenge directly the principles by which such convictions are protected. On this basis the Jones people pleaded that the case may appear to be about race and racial tensions, but down deeper, and more fundamentally, it concerns religious freedom. Because of the intrusions of human government, Jones believed that the primary threat to religious freedom is the government itself, and that, when government acts this way, Christians owe it to the God they worship to respond resolutely. In the end, the Jones people accused the U.S. federal government of trafficking in idolatry.

Devotion to dualism has enabled the Bob Jones community to separate the races from one another, religious from racial issues, and themselves from their menacing adversaries. It was a correct instinct to recognize, therefore, that when the government called their practices into question, the government was also inquiring about the legitimacy of a moral authority that rests on the firm belief that this world is under the dominion of two opposing principles, the one good, the other evil. Recognizing this dominion the Jones family knows that its vocation lies in keeping and protecting the sacred boundaries.

CHAPTER FIVE

A CHRISTIAN THEME PARK

It happens this way, at times, in the history of a movement. The general thrust of the effort can claim success, and the development can appear to be entirely on course, according to projections that seem expected and predictable. Then, suddenly, an intrusion occurs, interrupting the natural flow, setting the predictable decisively off course.

This is what happened to the New Religious Right movement early in 1987. Jerry Falwell had been having some difficulty raising sufficient monies, or so he said, to keep his "Old Time Gospel Hour" on the air. But he had sounded such warnings before. Pat Robertson, at the apex of his popularity, was consulting his advisers and followers about making a serious run for the presidency. Almost everyone expected him to do so, and understood such consultation to represent appropriate activity in the initial stages of his still-undeclared campaign. Other television evangelists were touring the country, writing and selling books, offering encouragement to their followers, and doing what they needed to do on behalf of the causes with which they were identified. Very few of these activities caught the attention of the press. None seemed out of the ordinary. The movement itself seemed strong and secure.

But then Oral Roberts, of Tulsa, Oklahoma, did something that appeared strange, bizarre. Roberts, telling his followers that his ministry was facing an extreme financial emergency, announced that God had told him that he would die unless he raised the necessary millions of dollars to keep his work sustained. In the same announcement, Roberts said that he was going to go into his tower, on the campus of Oral Roberts University, and adopt an attitude of fasting and praying until the money was offered.

Roberts's announcement received mixed reviews. Some called it a death wish. Robert Schuller, for example, offered that he had noticed that Roberts had seemed somewhat depressed; he believed he had been preoccupying himself more and more with the fact and significance of death. Others thought that it was simply another fund-raising ploy: Oral talks with God; God tells Oral what he needs; and Oral, like Moses coming down from the mountain, communicates that (his own) request to his people. Understandably, Oral Roberts's residence in the tower was the subject of cartoons, jokes, derision, and ridicule. And, as is the rule in this situation, when Oral Roberts was criticized so too was the brand of Christianity that he is understood to represent.

But if this were not enough to provoke questions among an already suspicious public, the next several events in this ongoing episode indeed were. Jim and Tammy Bakker, of the PTL Club, outside Charlotte, North Carolina, came upon very hard personal times. And, as outsiders watched the unfolding developments—like watching successive segments on some day-time television soap opera—many of them became more and more convinced that the entire story was ridiculous. Or, if they thought more specifically than this, they found themselves believing that the New Religious Right was actually less about viable religion than about what they had suspected it was about: sex, power, and money.

The first news of serious trouble in the Bakkers' PTL headquarters in Fort Mill, South Carolina, came in a headline in the *Charlotte Observer* on January 26, 1986. The headline read, in bold print: *Bakker Misled PTL Viewers, FCC Records Show.*[1] The story, written by Charles E. Shepard, of the *Observer* staff, alleged that Bakker had misled his supporters as far back as 1977 and 1978 about how contributions from PTL donors were being used. The supporters believed they were donating money for missions and relief work in South Korea and Brazil. The Federal Communications Commission investigators learned that none of the money was put to this purpose for at least a year, and that the bulk of it went to make payment on the ministry's regular bills.

Shepard also indicated that the investigation had raised some questions about the character of Jim Bakker. The initial impression of the PTL head was that he is a very dedicated evangelist and an enthusiastic money raiser, who loves his family and spends day and night working himself almost to total physical exhaustion on behalf of his ministry. The FCC investigation found some evidence, however, that Bakker really kept no accurate account of the amount of money raised in his appeals, was a rather careless administrator, and possessed a record of finding someone else to blame when situations did not always turn out to his (or to others') liking. Shepard noted that the FCC uncovered that the money that had been raised for missions and relief work in South Korea and Brazil had actually been used to help build Heritage USA, the Christian retreat center and amusement part that, along with the daily television broadcasts of the PTL Club, had come to identify the ministry of Jim and Tammy Bakker. It was a serious matter for it is against federal law, as Shepard records it, "to raise money over the air with false, fraudulent or deceptive appeals."

Bakker admitted to some improprieties, but condemned the *Observer* story for being filled with "lies and half truths." He added that he had been a bit exuberant by virtue of the optimism in his faith. "In those days, my faith was a little bit reckless. I believed God would do anything. We now have budget control," he explained. But he also pointed to mismanagement problems among persons working for him, particularly those who had been given the assignment regarding extensions of the PTL ministry into South Korea and Brazil.

But Shepard wasn't finished. In another article in the same day's issue of the *Charlotte Observer,* the staff reporter disclosed that Jim and Tammy Bakker had used significant portions of the PTL donations to buy an expensive sports car, a mink coat, a houseboat, and inordinant numbers of items designated exclusively for their personal use. Shepard indicated, too, that the Bakkers had used donors' money to buy a million-dollar house, on the lake, at Tega Cay, South Carolina, and had purchased a vacation condominium in Florida. Shepard added that Tammy Bakker had been drawing upon petty cash (donors' money) as a way of financing her frequent "personal shopping sprees." This, he said, he had learned from members of PTL's Board of Directors. He had also learned that Bakker would sometimes cash checks that had mistakenly been made out to him, though the money was intended for PTL. The money used to make the downpayment of $6,000 on the houseboat was a regular PTL check. A PTL check in the amount of $2,500 was used to purchase Tammy Bakker's mink coat. Shepard didn't know if the new Corvette had been purchased with a PTL check, but he noted that the Bakkers usually travel in PTL-owned automobiles. But this was just the beginning of the financial entanglement, for, Shepard learned, $375,000 of PTL money went to buy the Florida condominium, with another $81,000 from the same source used to purchase furnishings for it. In 1984, the Bakkers bought another home, this one in Palm Springs, California, for a reported price of $449,000, and, in the same year, bought two cars—a Rolls-Royce and a Mercedes-Benz—for purchase prices totaling nearly $100,000. Shepard thought it strange that in the very months that they were making the large purchases, Tammy Bakker told the PTL television audience that she and Jim "have given everything we have" to support the ministry. She made this declaration during the course of requesting funds from "PTL Club" viewers.

With the news about failed promises to the South Korea and Brazil ministries came a detailed chronological account, supplied by Shepard and printed in the *Observer,* of what happened. Acting under the influence of the promptings of the Holy Spirit, Jim Bakker asked the Reverend Cho Yonggi, whom he was interviewing at the time on the "PTL Club," if he would like to host a PTL show in South Korea. Though surprised, Yonggi said he would. Bakker later learned that it would cost approximately $500,000 to establish such a broadcast ministry in Korea. Bakker began trying to raise the money over television, and offered those donors who sent more than $100 a replica of Korean crown jewels. The initial interview with Yonggi occurred on June 13, 1977. News of the arrangement was issued in September of that year. And it was early in October that Bakker seriously began to request the necessary money during PTL television broadcasts. But, in the course of describing the South Korean program, he found himself exaggerating the progress. On October 6, 1977, on a regular broadcast, he announced that PTL was getting ready to ship a load of cameras to Korea to initiate the ministry. And between July and December 1977, he frequently described the ministry as something that was already "going on." By the end of the year, he told his supporters that PTL was building an $800,000 building in South Korea, and that broadcasts would start within a few weeks. The truth was that very little, if anything, had been initiated; the plans Bakker devised had met serious obstacles, and he lost his enthusiasm for the project. But it was difficult to explain this to supporters who had been led to believe that the project was a sound one, and that it was moving ahead on schedule. Consequently, on May 9, 1978, when Bakker was taken by surprise by a guest on his show, who asked him, "You are on in Seoul, aren't you?" he could only stammer a reply, "We are just. . . . We are building the studios there." This was not true. And, by now, Bakker's associates in South Korea were becoming annoyed. On June 16, 1978, one of Yonggi's associates sent Bakker a letter, indicating that Yonggi was "a little disturbed that things have been moving so slowly." He complained that when he travels about (in the words of his assistant), "everyone is always telling him how wonderful it is that he now has T.V. studios in operation, and all paid for, and provided by PTL." Some visitors even seek him out, asking to see the now famous new PTL studios. To make matters worse, by this time—June 1978—PTL owed the Korean church $5,369 for a satellite transmission. In September, Yonggi's assistant sent a telegram to PTL offices in Fort Mill, asking for payment of the bill and complaining that more and more visitors had come to see the new studios: "This has been a great embarrassment to us. It is an even greater embarrassment right here in Korea."

By now Jim Bakker had to do something decisive, so, in September 1978, he traveled to South Korea. Bakker returned, and reported that Yonggi had refused to accept some equipment that PTL had wanted to give to him, to enable him to finish the construction of the television studios. He explained that Yonggi's church was sufficiently well financed not to be in need of a gift of this kind. But the truth is that, by this time, Yonggi had lost credibility within his own church as well as in the eyes of those Americans who had donated monies to the "Korean PTL outreach" program, but had learned, by now, that they had been deceived.

Bakker was not able to offer statisfying explanations as to why he had behaved in this manner. He admitted that he had been late in getting the money sent, though he did arrange to have $350,000 sent to the Assemblies of God Church to be utilized for Christian television in Asia. He confessed that he hadn't been aware that the Koreans were so thoroughly upset; he was sorry about this too. But he pleaded that he was a minister of the gospel, and had been acting in that capacity: "I am a minister. I am not a businessman. And I think when the FCC is investigating a minister it must understand the thinking and the philosophy and the spiritual tenor of what we do." Bakker explained that he had been speaking "in faith" when he made the promises, fully expecting that "God is going to do the work." He didn't know quite why he had spoken as he did, he said, adding: "I speak spontaneously every day. I get excited. I have a lot of excitement. I enjoy life."

Shepard alleged in his coverage of this account that a similar story could be written about what happened—or, in fact, did not happen—in Brazil. And he provided documentation of similar consequences to monies that had been raised, through Bakker's television appeals, on behalf of missionary and relief work in Cyprus and elsewhere. In the latter situation, the goal was to build a transmitter for television broadcasts in the Middle East. But the transmitter was not built, for reasons that Bakker had an extremely difficult time explaining.

In subsequent days, the *Charlotte Observer* published other articles that provided even more information about the way in which PTL was being mismanaged. The articles provided detailed illustration of extreme financial overextension coupled with repeated pleas by the Bakkers to their viewers for continued support to meet real emergencies. The author of the article thought it particularly telling that, in periods when Jim and Tammy Bakker were spending the most on items to improve their own living conditions, Tammy would say: "PTL has a great financial need, and we are having to cut back, a lot . . . to where we are going to be able to support it financially, and not have to always have this terrible problem that we're having financially at PTL." The truth of the matter was that the construction on Heritage USA was costing more than had been projected, and these costs could only be covered, though never adequately, by monies that had originally been designated for other purposes. Eventually Bakker found himself selling what amounted to time-shares: where, for certain amounts of money, on a published scale, donors would be given so many free days per year in suites and rooms in the hotel complex.

But as soon as these articles were published, news about misspending and financial mismanagement multiplied rapidly. In addition to the examples already cited, the Bakkers were charged with spending large sums of money to finance their trips to Israel, and other locations. It was alleged that they had spent $6,000 to spend three nights in a Brussels hotel, this following their departure from India, where they had "shed tears" after encountering the widespread poverty there face to face. From other sources, it was learned that Bakker oftentimes hired and fired personnel on impulse (presumably under the influence of the Holy Spirit), and, as a consequence, had begun a number of expensive ventures, like building television studios and erecting transmission towers, that had to be abandoned before they were finished. From these sources it was also confirmed that such misadventures had resulted in large losses of money. Television stations that had been purchased for $2.5 million in one year, were sold for about half that amount some years later. All of the while the Bakkers were pleading for financial contributions, many of which arrived at their Charlotte offices in amounts of $10 and $15, sent by retirees, welfare recipients, people who were making sacrifices in order to be able to give anything at all. The Bakkers' goal, through all of it, was not merely to finance their ministry, which consisted primarily of their television show. Their larger ambition was to build the Christian "Disneyland" complex, the 2,300 acre Heritage USA, which was to include a 500-room hotel, a shopping mall, conference and meeting rooms, a single mothers' home, a water park, an up-to-date television studio, a church sanctuary, a variety of restaurants and snack shops, an amphitheater (built to resemble a Roman arena and intended to serve in the theatrical presentations of "The Passion Story"), several kinds of recreation facilities, campgrounds, houses for purchase as well as for both long- and short-term renting, food and clothing distribution centers for the needy, an adoption agency to care for babies of "unwed mothers," as well as the administration offices of the PTL ministry. The first buildings in the complex were erected in 1978, but the project was not destined to be completed.

After the *Observer* exposé had circulated extensively, and the Bakkers, in consultation with their trusted advisors had had an opportunity to react, Jim Bakker presented a defense in which he charged that the accusations were undocumented. In doing so, he offered some "documented" facts in a dramatic "Special Report" on his regular television broadcast, on Friday, January 31, 1986. Jim Bakker began the report by saying, "Tammy and I are undergoing the most vicious attacks in the history of this ministry." And after supplying explanations in defense of his behavior, Bakker commented:

> We were tried in the press once. We were tried by the FCC. We were tried by the Justice Department and we were cleared. And now they said, "We're not satisfied with what two agencies of government have done, we're going to try you this time by public opinion."

To make matters worse, in Bakker's judgment, the *Charlotte Observer* had been given an opportunity to hear the other side, that is, to benefit from the information the Bakkers wanted to provide, but, in Bakker's words, "they passed up the chance." In response, executives of the newspaper said that they had pleaded with PTL officials to sit down and talk with them before they published their stories, but that the officials "did not respond to the offer." Bakker used the situation repeatedly, on his broadcasts, to illustrate that true followers of Jesus Christ are both misunderstood and mistreated by detractors of the gospel message. In his view, the *Charlotte Observer,* as might have been expected by people who know that the devil is constantly working to frustrate the work of Christ, was on a crusade to do the ministry in.

The following year, beginning in March 1987, the situation for Jim and Tammy Bakker, and their already controversial PTL ministry, worsened dramatically. On March 17, from his Palm Springs home, Bakker asked Jerry Falwell to take over PTL. Bakker was in Palm Springs at the time to be with Tammy, who was undergoing therapeutic care at the Betty Ford Center for drug dependency. On March 19, Bakker announced the decision during the regular broadcast of the "PTL Club." He explained that he was unable to muster the strength to fight anticipated disclosures of his sexual liaison, some years before, with church secretary, Jessica Hahn. Bakker intimated that rival television evangelists, after robbing him of his good reputation, were planning a "takeover" of his ministry. What he didn't say, but was fully aware of, was the fact that his own denomination, the Assemblies of God, had begun an investigation of Bakker's sexual misconduct.

Following this startling news, other distrubing facts came to light. First, the ministry was facing serious tax challenges from the Internal Revenue Service. Secondly, though reaching nearly 13 million viewers daily and bringing in about $129 million in revenues annually, the ministry had acquired over $67 million in debts. Approximately $14 million was owed to Roe Messner, a Kansas-based contractor, who had been building Heritage USA for PTL. Thirdly, since 1980, when the sexual encounter between Bakker and Hahn took place, PTL had paid her $265,000 to purchase her silence, an arrangement that had been made by Richard Dortch, Bakker's top assistant and key associate. Fourthly, it became known that the Bakkers were paid about $1.6 million, including bonuses, in salary in calendar year 1986, and $4.6 million over the most recent thirty-nine-month period. In addition, the Bakkers' expense accounts provided them with free utilities, food and clothing, and, by now, they had homes in Tega Cay, South Carolina; Gatlinburg, Tennessee; Palm Springs, California; and Highland Beach, Florida. Fifthly, an audit uncovered that the PTL ministries had been running a deficit of approximately $2 million per month since July 1986. In spite of this deficit, PTL paid Richard Dortch approximately $350,000 in salary in the previous year. And, when building the hotel complex, the planners asked for a suite that included several bedrooms, together with 14-karat gold-plated fixtures in the bathroom. The suite had been the Bakker's when the hotel was first built. During a ten-day stretch in February 1987, the Bakkers themselves received $480,000 compensation. And, finally, auditors of the Arthur Andersen Company were unable to trace $12 million from PTL accounts. Before they were finished, the accountants (appointed by a new PTL board of directors) raised that figure to $92 million.

Following these disclosures, the spotlight was focused on Jim and Tammy Bakker, who remained in seclusion in their Palm Springs home, on Jessica Hahn, and on Jerry Falwell, who was trying to restore order at PTL. Hahn was worried that some, particularly some among the Christian faithful, might assume that activities of the kind in which she was involved are commonplace within the evangelical world. "I feel deeply concerned about the people that attend all these churches," she told reporters. "I don't want people under the impression that this goes on everywhere. It does not go on everywhere." She was asked to provide some of the details regarding the money she had received to keep the matter quiet. She refused to discuss the particulars, emphasizing that her primary concern remained those Christians, particularly those who have supported such ministries, who might jump to conclusions. "My feeling right now, the only thing I can really discuss, is that I feel deeply concerned about the people that attend all these churches," Hahn repeated. "I hope they see this will pass, and this has no reflection upon the Lord." Then, hoping to be reassuring, Hahn added, "God is still there for them and always will be. I am all right, but would like for this to end. I don't want to see innocent people hurt." But, when pressed, Hahn said that she had only received "a few dollars" of the money Bakker, through intermediaries, had promised to send her. Choking up, she switched back to her main theme, "My greatest concern is people I love, who are very dear to me, and innocent bystanders who have been hurt. That to me is more devastating than anything else. I can handle a lot, but I can't handle that." Noting that she was referring to members of her own family, Hahn added, "there are a handful of people who are my life, and they have been hurt by this."

Attempting to restore order at PTL, Jerry Falwell was acting like a man who had just received a new lease on life. In recent months, until he was invited to clean up the Bakker mess, he had been less than prominent in television evangelism circles. His fellow Virginian, Pat Robertson, had been attracting attention because of his expected bid for the presidency. In Oklahoma, Oral Roberts was threatening to die if he didn't raise sufficient funds. True, Falwell had been raising money to support a Lynchburg home for young· mothers and infants—his major antiabortion offensive. But this was not the kind of effort that could compete with the dramatics that were occurring elsewhere within the electronic church. And besides, Ronald Reagan, with whom Falwell enjoyed a closer personal and working relationship than any other evangelist, was experiencing some unusually rough times of his own. By this time, the President was enmeshed in the Iran-Contra scandals, and was facing the prospect that the details of all of it would be made available for public consumption much in the style of the Watergate hearings a little more than a decade before. Although not looking for a new agenda, when the opportunity presented itself Falwell recognized its potential.

The first order of business was to bring some semblance of order to PTL operations. Falwell met with the board of directors, on March 26, then with the staff. He held a press conference, admitted that the Bakker affair had been "a severe blow, a broadside, to the cause of Christ." But, after an initial examination of the situation at Heritage USA, he affirmed that "we do not feel the organization is in critical condition." He also wanted to reassure everyone that he had no intention of taking over, or of wanting to stay in his new position very long. "I'm not here to stamp Jerry Falwell on this ministry or to create an independent Baptist empire," he said. "We are trying to close ranks and prevent the enemy from having a field day." Identifying the enemy, he urged PTL supporters not to "let Satan win the day." And as far as the Bakkers were concerned, Falwell announced two policy decisions. First, the Bakkers were asked not to return to the premises of PTL, at least not for a while. Pointing to the need to restore confidence and stability, Falwell reported that it was the opinion of the board that "we could not do it if Jim Bakker were here on this campus." Second, the Bakkers were to continue to receive their current level of compensation. Reported that the PTL board felt it would be "less than Christian" simply to cut the salary altogether.

But the issue could not be put to rest easily. On March 28, Baton Rouge-based television evangelist Jimmy Swaggart called for Richard Dortch, Bakker's top assistant, to quit the ministry because of his involvement in the scandal. Swaggart used the occasion to chide Bakker, drawing a parallel to the biblical story of David and Bathsheba. "David never blamed it on Bathsheba," Swaggart reminded his hearers. "He never blamed it on a hot, sultry night. He just said, 'Lord, I have sinned, and it is my fault.' Jim Bakker, as I see it, has not done that yet." Swaggart used the occasion to defend his own role in bringing the incident to light: "I put my ministry on the line. I went public . . . in no uncertain terms. I don't know how it will affect my money, my image. But if the whole church turns against me, I still got to preach what I believe is the truth."

And, as the investigation widened, and as more facts became known, even Jerry Falwell's position toward the Bakkers became increasingly more hard line. Writing in his *Liberty Report,* the Lynchburg evangelist complained: "It is doubtful that the cause of Jesus Christ has ever suffered a greater tragedy than during the past several weeks. The credibility of every Bible-believing pastor, evangelist and church in America has been greatly damaged." Falwell was saddened too that the liberal press was making ideological capital out of the episode: "They would like to convince the American public that *all* evangelical and fundamentalist Christian ministries on television and radio are dishonest and unworthy of the financial support of Christian people."

Within days, Jim Bakker was accused of "moral failure" by the leadership of his church, the Assemblies of God, and was formally dismissed from its ministry. Within days, public respect for Christian television ministries plummeted, and financial support dropped to the lowest point in several years. A Louis Harris survey, released on April 20, 1987, confirmed that by a decisive 69 to 25 percent the American people are convinced that the television ministers "do more harm than good." The Harris poll also brought empirical evidence that "the size of the following of the evangelicals may also be slipping rapidly." In similar surveys conducted over the past several years, approximately 21 percent of the American public said they were followers of the television preachers. That number dropped to 16 percent, according to telephone inquiries conducted between April 10 and 15. And the same polls disclosed that approximately 40 percent of those who consider themselves followers of the evangelists are seriously rethinking their commitment. And on specific matters: (1) by 60–36 percent, the persons queried feel that Bakker's affair with Hahn is "an indication of the lack of moral standards in the TV evangelical movement"; (2) by 60–34 percent, those asked believe that Tammy Bakker's need to be treated for a drug problem is also "an indication of the lack of moral standards" within the television evangelism movement; (3) by 72–22 percent, those asked "condemn payment of $265,000 in hush money by Bakker's successor to keep the church secretary from publicly revealing the story of her affair with Bakker"; and (4) by 72–23 percent, the same respondents believe "it was an indication of the lack of moral standards" for Oral Roberts to declare that he would die unless he received $8 million in contributions. The same poll disclosed that a 52–39 percent majority believed it "indicative of the moral corruption among the TV evangelists" for Pat Robertson, the Bakkers' former boss, to have asked for his father's assistance to get him out of combat duty during the Korean War. The significance of the Harris poll was twofold: in the first place, it underscored that there was little sympathy for Jim Bakker among the American public; and, secondly, it illustrated that indignation against Bakker was also directed against the other Christian television evangelists (Roberts, Robertson, and Swaggart being the ones mentioned most often) and against television evangelism itself.

And the unraveling continued, as more and more details of the Bakkers' lavish lifestyle and of the spending patterns at PTL became known. And the Bakkers themselves, whose livelihood required that they make themselves visible, several times per week, before millions of television viewers and thousands of members of the live audience, were not enjoying the enforced seclusion. Jim Bakker telephoned a newspaper reporter of the *Muskegon Chronicle* (Michigan), in his hometown, to explain to his family and friends what had happened, and to complain about their treatment in Palm Springs. Our world has been reduced "to the size of a postage stamp," he told the reporter, and their house was under constant surveillance. "Do you know they're taking pictures of us with telephoto lenses now?" Bakker asked. "They're getting on the tops of buildings a half-block away and trying to get our pictures. This is a Spanish-style house, and there are no drapes on the windows. They can see in every window except a little corner in our living room and the bedroom." He called it "free-for-all time right now." He said that he had anticipated that television and newspaper reporters would be trying to get pictures and writing stories, for this, as he put it, is "their job." But, he added, he was "surprised by people in the ministry . . . to hear such hatred directed toward me." The point of his telephone call, however, was to apologize to his friends and supporters. "I am so very, very sorry," he repeated. "I am so very sorry this happened. I ask God to forgive me every hour of every day."

William Michaels, an executive with an investment firm in Tulsa, Oklahoma, Oral Roberts's headquarters, published an op/ed piece in the *New York Times,* on April 2, under the title "Oh, to Be Rid of TV Evangelists."[2] Michaels, who was distressed that the city of Tulsa had allowed itself to be exploited by Roberts for the past twenty-five years, offered this scenario regarding the way in which the television evangelists operate. First, he said, "they decide which charitable causes people will be eager to donate money for—a church, a school, a hospital." Then, after raising the money for such causes, they donate some of it to support the designated charity, "while the rest is placed in so-called outside investments, many of which are in effect controlled by companies owned by the evangelist or his family." In Michaels's view, though such practices do not necessarily violate the Internal Revenue Code in any technical sense, the intention clearly is to enhance the evangelists' "own personal pleasure and their self-aggrandizement." Furthermore, finding protection under constitutional principles regarding freedom of religion, the television evangelists have a successful record in warding off would-be investigators. Incensed that his own city has been exploited this way, Michaels concluded:

> As a resident of Tulsa, I believe this city has a far higher destiny than to be simply the headquarters for electronic beggars. Consider how much money has been diverted from Tulsa's good established churches by the divisive influence of Mr. Roberts over the last 25 years.
>
> Tulsa's future should not be to remain a vortex of electronic panhandling, peopled by false prophets who gather around fortunes used not to aid the less fortunate. . . . We should rid ourselves of these parasites of the Lord and turn our energies instead toward improving our education system and promoting friendlier laws that would attract other people and new businesses.[3]

Meanwhile Jerry Falwell was receiving much criticism, some of it from members of his own Thomas Road Baptist Church congregation in Lynchburg, for getting so fully and visibly involved in the case. Though much of the "outside world" would simply view Falwell and Bakker as belonging to the same group of conservative Christians, if for no other reason than that each is a prominent television evangelist personality, it is important to note that Christian fundamentalists (which Falwell is) and Christian Pentecostalists (which Bakker is) have not always enjoyed amicable relationships with each other. Bakker had been criticized for asking a fundamentalist—and, therefore, someone outside the sanctionable PTL camp—to take over the operations of his enterprise. Now Falwell was being severely criticized for accepting involvement in the controversy.[4]

The Lynchburg evangelist understood the criticism.

Previously he had shown little tolerance for Pentecostalists, even observing that Christians who speak in tongues "are people who ate too much pizza last night." And there were many within Falwell's following who were openly pleased that the Jim and Tammy show—which, by this time, was being strongly ridiculed and satirized—was suffering so openly and extensively. PTL, some were saying, stands for "Pay the Lady," or "Pass the Loot."

"My soul," Falwell exclaimed to the members of his church, "in 1980, when we had a part in electing a President and throwing out twelve Senators, there was nothing like the backlash we've had with this." Falwell explained that he had received "fifty hot calls from my Baptist preacher brethren who called us everything but gentlemen. I don't know what their philosophy is—to bomb it, to napalm it, maybe. But it's not mine." Then, pleading with his friends (and with his colleagues in the Baptist faith) for understanding and cooperation, Falwell requested, "Please, please trust me to follow the Lord's leading in this matter. This is an unprecedented happening. I need divine wisdom." Following the plea he enunciated the principle upon which he had been drawing to guide the character of his involvement in the undertaking: "We ought to be friends to all who are friends of Christ," he said. "We don't have to preach what they preach or believe what they believe, but we ought to be their friends."

The outlook in Palm Springs appeared bleak, but the Bakkers' situation worsened further by virtue of a disclosure that Jessica Hahn was not the only person with whom the PTL evangelist had had a questionable sexual relationship. On Friday, April 24, 1987, the Reverend John Ankerberg, another television evangelist of the Assemblies of God faith, charged that Bakker had used prostitutes and had engaged in homosexual acts. Ankerberg offered evidence consisting of tape recordings of interviews with witnesses. On April 26, the *Washington Post* carried an article alleging that one of Ankerberg's tape recordings was of a woman identified as a prostitute in Charlotte, who had told television station WSOC (Charlotte) of three sexual encounters with Bakker for which she was paid $40 each. It was also alleged that on one occasion Bakker had donned a wig to protect his identity in a Charlotte massage parlor. And there was talk of "wife-swapping" among PTL officers.

Bakker responded on Saturday, April 25, via a statement read by his wife. "I have never been to a prostitute, and I am not or have ever been a homosexual," it said. "Those who say such things should have those accusers come forward and give their names and prove their accusations."

Well, some did come forward. On Sunday, April 26, Baton Rouge-based television evangelist Jimmy Swaggart appeared on CBS's "Face the Nation" broadcast, and said that he had seen some of the evidence. Moreover, in Swaggart's judgment, Ankerberg was a trustworthy person, a man of integrity. "I have seen some of the proof," Swaggart testified, "and I don't know all of the charges, but I do know about some of them, and I do believe that they are true."

Oral Roberts didn't know if the charges were true, but he wanted to defend Jim Bakker. "I stand by that man who sinned and said, 'I sinned and now I repent,' " Roberts declared. "I stand by those who want to forgive him—that's where I stand."

Jerry Falwell, also appearing on "Face the Nation," didn't want to get into the specifics of the accusations. He was willing to say that the Reverend Ankerberg "is a very highly respected church leader in America." And, speaking on behalf of the PTL board of directors, he added that "we do take seriously what he is saying." But he wanted it to be a matter that the board took up in its regular session, in private. He offered, though, that in the judgment of Assemblies of God philosophy, it is regarded as being more serious to be involved in homosexual activity than to be involved in an adulterous relationship with someone of the opposite sex. Restoration is possible in the latter instance, Falwell explained, but the Assemblies of God "allow no recovery" for those engaged in homosexuality.

But Falwell wanted to stay away from the Ankerberg accusations. His own preference was to use his "Face the Nation" appearance to talk with his own accusers, to explain to them why he was doing what he was doing, and to reassure them that he would stay in his new position only as long as he believed it to be absolutely necessary. He repeated that he "really [is] praying about how long I should be involved there," and said that he might even resign at the next meeting of the board, scheduled to begin the next day.

At that board meeting, Falwell learned more of the details of the PTL operation, and all previous expectations of an early and positive outcome to the difficulties had to be thoroughly revised.

On Tuesday of that week, during the second day of meetings, the board voted to cut off the salaries paid to the Bakkers. Falwell urged the board to take this action after receiving a letter from Bakker in which the latter threatened "a holy war" if Falwell interfered with Bakker's planned return. After the announcement was made, Tammy Bakker again made a brief appearance on the driveway of the Bakkers' Palm Springs home. "We are very sad right now," she said. And then, with tears flowing, she promised that "Jim will be back soon, and will explain our side of what happened."

The board also voted to remove Richard Dortch from the PTL payroll. Dortch, Bakker's top assistant, had been working as the television host of the "PTL Club." The board took this action because of Dortch's role in the coverup and because of the excessive salary that he had helped arrange for himself.

The board also declared that they would ask Jessica Hahn to return the portion of hush money she had received. By talking with reporters, they said, she had violated the terms of the settlement. Hahn, appearing outside the door of her house in West Babylon, New York, like Tammy Bakker, also in tears, denied that she had violated any terms. "I have done everything I've been asked to do," she pleaded. "I've kept quiet. I have not been hostile to Jim Bakker or the ministry. I have not even commented about Jim Bakker."

Falwell admitted that his involvement in PTL matters had become far more extensive than he had anticipated, but he reiterated that he sought no "permanence" in the organization. Speaking directly to the gathering of PTL employees, after receiving their sustained applause, Falwell declared, "I love every one of you. I don't have a hit list. I'm not mad at anyone. I believe God led us to assume this responsibility at this hour." And, on the same day, the Internal Revenue Service announced that it was considering revoking PTL's tax-exempt status for 1981–83 because "a substantial portion" of the organization's earnings directly benefited the Bakkers, other officers, and their friends and relatives.

Then the Assemblies of God church became formally involved in the drama. After investigating charges, the executive presbytery of the church ruled that both Jim Bakker and Richard Dortch should be dismissed as ministers. Bakker was dismissed for his encounter with Hahn and "for his alleged misconduct involving bisexual activity." Dortch was dismissed for the role he played in the coverup, or, in the words of the committee, for "conduct unbecoming to a minister." Although the two ministers had submitted resignations on March 19, when the disclosures first became public, the decision was not reached until May 6, 1987. Church protocol for Assemblies of God requires that resignations are not accepted immediately, pending investigation of churches and reasons by a committee appointed at the district level. That committee completed its work, transmitted its recommendations to the national church body, and the national organization concurred in the recommendation.

Informed of the decision, Jim Bakker, accompanied by his wife, met reporters on the driveway in front of his Palm Springs home. "Right now, without a miracle of God, we will never minister again," he said. "We don't know what the future holds. We really don't—that's in God's hands."

Meanwhile, back in Fort Mill, South Carolina, Jerry Falwell announced that the financial strains were so great that the PTL ministry might be forced to shut down *unless* supporters sent in a minimum of $7 million by the end of the month of May.

It was a variation on Oral Roberts's plea that his own life would end *unless* his followers sent him $8 million by a designated due-and-payable date. Calling this the "May Emergency," Falwell explained that this was only the beginning: the ministry would need between $20 million and $25 million within the next ninety days to pay creditors, the majority of whom were the television stations who carry the PTL Club. Without this, he reiterated, "the entire ministry will be in dire jeopardy."

The board also announced, with regret, that 200 PTL employees would be dismissed to reduce the monthly payroll of $1.2 million. Falwell explained that the financial situation was much worse than he had believed at first. For over a year, he explained, the ministry had been losing between $1 million and $4 million per month. And the building contractor, Roe Messner, to whom more than $10 million was owed, ordered his workers to board up the unfinished portions of the hotel, and to engage in no more construction. Reiterating the necessity of strict financial accountability, Falwell pledged that he would provide details of a complete financial audit to every PTL contributor.

Though Roe Messner was owed approximately $10 million, he and Jim Bakker remained good friends. Consequently, Falwell had dispatched Messner to Palm Springs, following the meeting of the board on April 28, "to sit down with Jim and ask what can we do to help you." Messner returned with a list of particulars, on Tammy Bakker's personal stationery. He transmitted the list to Falwell on May 6, explaining that "Jim and Tammy gave me this list of things they would like to receive. Jim said they would accept whatever you decide. They both looked great and had very good attitudes." Messner added, "Jim said he would not do anything to hurt you, or the PTL partners. His desire is that the ministry will succeed." The list that Messner brought back included requests of $300,000 (for Jim) and $100,000 (for Tammy) annual salaries ("lifetime"), a PTL-owned and furnished house at Tega Cay, a paid secretary for one year, two cars, all stock that is left from sales of books and records, hospitalization insurance, rights to proceeds from books and records sales, a maid for one year, paid telephone expenses for one year, a security guard (Don Hardister is specified), and attorney fees for whatever costs are involved in responding to the IRS and other audits.

Until this point, Jerry Falwell had been trying to maintain something of a conciliatory attitude. When he was asked to take over the ministry, in mid-March, he and the Bakkers had discussed the terms of the arrangement in a demonstrably amicable way. In the course of his developing involvement, he learned more and more about the Bakkers' mismanagement of PTL, and found it necessary, first, to ask Bakker not to return to the PTL ministry (at least not until the situation could be clarified), and, second, to stop payment of his salary. But, even to this point, he was still trying to function as a reconciler, that is, to make the best of a bad situation, and to go on from there. He would leave—such were his intentions—as soon as the mess could be cleaned up. But when Falwell received the list of requests from the Bakkers, including the one for a $400,000 annual salary for life, he became incensed. And what had been a conciliatory attitude, and an increasingly difficult friendship, degenerated into open hostility, and the hurling of accusations, charges, and counter-charges.

All of it was brought explicitly to public attention on Tuesday, May 26, when Ted Koppel, host of ABC's "Nightline," asked Jim Bakker to respond to questions. Appearing on live national television for the first time since his resignation on March 19, Bakker was anxious to tell his side of the story. He gave a different version of the March 17 transaction with Jerry Falwell. It wasn't he (Bakker) who had gone to Falwell to ask him to protect PTL from an anticipated hostile takeover. Rather it was Falwell who approached Bakker and offered to be a caretaker, to protect PTL from the threat of a takeover by Jimmy Swaggart. In trying to set the story straight, Bakker accused Falwell of trying to steal his ministry.

Jerry Falwell was angered by Bakker's accusation, and called a news conference for Wednesday morning at Heritage USA. He told of his "concern for the welfare of Reverend Bakker and his family," and asked that "all of our people would continue praying for him." But Falwell wanted it known that Bakker's accusation was completely without foundation. "No one, no one, not Jerry Falwell or anyone associated with Jerry Falwell, has ever attempted to take over his ministry, whether in a friendly or hostile takeover." And on the other matter, about who contacted whom, and who raised the prospect of a Swaggart takeover bid, Falwell stated unequivocally: "At no time did Jerry Falwell suggest to him that Jimmy Swaggart or anyone else was attempting to take over his ministry."

Falwell wanted to set the record straight. He stated that the Swaggart takeover possibility was first mentioned not by Falwell, but by Richard Dortch. Dortch had discussed this possibility with PTL's Washington attorney. And the conversation had occurred on March 4, about a week before Falwell or his associates contacted PTL to talk with Bakker about Jessica Hahn. As early as November 12, 1986, Dortch had told Jerry Nims, and another Falwell associate, about the alleged Swaggart-takeover plot, at a meeting in Tampa, Florida. One of Falwell's associates remembers that Dortch "broke down and cried during the meeting at Tampa's airport." Dortch believed that Swaggart was carrying a "personal vendetta" against him. And, by the close of the meeting, Dortch asked Nims to ask Falwell to meet with Bakker. This was the meeting that occurred in Palm Springs on March 17, the meeting at which Bakker says that Falwell fooled him with warnings of the supposed plot, the meeting at which Falwell says that Bakker asked him to take over the PTL ministry.

Furthermore Falwell explained that wanting to steal Bakker's ministry is "like accusing someone of stealing the Titanic just after it hit the iceberg." He pointed out that Bakker's ministry, "absolutely from the moment we obtained the responsibility to lead it, has been in horrendous condition."

But Falwell did reveal that Bakker had telephoned him on the night of May 17, and asked to have his ministry back. Believing that the conversation might be recorded, Falwell chose his words carefully. He rehearsed the entire episode, from the time he confronted Bakker with the information he had—"I had heard that you raped some girl in a Florida hotel"—to the additional information he had acquired regarding alleged homosexual encounters.

> I said, "Jim, here's what I want to say to you. When I was there March 17, and confronted you with the story I had heard . . . , you advised me in a private meeting that you did not rape anyone, that in fact, your wife at that time was in love with another man, and you were trying to win her love back, and hoping to make her jealous.
>
> "John Wesley Fletcher, per your request, brought a 19-year-old girl down from New York named Jessica Hahn. You told me that when the door was closed and you and Jessica were in that room that if anyone raped anyone, she raped you. She began to undress you. [You told me] you were at that moment temporarily impotent, so obviously you could not have intercourse with her.
>
> "You told me that 15 minutes later you were in the shower, weeping and saying to God, 'Oh, God. I've been with a whore. . . . '"
>
> But I said, "Jim, since that time I have learned that not only did you have sex with Jessica Hahn; so did your associate John Wesley Fletcher; and a third person, a member of your team, went in with the intention of having sex with her and she was prostrate and on the floor and unable to respond and could not accommodate him.
>
> "And I've learned, Jim, that two weeks after that, in Hawaii, you went to that person and asked the question, 'Did you get her, too?' And, Jim, that made my blood boil.
>
> "Later I sat across the table from men who told me of your homosexual advances. And since then, of course, I have learned of the fiscal irregularities. And, Jim, I must tell you I would be doing a disservice to God . . . and to the church at large to allow you to come back here, now or ever. . . . "[5]

Then, finished with the recitation of what he had told Jim Bakker over the telephone, Falwell provided those at the news conference with his list of recommendations. "Number one," he began, "he

(Bakker) needs to come clean about Jessica Hahn and repent. That little girl, 19, 20 years of age, in my opinion, was injured for life by that terrible travesty in Florida." Falwell explained that Bakker needs to ask God's forgiveness, and "he needs to say to Jessica, 'Please forgive me.' " Secondly, Falwell continued, Bakker "needs to acknowledge these homosexual problems dating back from 1956 to the present time, as they've been alleged to us." Here too, in Falwell's counsel, Bakker needs to say, "Yes, I've been wrong. I've made a mistake. I have sinned. But I ask God's forgiveness." And finally, in Falwell's judgment, Bakker needs to "return the millions of dollars that have been taken from the coffers of this ministry at the cost of widows and supporters and people who've sacrificially built this Christian ministry." Not until he has done all three, in Falwell's view, will he have demonstrated that "he has genuinely repented and deserves the right of fellowship."

Falwell was conscious of the fact that the viewers and hearers might simply be comparing his word with Bakker's, and would have difficulty knowing which of the two was telling the truth. "How do I expect people to believe me instead of believing Jim Bakker? I don't know," he stated. But he wanted it understood that in a ministry of thirty-five years, he had never once been "charged with immorality or confiscation of funds. . . . I would suggest that a 35-year track record may mean something."

Bakker was given an opportunity to respond that same evening, Wednesday, May 27, when both he and Tammy were the invited guests of Koppel's "Nightline." Koppel initiated the interview by asking Jim Bakker "why in heaven's name did you agree to come on?" Bakker said that he and Tammy had remained quiet for "these many, many weeks," but now they wanted to respond to the thousands of people who have written them to say, " 'We really want to hear from you, Jim and Tammy. We want to know what went on. We want to know where you are, how you feel. . . . ' "

Koppel's first question was the obvious one. What about the statement Jerry Falwell made earlier in the day? Koppel paraphrased it: " . . . forget about the precise words, forget about the precise charges for a moment—he is saying, 'Jim and Tammy Faye, don't you ever set foot down here again. Don't you give us anymore trouble. Get back in your hole and stay there if you know what's good for you.' Do you read it any differently?"

Bakker told Koppel that the entire situation saddened him, that this "thing just hurts us so deeply." And he reiterated that they would like to return to PTL if the people there wanted them back. "It's our love. It's our baby. We built it," Bakker declared. "I want my ministry back."

Bakker told Koppel of the plans he had been contemplating. He said that he had put together a list of twenty-five directors for a reconstituted board of directors. He would give this new board the power to decide what his salary should be, what cars he should own or drive, and what the other terms of his employment would be. He repeated that he was sorry for the mistakes he had made in the past. "We felt we dealt with our sins seven years ago," he stated. "God forgave us. Now we are asking the people to forgive us." And in response to questions about huge salaries and excessive spending on items of personal luxury, Bakker countered that a generous board of directors had made all of this available to them, and urged them to take advantage of it. "They told us we were worth it," Tammy added. In retrospect, Bakker confided, it was "a mistake." Looking back, "if I had to do it over again, we would just say 'No.'" But he explained that the board made additional offers to him that he had refused. And, as to the $400,000 annual lifetime salary that he was requesting of Falwell (in the list of desirables he had given to Roe Messner), Bakker explained that he had simply "started at the top" in what he anticipated would be negotiations with PTL's board. On the matter of his alleged homosexuality, Bakker challenged his accusers to supply the proof. "I think if people have these charges, instead of shooting at us from behind the bushes they ought to come out and give documented proof." And regarding fiscal management at PTL, Bakker acknowledged that he should have been more attentive to the details of the operation, but he had been very, very busy in doing what he felt obliged to do. "Tammy and I were interested in building our ministry and working for the Lord," he explained. "I did not handle my own finances. I did not handle even my own checkbook. It's a flaw. But anyone who knows me knows I worked day and night."

Bakker reiterated for Koppel that he didn't want to engage in vitriolics with his accusers, with Jerry Falwell, specifically, or with anyone else. But he had been upset by the comments Falwell made about him earlier in the day, though he continued to want to avoid an open quarrel. "I don't want to throw stones at anyone. We don't want to fight," he repeated. "If God cannot deliver us and restore our ministry, then we wouldn't really want it back anyway." He cited the biblical verse, "ye without sin cast the first stone." He commented, "it's just such unscriptural activity for all of us to be debating back and forth publicly; we're supposed to do this privately."

Jim and Tammy Bakker were not invited to take up their former ministry again. Falwell's "May Emergency" was renamed the "May Miracle," by virtue of the fact that the announced objective was accomplished. But in congratulating PTL supporters for their generosity and dedication, Falwell repeated that the month of June would require a similar effort, and every month thereafter, for the foreseeable future. In the meantime, the new PTL board of directors tried to sell as many of the expendable items as they could. Toward this end they invited Jim and Tammy Bakker to return to their former home at Tega Cay, to remove their belongings before the house was sold. The Bakkers did this, traveling from Palm Springs to Charlotte, then to their former home on Wednesday, June 10, 1987, enjoying a triumphant reentry. And if the Bakkers had returned simply to remove the belongings from their former home, this wasn't apparent from the explanations and descriptions both Jim and Tammy offered. Minutes after arriving, Jim told a reporter from the *Charlotte Observer:* "We just feel that God wants us to continue. If the people I minister to are satisfied and happy, and all is fulfilled for them, then Tammy and I are more than happy to start over." But the understanding was that the Bakkers would vacate their home by June 15.

On June 11, the two of them, with friends, journeyed by boat from their home—a distance of less than five miles—to Heritage USA, where they were greeted warmly and excitedly. Bakker reiterated that he would be back in a television ministry "within thirty days." Cheering supporters swarmed the Bakkers' black Mercedes as it pulled in front of the Heritage Grand Hotel, and Bakker shouted to them that he had returned to stay. Taken by surprise by the Bakkers' attempt to make a triumphant return, Harry Hargrave, PTL's chief executive officer, affirmed that "this is a free country. We welcome them back to this part of the United States," Hargrave declared. Then, signaling that their status had been radically altered, Hargrave added: "They can come back any time as paying guests." And he made it clear that PTL had no intention of letting the Bakkers take up residency in their former home.

The next day, June 12, PTL filed for protection under the federal bankruptcy laws provided under Chapter 11. The officers of the board explained that the organization was $70 million in debt, including $23 million in delinquent payments, most of these to television stations. They insisted, however, that PTL was not bankrupt. And Jerry Falwell, speaking on the "Larry King Show," predicted that PTL would emerge successfully from Chapter 11 "in a year or less."

The next day the Florida State Attorney's office disclosed that Mildred Dortch, wife of Richard Dortch, was under investigation for claiming property tax exemptions for which she might not have been eligible. On June 17, in St. Louis, the Reverend Bailey Smith—the one who had told the 1980 Religious Roundtable rally in Dallas that "God does not hear the prayer of a Jew"—was back at it again. Speaking to more than 2,000 Southern Baptist evangelists, Smith said, "I'm not against the Jewish people. But unless they repent and get born again, they don't have a prayer." Paige Patterson, a friend of Smith's, explained that Smith is "a friend of the Jewish people" while being "unequivocal in his conviction that nobody comes to God other than through Jesus." The incident had nothing directly to do with either Jerry Falwell or with the trials and tribulations of Jim and Tammy Bakker, but it served to encourage a further deterioration in the regard by which fundamentalist preachers and television evangelists are held in the eyes of the public.

Meanwhile, the situation of Jim and Tammy Bakker had not been resolved. To raise money for the PTL ministries, an auction had been held, many of the Bakkers' worldly goods and possessions had been sold to the highest bidders. Someone paid $2,900 to purchase a six-foot brass and copper giraffe that had graced the office of Jim Bakker, and the family doghouse was sold for $4,500. Yet, after having missed the June 15 deadline for vacating their former home—which deadline the new PTL officers were not insisting upon rigidly—the Bakkers began giving every indication that they wanted to stay. When asked when he would be leaving, Bakker admitted that their departure was imminent "unless Jerry Falwell changes his mind." Then, with the full dramatics for which she had become known since the difficulties began, Tammy Bakker appeared in front of her house on Wednesday, June 17, to complain about the way the two of them had been treated. Lashing out at Jerry Falwell, Tammy Bakker said that the Lynchburg evangelist had been trying "to take our home away." She mentioned that her son's toys had been sold. Their dogs had been taken to a dog pound. She had a list of particulars.

Mrs. Bakker was also critical of whatever operational decision had been responsible for PTL's ministry to land in bankruptcy court. "He [Jim Bakker] just never would have done that. And we're so sad it happened," she said.

But her venom was mostly directed against Jerry Falwell. "I would like to say I hope that Jerry Falwell and his family never have to suffer the way they made our family suffer," she began. "I know what it's like to be hunted like a little scared animal and running all the time and not be able to get in your car and go anywhere without the cameras pressing up against your car," she complained. And then, with the moving van standing outside their house, owned and operated, significantly, by "Christian Moving Company," Tammy Bakker declared that she and her husband would fight to keep the parsonage. "They keep threatening us they're going to take our home away," she stated. "We're going to get a lawyer, and we're going to try to keep our home."

Even with the pledged assistance of the well-known defense attorney, Melvin Belli, the Bakkers were unable to regain the power and prominence they once enjoyed. Instead of having their television ministry restored, they were forced to live in relative isolation in Gatlinburg, Tennessee, while facing the prospect of a Congressional probe into the funding of television ministries. And, as they waited, they suffered the further indignity of a grand jury investigation into the legality of payments made to Jessica Hahn by the PTL ministries. But, if this were not enough, Hahn was also given opportunity to "tell all" both to the grand jury in Charlotte, North Carolina, and through *Penthouse* and *Playboy* magazines. In the former, she was described as "the woman at the center of America's most sensational sex scandal." And her story in *Playboy* was accompanied by a ten-page picture layout, some of which photographs show her topless in the water, under the title "Jessica Hahn. Born Again. In Words and Pictures." Ms. Hahn explained that "these pictures are a celebration of a new life for me, a new beginning," while admitting that to pose this way is "probably the most ironic, the most far-fetched idea for a church secretary." After telling her story in lurid detail, Jessica Hahn became somewhat of a media personality and was invited to spend time with Hugh Hefner in his Playboy mansion.

In the end, the Bakkers were not successful in their attempt to reclaim their home or recapture their ministry. But their story became real soap-opera material when it became known that Jimmy Swaggart, one of Jim's principal accusers, also fell victim to "moral failure" by virtue of having been photographed leaving the motel room of a prostitute. Through all of this, Heritage USA stayed open, continuing to operate, but a number of individuals and groups made overtures to purchase it, one group wanting to transform the park into the site for a baseball stadium that would help lure a major-league franchise to the Charlotte area.

For Jim and Tammy Bakker, the worst was still to come. In August 1989, Jim was brought to trial—on fifteen counts of wire fraud, eight counts of mail fraud, and one count of conspiracy to commit mail and wire fraud—in the Charlotte courtroom of U.S. District Judge Robert Potter. In pre-trial deliberations, Richard Dortch employed a plea-bargain agreement to testify against his former boss, and was then sentenced to eight-years imprisonment and fined $200,000. Hoping for leniency from Judge Potter, former Bakker assistants David and James Taggart also agreed to testify, as did former PTL vice president Steve Nelson. David Taggart told the court that Bakker once ordered him to install an air-conditioning unit in his son's tree house, and once fired a cook who had served him a hamburger without mustard. Nelson told the court that he had warned Bakker that "someone could go to jail" over PTL's fund-raising practices.

But, after completing his testimony, Nelson collapsed in the court, whereupon Jim Bakker knelt by his side and prayed softly before paramedics took the stricken man to the hospital. The next day Bakker himself began trembling and sobbing, and had to be placed in handcuffs and leg shackles after a psychiatrist and his defense lawyer testified that he had been hallucinating and cowering in a fetal position on the floor of his lawyer's office. Still sobbing, bent and broken, Bakker was led by federal marshals from the courtroom to a car, where he again curled up in a fetal position in the backseat, to be driven to a psychiatric ward in the federal prison in Butner, North Carolina. The validation that this behavior represented a true mental and emotional collapse, and was not premeditated theatrics or histrionics, was given by Tammy Bakker, who, after visiting her husband, confided that "he told me that he wasn't acting." Jessica Hahn, on the other hand, saw it as planned drama. Bakker had "been acting" his entire career, Hahn commented; this was simply "more of the same." Judge Potter postponed the trial for a few days to give Bakker time to recuperate.

Bakker sat through the rest of the trial as a model of composure as he listened to witnesses confirm that "lifetime partnerships" had been sold to finish construction of the park's Heritage Grand Hotel. An initial limit of 25,000 memberships had been set, but PTL actually issued 68,000 memberships, the proceeds from which were diverted into operating expenses from which the Bakkers received large bonuses. If convicted on the 24 counts against him, Bakker faced imprisonment of up to 120 years and a fine of as much as $5 million.

When it came time for him to testify on his own behalf, Bakker explained his administrative style. "You live by faith in God," he said. "Faith is the supplier of things hoped for, and the evidence of things not seen." He told of the pressure of having "to raise funds for the next week, the next month, the next year." Describing his work as a response to a vision from God, he explained that he was so thoroughly caught up in this vocation that "I did not look at my checkbook for many years."

After two days of deliberation, the jury found Bakker guilty on all counts. Following the announcement of the conviction, Tammy Bakker came out of the courthouse, stood on the steps to sing "On Christ the solid rock I stand; all other ground is sinking sand." Bakker himself emerged to declare his innocence and his continuing faith in God. And Bea Martin, one of the Bakkers' devoted followers, predicted that "Jim will clear out the prisons, and will get the prisoners saved." More soberly, Bakker's attorneys announced that they would appeal the jury's decision.

The potential for grand soap-opera melodrama was not the most obvious characteristic of Heritage USA when I visited the place a few weeks before the scandal broke. Instead Bakkers' park presented itself as a gentle, pleasant, innocuous place. On my visit I was greeted by numerous senior citizens. I found them walking about, sitting on benches reading devotional literature, having cups of coffee and munching on pastry-goodies at tables in front of various gift shops, and participating in scheduled workshops on religion, health, current affairs, and financial planning. As I walked about the place and talked with those who had come there, I had something of the same impression that I had had when frequenting Christian monasteries; much of Heritage USA belonged to the institutional category of "retreat and conference center." It was an intentional Christian community, on a large public scale, dedicated to fostering spiritual growth among individuals who had acquired sufficient time to be able to devote some attention to this subject.[6]

The Bakkers had gotten their start in Christian television broadcasting while working with Pat Robertson in Virginia Beach. The Bakkers offered a "Jim and Tammy Show" for children, and assisted in the production of the "700 Club" in a variety of ways. While working with Robertson, the Bakkers developed a "Friendship Club" (the predecessor to the "PTL Club") which became a successful fundraiser. After several years of functioning as an understudy, Jim Bakker understood himself led by the Lord to resign his position with Robertson. Robertson's response, after hearing the news, was simply, "Jim, if God has told you, I can't argue with that. In my heart, I don't want you to go. In fact, the board of directors has just voted you a salary increase." But the divine directive was insistent. After listening to what Bakker reported had been spoken to him, Robertson said, "You've got to do what God says. As much as I'd like to, I can't hold onto you. But I want you to know that you always have a place here." And the Bakkers went off to establish their own television show, and attendant activities, in Charlotte.[7]

Jim Bakker had envisioned the enterprise as a Christian version of Disneyworld. The idea had come to him when he visited Disneyworld near Orlando, Florida, with his son. He wanted to create a place where persons of Christian sensitivity would have a good time and would find assistance in cultivating their spiritual lives. At the same time, he calculated that this could be the kind of venture, if it caught on, that could bring in adequate financial returns to support an effective television ministry. If it worked well, Bakker would no longer have "to beg and plead for money" (his words) to be able to do what he wanted to do.

For a time the idea appeared to be working. The concept

inspired the gifts to flow, and the people came by the thousands to enjoy the wide variety of programs that had been created. The venture did indeed tap into certain perennial resources of individual spiritual life. When it functioned this way, Bakkers' park became a kind of retreat center, at least in part. It offered daily opportunities for worship, frequent opportunities for devotional reading and prayer, and ample opportunities for the balancing of physical activity with instruction in contemplative discipline. It would not be inaccurate to approach the project as a temporary or semi-monastic undertaking for those who had become serious about the deliberate cultivation of the spiritual life. Indeed, in the end the Bakkers were accused of having fallen victim to "greed, lust, and power" which stand as opposites to the vows of "poverty, chastity, and obedience" that belong to the monastic ideal.

Jim and Tammy demanded disciplined commitment on the part of their devotees, but flaunted such commitments for themselves. They claimed to be working "day and night" on behalf of their cause. And yet, much of the time—perhaps most of the time—they did not hold themselves to high principles. They made numerous religious claims and boasted of their spiritual prowess, but did not honor the requisite religious vows. Monastic tradition, on the other hand, enjoins obligations designed to keep human aspiration in proper alignment with divine agency. Those who have been guided by this trustworthy way of life are acutely sensitive to the fact that any violation or diminishment of a vow brings significant violation or diminishment to the individual(s) as well as to the institution. The violation of the vows makes a mockery of the way of life.

Because they operated as individuals for whom there is no higher authority than the God of charismatic experience, the Bakkers made decisions on their own. But, without benefit of some necessary institutional system of checks and balances, they had no real way of measuring the integrity of their actions, except on the basis of balance sheets (which they hardly knew how to read) and their own individual spiritual ingenuity. Through the centuries, Pentecostalism has been particularly vulnerable to the excesses of whims of personality and the exploits of talented, magnetic charismatic leaders. More than once, those who have claimed to know the will and ways of God with utter assurance have been shown to be honoring their own ambitions. In the Bakker situation, such ambitions broke faith with the spiritual disciplines.

Thus, in addition to violating the vow of obedience, Jim and Tammy violated the vow of poverty. Instead of making themselves poor, they were extravagant in assuming that institutional resources belonged personally to them. Their faithful bodyguard, Don Hardister, found it necessary to resign, on June 17, 1987, for example, after learning that the Bakkers planned to fight for the retention of the lakefront "parsonage" at Tega Cay. Hardister objected to this tactic, he stated, but his deeper anxiety came from the "serious doubts" he had developed about the Bakkers' lifestyle. He cited the need for Mercedes-Benz automobiles and expensive homes. Pat Robertson once explained that the Bakkers desired to live like Johnny Carson. There is something terribly non-authenticating about such ambitions when they characterize persons who profess to be "true servants of God," and who request the financial support of others on the basis of such professions.

And we need hardly say anything about the workings, or misworkings, of the vow of chastity. Here the monastic literature attests that something more than a technical or legal moral code is at stake. The fundamental issue is the posture of self-aggrandizement that seeks satisfaction and confirmation through sexual agency.

I am suggesting that the Bakkers' venture did derive some sustenance and direction from the resources of a distinctly religious mode of life, but only to a point. The sustenance ran out when authentic spiritual nurture came in conflict with the dictates of a contrary spirit. Thus the episode describes a contest between two competing forces. It is not that God is fighting Satan for control of a well-intended enterprise. Rather, it is a story about a venture that, virtually from the first, was motivated and guided by contradictory aspirations. Throughout the saga, the question was not which one of the two forces would eventually dominate, but how long any semblance of order could be maintained when there was conflict at the core of the operation.

Eventually, as could have been predicted, PTL came apart from within. What Jim and Tammy were able to create together they were also able to destroy together. And the really arresting element in the story is that they appear to have behaved exactly the same way in both circumstances.

CHAPTER SIX

A CANDIDATE
FOR PRESIDENT

From all outward appearances, he appears to possess most of the right stuff. His father, J. Willis Robertson, was a U.S. Senator representing the state of Virginia. He himself is a descendant of the first group of settlers to establish a permanent colony in the New World. He is well educated, a Phi Beta Kappa graduate of Washington and Lee University in Lexington, Virginia, and a graduate of the Law School at Yale. He seems remarkably well trained for the era of telecommunication, having served for years as host of the "700 Club," president of a television network, and head of a steadily expanding university that trains Christians for involvement in evangelism and politics. Furthermore, he is the most successful of the nation's television evangelists. Each year for several years he raised more than $200 million for his vast and expanding operation. In the month of May 1986 alone his "700 Club" claimed 15,000 conversions to "the cause of Christ." Though his way has not been easy, his story is primarily one of success. And he has the look, the bearing, the easy rapport with an audience to be able to achieve what Jerry Falwell could never seriously contemplate: to make a serious run for presidential office, perhaps as the one who would claim to be Ronald Reagan's political and spiritual successor.

His enthusiastic supporters frequently refer to him as the Lee Iacocca of the evangelical world. When one observes what he has accomplished, it is difficult to think of him as a small-town Baptist preacher who somehow, someway became so successful at his calling that he attracted national attention. There are ways of looking at him that convince one that he would have been successful at anything he undertook. One can see him as the chief executive officer of a major corporation, or as the president of an international industry. One can even perceive him as a television personality—the host of a talk show, a commentator on the formative political events of the day, or a master of ceremonies for the large, sweeping patriotic extravaganzas that are broadcast in commemoration of national holidays. He has an easy way about him, giving the impression of not often being caught off guard, of being in control, self-assured with finesse and authority.

His is a Pentecostalist, charismatic Christianity that is not as doctrinally belligerent as Falwell's fundamentalism, because of its lighter touch. At the same time, its intrinsic charismatic quality carries few safeguards against lack of rational and institutional control. And this creates difficulty for him, for his intention is to fashion this form of Christianity consistently with a particular rendition of the story of America. It is a ready-for-prime-time portrayal of the Christian faith. Television is its instrumentation, and updated, revisionist American history is its primary material. A blending of American aspiration and Protestant Christian faith, Robertson's message is calculated to be strongly appealing to an electorate that cherishes boldness, strong conviction, resolute authority, and the promise of sanctions and protections of the American way of life.

It wasn't always this way, of course, for Pat Robertson. Most accounts of his successes and enduring promise point to the positive political elements that he represents. They tend to overlook the fact that though his academic career at Yale was respectable, he nevertheless failed to pass the bar exam, and became so discouraged after decisively failing it that he decided not even to try it a second time. Such accounts also tend not to dwell on the host of uncertainties and signs of vocational unsteadiness that marked his early years. Yes, he did indeed find the resources, cultivate the personal talents, and master the technology of Christian television evangelism. But it certainly didn't happen overnight, nor outside an extended process of trial and error that exhibits nearly as much failure as success.

One can read all about this in two autobiographical treatises, one by Pat Robertson himself, entitled *Shout It from the Housetops*

(1972),[1] and a companion piece, *My God Will Supply* (1979),[2] written by Dede (short for Adelia E.) Robertson, Pat's wife. The two accounts chronicle the interweaving of the lives of the husband-and-wife team, from the days they were students together at Yale—she in the master's program in nursing—until the time that the Christian Broadcasting Network (CBN) became a major religious and political success story. Their story is a Christian story, an impressive and forceful illustration of what can happen when the indwelt spirit of God comes to rule a dedicated life.

There is a dramatic before-and-after in both chronicles. Before he was converted, Pat was "a swinger," who enjoyed alcohol and was intent on finding success in business in New York City. Before she was converted, Dede was an aspiring aristocratic woman, having been shaped toward such objectives by her sorority experience in a midwestern college, who had been captivated by the verve, drive, and apparent energy and optimism of the handsome son of a respected U.S. Senator from Virginia. After conversion, both were taught to temper their worldly ambitions. Though they lived for a time in the sparsest of situations (in shared tenement housing in the Bronx, in one-room dwellings—with their three children—when first settling in the Tidewater section of Virginia), they were confident that they were being undergirded by the power and grace of God, and sensed that their corporate experience was preparing them for a large and mighty apostolic work. Both view their lives as a kind of miracle story in which the spirit of God was palpably and impressively present to them in the most unexpected but crucial moments, by whose leading they were privileged to enjoy an evangelistic vocation that is designed, from top to bottom—as St. Paul's of Tarsus was before them—in this precise period of human history. Consequently, both give evidence of a wide-eyed attitude to life that continues to be awestruck by the perpetual surprises of what God can do with lives that are thoroughly dedicated to his service. Both Pat and Dede believe thoroughly and resolutely in the power of miracles because their own stories can be explained in no other way.[3]

The same is both plot and subplot. Indeed, the story about the origins and development of the Christian Broadcasting Network, with all of its satellite activities, is understood to be a story about the New Pentecost that is occurring in what may be the final period of human history before the Messiah returns and the end comes.[4]

This is a serious observation. Robertson believes that the reality of the Holy Spirit is the most important element in the life of a Christian, and is the most important potentiality, by far, for human life itself. Consequently, individuals are distinguished not only on the basis of whether or not they have truly had a born-again experience, but, more definitively, on whether or not they have experienced the baptism of the Holy Spirit. In the months after he became a Christian, in spite of the power and authenticity of what he was later to describe as his "Damascus Road experience," Pat Robertson knew there was something vital and essential that he lacked. What was lacking, the baptism of the Holy Spirit, he received in 1958.

He was living in New York City at the time, but had been invited to the Presidential Prayer Breakfast in Washington, D.C., because his father was a member of a Senate prayer group that was functioning as one of the event's sponsors. At the end of the breakfast, one of the organizers, Bob Walker, editor of a periodical called *Christian Life,* asked Robertson if he heard of the baptism in the Holy Spirit.[5] Pat responded that this was the very experience he had "been searching for." When he returned to New York City, he went directly from Penn Station to a meeting of a group called Christian Soldiers, Inc., where he met Harald Bredesen, who, at the time, was public relations director for the Gospel Association for the Blind. Early in their conversation, Bredesen asked Robertson if "he knew anything about the baptism in the Holy Spirit." Struck that the same question would be addressed twice in the same day, Robertson replied, "Funny you should ask," then explained: "Just today in Washington I met a fellow named Bob Walker, and he asked me the same question." Also startled, Bredesen acknowledged that Walker was one of his best friends. He told Robertson that Walker was eager to talk of the experience because he had just received the baptism. Robertson was "awed by the providence of God," and recalls having these reflections as he left the meeting:

It was time to leave, and as the doors of the car swished shut behind me and the train roared off into the darkness, I sensed that this crew-cut cleric was destined to play a profound role in my life. I was soon to learn that earlier that evening, on the way to the banquet, he had asked, "Lord, you must have some reason for taking me to this dinner. What is it?" The moment he walked into the room and saw me, it was as if God said, "This man is the reason I have brought you here. He is open to the baptism in my Spirit."[6]

Bredesen, in his autobiography, *Yes, Lord,* also speaks of the significance of the meeting with Robertson. He recalls meeting the young man who was "tall and lean with a mop of dark hair and an All-American football-hero smile." He agreed with others who commented that Robertson "resembled John F. Kennedy" since "they shared the same charisma, the same inborn qualities that make a man a leader of men." He also vividly recalls meeting Dede Robertson, Pat's "attractive auburn-haired wife, who was obviously in love with him as he with her." Bredesen remembers his conversation with Robertson: "He started to tell me about all the ups and downs of his life, and it was the perfect description of my own. But he said something tremendous had happened to him, and he was just going to tell me what this experience was when somebody interrupted."[7] The "something tremendous" was Robertson's meeting with Bob Walker earlier in the day.

After the initial meeting, Bredesen journeyed by bicycle to Robertson's house to bring him a book on the Holy Spirit. He explained to Robertson that he wanted to bring the book, and, besides, he had needed the exercise. After Robertson said "That's fantastic. 1 can't get over it. You biked ten miles just to bring me a book?" Bredesen remembers thinking: "I learned that day that Pat had a way of making the ordinary seem spectacular."[8]

Pat Robertson and Harald Bredesen spent much time together in the next weeks. Soon they were going to the same prayer meetings together. Eventually Robertson asked Bredesen to baptise him. Though he had received water baptism in the Baptist Church as a boy, he recognized that he still needed "a believer's baptism." Bredesen performed this rite in the First Baptist Church in Flushing, New York, but Robertson knew immediately that it was not a baptism in the Holy Spirit. In the next several weeks, Robertson's and Bredesen's friends and family became friends and close associates of each other. On regular occasions they met for prayer. During one of these prayer meetings, in the Flushing Full Gospel Church, something dramatic occurred. Robertson reports that Bredesen "suddenly leaped to his feet," and began expounding in "a torrent of beautiful words in a tongue I had never heard pouring from the depths of his being." Robertson remembers recognizing that Bredesen "seemed transported into another realm of experience. I didn't know what had happened to him. I only knew that God had touched his life."[9]

Bredesen's version of the event is recorded as follows:

> . . . I was praying with Dick and Pat and the rest of our group when I felt the hand of God upon me. There, as I was praising God with my friends, the glory of God came down upon me so strong that I couldn't kneel. I leaped to my feet while a torrent of words in a tongue I had never heard before poured out of the depths of my being. I was overwhelmed with a sense of the marvelousness of God's love and His grace. I wanted to proclaim the Gospel everywhere. I had always dreaded going into the ministry, because of having to preach; now I longed for the chance to tell everyone about Jesus."[10]

After discussing this event with Robertson, Bredesen went home to ponder its implications. The next day a friend telephoned to communicate a vision that she had had which pictured Bredesen as the pastor of a church. Two days later Bredesen was invited to accept a call to be pastor of First Reformed Church in Mount Vernon, New York. Bredesen accepted, asking Pat Robertson to be his assistant pastor. Robertson accepted, and the two interpreted the unusual spiritual occurrence to signify that God had wanted them to work together.

Robertson's own experience of being indwelt by the power of the Holy Spirit came one night, in his own home, a few weeks later, when he was anguishing over the severe illness of his son, Tim, who was suffering a high fever, and had become unconscious while experiencing muscle spasms. Fearing that the boy would not make it, Robertson fell to his knees in desperation, "God, do something!" he pleaded, then tried to resign himself to the omnipotent will of God. "Instead of begging anymore," he reports, "I just consciously lifted Tim up to the Lord. I gave him back to God." Next, "suddenly I was aware of the love of God enfolding him, and the power of God going through him." At this point, the boy opened his eyes, looked at his father, and said, "Daddy, I gotta go to the bathroom." Robertson was so thoroughly relieved and overjoyed that he simply shouted "Praise you, Jesus. Praise your holy name." And in that moment he became aware that his speech was garbled, and that he was speaking in another tongue: "Something deep within me had been given a voice, and the Holy Spirit had supplied the words. I was aware of the sounds, but they were not of my own creation. It sounded like some kind of African dialect, and the flow of words continued on for five minutes or more."[11]

Robertson was so caught up in what was transpiring that he didn't realize that his wife was in the room. "How long has this been going on?" Dede asked. Pat wasn't sure what she meant. "Speaking in tongues," she responded. Pat said that this was the first time this had happened. His wife said, "You remember I said you didn't need to go running around all over the city seeking; I told you that God would give you the baptism right here in your own living room." Within months Dede Robertson had experienced the same for herself. She had been kneeling beside her bed, thanking God for her family, for good health, for freedom, for the necessities of life, then: "While I was praying, just as naturally as if I were speaking in my own language, I began to pray in the Spirit. The tongue sounded like beautiful French to me, but it wasn't my French, for sure. My French was anything but beautiful."[12]

It was in the period of time immediately following that Pat and Dede Robertson understood themselves to be led by the same indwelling Holy Spirit to buy an inactive, defunct television station in Virginia, which was the beginning of the Christian Broadcasting Network. When they sensed that this is what God had wanted them to do, communicating his will for them through the Holy Spirit, they began to laugh and dance. Pat prayed, "Oh Lord, this idea of buying a television station is so crazy. We have no money and no television experience. We're not sure what to do with the station. But we know for sure that You are sending us forth." And they took off from New York City with a U-Haul trailer, their belongings, their children, and $70—the $100 that Pat received as a gift from his mother, minus $30 that was spent for gasoline and groceries. In their view, the remainder of the success story is a miracle too. By 1986, the Christian Broadcasting Network had become the second largest satellite-to-cable service in the nation, servicing some 30 million households with a potential viewing audience of 70 million persons. Robertson's daily "700

Club" is carried on close to 200 television stations, and is broadcast in over 60 countries, including mainland China and Lebanon (from where it is beamed throughout the Middle East). The Network also owns and operates television stations in Dallas, Boston, and the Virginia Beach area, and maintains telephone counseling centers in 60 American and 25 foreign cities. In addition, CBN offers graduate degrees in five fields of study: Biblical Studies, Public Policy, Business Administration, Communications, and Education. Through a CBN program, called Operation Blessing, more than 5 million Americans and an equal number of persons overseas are assisted each year with food and housing needs. In addition, the Robertson operation also includes a national grass-roots organization, called Freedom Council, which although it functions throughout the country like a political action committee, was established to "protect religious liberty."

When one talks with the people involved, one encounters two strong thematic emphases. The first is the confidence that the Holy Spirit is at work in the world, the signs of whose presence are in evidence around every corner. CBN workers understand that Pat Robertson was the willing instrument who assisted at the birth of their organization. He was instrument, but neither founder nor creator. God is founder and creator; thus, he who is singularly responsible for CBN is the God who created the world and gives of his spirit to those who submit to his will.

The second underlying theme—a strong injunction—is that the time has come for Christians to reclaim the world. Laura Walker, a staff person at CBN University told me confidently that "Christians have been appointed to take the land back." I asked for explanation, and heard Dr. Jerry Horner, Dean of the School of Biblical Studies at CBN University, say:

> Well, for too long we Christians have allowed everyone else to set standards for us. The world sets standards regarding what we are to hear on the radio, what we are to watch on our television screens, what we are to read, how we are to dress. The world has been telling us how to measure success. And we've tolerated it too long. It is time for us to set our own standards, to establish our own dominion, to bring our exile in the land to an end.

Agreeing with Laura Walker, Horner reiterated, "Yes, God wants us to take the land back."

And when Robertson followers talk this way, they point to the fact that in recent years Christians have established their own television stations, newspapers, styles of music, modes of fashion, art forms, analyses of culture, hospitals, educational institutions, political action committees, and candidates for office. In addition, they have cultivated their own sense of what it is to be an American, their own version of human destiny, and their own interpretations of the significance of national and international events. When they do this they are simply exercising their obedience to God's intentions.

The two thematic emphases are thoroughly interrelated. The work of the Holy Spirit is understood to be the prime cause of that process through which Christians are claiming dominion over the land. Several implications follow. Emphasis upon the work of the Holy Spirit brings emphasis to the process of creativity as well as to the theological doctrine of creation. Creation is God's activity, but creative human beings (if such creativity is being prompted and guided by God's spirit) can be sure that their activities and God's are interrelated. Emphasis upon creation brings emphasis to the status of the land—specifically *this* land, as in the phrase "this land is our land." A Christian can hardly think about the meaning of the land without thinking about the purposes of creation; and, through the nexus of ideas and convictions that pertain here, it is difficult to think properly about either without contemplating the role and presence of the Spirit. To create, in all of these contexts, is "to breathe life into," as in the opening passage of the Book of Genesis in the Hebrew Bible: "In the beginning, God created the heavens and the earth. The earth was without form and void, and darkness was upon the face of the deep; and the Spirit of God was moving over the face of the waters." The connections between these conceptions enable the Robertson group to link reverence for the *Holy Spirit* to the act of *creation* as well as to the status of the *nation* (being a principal focus and recipient of God's creative activity), since God's creation and land as creation belong together. Thus by a series of steps in theological reflection, Robertson's understanding of the presence of the Holy Spirit is thoroughly compatible with his convictions concerning the nature and destiny of the United States.[13]

Furthermore, there are strong and direct conceptual and convictional linkages, in Robertson's understanding, between the work that is effected by the Holy Spirit and the reality of the Kingdom of God. Robertson frequently refers to the latter as "the secret kingdom," which, to a remarkable degree, is the life-world that is reestablished when Christians reclaim dominion over the land. When the Holy Spirit breathes life into an individual, in Robertson's view, he also places that person in responsible access to the fullness of the world where God is present. He uses such phrases as, "we are standing on holy ground, my friends, for we are in the very center of God's purposes." Robertson recognizes, in this regard, that individuals, families, and nations live out their lives and conduct their behavior according to specific attitudinal and dispositional sets. He believes that this is why the contest between a prescribed Christian way and the way that is identified as being "secular humanism" is so crucial. The same can be said of the competition between a democratic/capitalist system of human governance and that which rules the communist world. Human lives are principled in very specific ways. Such principles are expressive of certain conceptions, as it were, of the nature of reality. All such views and principles are unable to measure up to those that pertain to the Kingdom of God, a realm or region of life that runs according to certain fixed and immutable laws. And Robertson confesses that he didn't know all of this after experiencing the baptism in the Holy Spirit:

> Having been trained and surrounded by Christians who did not concern themselves especially with the Lord's teaching on the reality of the kingdom here and now, I didn't begin to catch glimpses of this reality in any meaningful way until the mid-seventies. I, too, had dwelt pretty much on the good news of salvation and the work of the Holy Spirit in believers' lives, and that truly is good news. But there is much more.
>
> By mid-decade, I was wrestling with John the Baptist's insistence that "the kingdom of heaven is at hand." As I have said, I soon saw he was reporting that the kingdom was here—here on earth—obviously because Jesus Christ was here.

Robertson continues:

> I mused over this for many weeks and months, tracking through the Scriptures, praying for wisdom, and talking with one or two friends. As I badgered the Lord for wisdom, I began to realize there are principles in the kingdom as enunciated by Jesus Christ and that

they are as valid for our lives as the laws of thermodynamics or the law of gravity. The physical laws are immutable, and I soon saw that the kingdom laws are equally so.[14]

Thus, the ways of the secret, invisible Kingdom of God—an ever-present reality—are as dependable and law-like as the laws that pertain anywhere else.

Robertson employs this comprehensive understanding of the nature of things to affirm the unique status of the Holy Bible. The Bible, in Robertson's view, is the sacred Word of God in which the principles of the secret present kingdom are to be found. The Word of God is the truth, and it also has an indispensable practical function. Robertson comments:

> Once we perceive this secret, we realize anew that the Bible is not an impractical book of theology, but rather a practical book of life containing a system of thought and conduct that will guarantee success. And it will be true success, true happiness, true prosperity, not the fleeting, flash, inconsistent success the world usually settles for.
>
> The Bible, quite bluntly, is a *workable guidebook* [emphasis mine] for politics, government, business, families, and all the affairs of mankind.[15]

The formula can be stated succinctly. The Kingdom of God, over which the Spirit rules, is fundamental reality, though it is not perceived or recognized this way except through the guidance of the Spirit. This fundamental reality is governed by unchangeable laws, which laws are revealed and elaborated upon in the Bible. Lives lived in accordance with the guidance of the Spirit will also conform to the laws and principles that are revealed in sacred scripture. Such lives are bound to be successful, since they have been principled by the only sure and "workable guidebook." Robertson paraphrases Jesus' injunction from the Sermon on the Mount: "Seek the kingdom, under the way it works, and then, as day follows night and as spring follows winter, the evidences of earthly success will follow you." Robertson's counsel is "to reach into that kingdom" and allow its principles to govern one's life right now. And the promise is that "God will inaugurate the visible reign on earth of His Son and of those who will rule with Him." His purpose for them now is that they come to "know Him and learn how His secret kingdom functions."[16] Such functions are applicable in every area of human life. And they are particularly prominent in education. "The mission of" CBN University, for example, as stated in its catalog, "is to restore God's word to its rightful place in the university by bringing Biblical truth to bear on every discipline, in every area of life."[17]

I spoke with Dr. Herbert W. Titus, Vice President for Academic Affairs and Dean of the School of Public Policy at CBN University, about this very point. Before moving to Virginia Beach, Titus had served on the faculties of the Universities of Oregon, Colorado, and Oklahoma. While teaching in the Law School at the University of Oregon, he had experienced a radical conversion to Christianity. "Simply put," he said, "I got saved. I know it sounds corny, but this is exactly what happened." Titus not only believes that biblical truth is the fountain and safeguard of all truth, and particularly of the kind that gets disseminated through the fields and disciplines that lend constitution to a college and university curriculum; but he is also confident that this principle was understood by the nation's Founding Fathers. Titus argues that when the framers of the Declaration of Independence affirmed that the nation was founded upon the "laws of nature and of nature's God, they were thinking specifically of the attitudes of John Locke and William Blackstone, the basis for much of which was the thought of Samuel Rutherford who had derived such ideas from the Hebrew Bible. This, in Titus's interpretation, implies that the principles that govern the land are the laws of the Bible, which laws are the only guarantee of the freedom of the people. But Titus is more indebted to Blackstone than to either Locke or Rutherford (in whose interpretation of the latter he follows the lead of Francis Schaeffer). He loves Blackstone's comment, in chapter 2 of his *Commentaries on the Law of England,* that God, the Creator of the heavens and the earth and of all living creatures, "created the rules of action that all creation was bound to obey."[18] The emphasis upon necessary obedience is in keeping with the idea that the Bible is a "workable guidebook." Put all of it together, and one comes to the conclusion—strongly enjoined—that only when the American people live in accordance with these laws will they "enjoy the blessings of their God-given rights to life, liberty, and the pursuit of happiness." The direct implication is that if Americans are not currently enjoying such blessings, it is due to the fact that they have broken the laws. It follows, therefore, that when the reality of the Kingdom of God comes afresh, it brings those immutable laws with it. The Kingdom is accessible only through the power of the Holy Spirit, which in turn is accessible only through baptism, which is accessible only through a born-again experience, which is the key and point of entry to all that is most significant.

The inescapable conclusion is that the signers of the Declaration of Independence and the framers of the Constitution both intended that the United States of America be *a Christian nation*. Titus contends that there are impressive texts that support this interpretation. In a February 29, 1892, ruling of the U.S. Supreme Court, for example, he discovered this line: "If we pass to a view of American life as expressed by its laws, its business, its custom, and its society, we find everywhere a clear recognition of the truth that this is a Christian nation." He is also impressed that Emilio Castelar, a Spanish statesman, attributed the strength of the United States to "its founding on one book, the Bible" in a celebrated speech before the Constitutional Assembly of Spain on March 12, 1870. He finds it instructive that most of the charters for the colonies identify "propagating of the Christian faith to people who as yet live in darkness and miserable ignorance of the true knowledge and worship of God" (a phrase taken from the First Charter of Virginia) as the purpose of the new settlements. And he recognizes that the Mayflower Compact draws upon certain central assumptions regarding covenant, chosen people, New Israel, and the like. It is selected evidence that enables Titus and the other Robertson spokespersons to ascribe legal authority to certain religious and political objectives. Since the First Charter of Virginia identifies evangelization as the *raison d'etre* of the commonwealth, and since M. G. (Pat) Robertson is a descendant of those first settlers, it is fitting—his followers would say—that he is leading an undertaking that was explicit from the beginning. Now, through the power of television, the propagation of the Christian faith to all who live and walk in darkness is a real possibility. And the verses also stand as partial historical evidence that the Robertson theorists are not simply imposing ideas of their own. At least, this is their claim, their intention, their hope.

However, the truth is that the body of legal documents, taken in their own terms, are not capable of producing or sustaining such an interpretation. Certainly selected statements and phrases can be read as being reflective and/or supportive of a Christian fundamentalist view regarding the status of the nation, that is, if the interpreter has such a view in mind and is intent upon finding confirmation of it. But the same documents can be interpreted more fully and cogently apart from such intentions. No matter what arguments Robertson or Falwell enthusiasts mount, the fact is that the signers of the Declaration of Independence in 1776 as well as the framers of the Constitution in 1787 were neither Christian fundamentalists nor fundamentalist precursors, and no distillation of their religious convictions can ever be interpreted as lending explicit support to the fundamentalist cause. One comes much closer to an accurate identification of their creedal affirmations when one studies their remarkable and perhaps startling association with Freemasonry, a movement whose teachings and practices do not even qualify as being explicitly Christian. The father of the country, George Washington, our first President, was a Freemason. In 1734 Benjamin Franklin was elected grand master of the Masons in Pennsylvania. Thomas Jefferson, the intellectual inspiration behind many of the very documents on which current fundamentalist claims are based, was a Freemason too. We are not proposing that the religious content of the formative documents of the republic can be accounted for in Freemasonist terms. But we are suggesting that they are profoundly more compatible with the teachings of this secret fraternal order—whose prominence in the eighteenth century is directly associable with the rise of anticlericalism and freethinking—than they could ever be with Christian fundamentalist teachings. The spirit of tolerance with regard to political and religious ideas that Jefferson championed— the conviction that laws, institutions, and truths develop in accordance with "the progress of the human mind"— is antithetical to the fundamentalist penchant for theological dogmatism. If Titus, Bob Slosser (president of CBN University), Robertson, or all of the CBN spokespersons collectively believe that the United States will never again enjoy the blessings of the Almighty unless it conforms to a fundamentalist Christian translation of its founders' expressed intentions, they are bound to be disappointed—or, perhaps, surprised. While Titus's and Robertson's efforts to read the documents this way are moderately impressive, they will never be able to prove that their late twentieth-century interpretation is identical to what the Founding

Fathers had in mind. Nor will they ever be able to demonstrate
that the presidents before Ronald Reagan ever read or saw the
situation that way. While some of those presidents may have been
willing to ascribe to a concept like "Christian nation," they would
not have chosen to be religiously or politically specific. One cannot
read the legal documents in strict fundamentalist terms, even
though words and phrases here and there may whet such an
interpreter's appetite. (The same is true, I believe, concerning the
scriptures—though I have chosen not to address this issue here.)
The conclusion is that the contemporary fundamentalist reading of
the national founders' documents is made in light of post-World
War I theological debates. I don't expect Robertson's supporters to
accept this judgment, but the historical evidence is voluminous.
Yet, it may not be very important. The Pat Robertson movement
is only partially about textual interpretation. Its more basic claim
is to the presence of a living, transcendent spiritual reality—a
kingdom of light and infinite resourcefulness—that is accessible
through the awakening of the Holy Spirit. Robertson's emphasis is
much more on the necessity of this religious experience than on
the correctness of doctrinal formulation.

But the questions are prompted nevertheless. Will Pat
Robertson, the debonair son of a Virginia Senator, with all of his
charm and abilities of persuasion, ever be able to convince the
American people that he holds the meaning of a portion of their
history and destiny? Could they choose a man as candidate for
President who regularly speaks in tongues, is a frequent instrument
of healing (or so he and others say), and confidently believes that
the day-to-day activities of the nation should be dictated by laws
and principles that are integral to the "invisible kingdom" of the
Holy Spirit? Can they turn over their own future to a man who, as
commander-in-chief of the nation's military forces, makes
decisions on the basis of tangible communications and prophecies
that "come to him" through prayer, while he is waiting diligently
to "know the mind of the Lord?" Will they want their leader to be
a person who fully expects this world to cease, perhaps soon, and is
anticipating this eventuality with excitement and enthusiasm, so
that the heavenly world ruler can return to establish the real
kingdom? Could they select a man who not only believes that his
religion is the only religion of salvation, but whose enduring
vocation is to convert "thousands upon thousands" of individuals

to Jesus Christ? And what if he does possess a prophecy that God desires him to take up residency at 1600 Pennsylvania Avenue? How important should such considerations be? What difference, if any, should they make? If a Jeremiah were available to run for office, would the people be well served were he nominated and elected?

Robertson has regularly appeared before the annual meetings of the Full Gospel Business Men's Fellowship International organization, and has made statements, or has presided over religious services, that have become politically troublesome for him among voters who do not share or honor Pentecostal Christian aspirations. What is worse for him, through the abilities of television technology, his performances in these international meetings have been recorded for the world to view. In one of these meetings, in 1981, Robertson led a revivalist faith-healing service in which he proclaimed that members of the audience could claim to be cured for almost everything that ailed them, including cancer and other serious illnesses. The videotape of the meeting shows Robertson holding up his Bible, and saying, "If I am reading this book right, tonight is the night that you get those prayers answered. Tonight is the night!" And what are the prayers that are to be answered? Robertson's summary runs as follows:

> How many people in this audience, right at this moment, still haven't had a prayer answered? You're praying for relief from sickness and you say God hasn't answered me. You've prayed for financial help, and God hasn't answered you. You're asking for guidance or wisdom, and you don't feel like you've been answered.

And then he declares that God has healed persons present in the auditorium of a wide assortment of diseases and ailments:

> God has just healed someone of a concussion, a fractured skull. The Lord has healed him of it. Where are you brother. . . . Aw, there are so many people, I just can't see. But God is healing somebody right now. Thank you, Jesus. Thank you, Jesus. God is healing people all over this place. An inguinal hernia has been healed. If you're wearing a truss, you can take it off. It's gone. . . . Several people are being healed of hemorrhoids, and varicose veins. Thank you Jesus.

He continues:

> There is a woman here with cancer of the womb. I don't think it's

been diagnosed. She didn't know what it was. There has been excessive bleeding. God has healed that right now. It's healed.

And more:

Many people, their eyesight is being opened right now. You're seeing when you couldn't see well before. Your eyes, your vision, is being restored. People can hear. In the name of Jesus, their ears are being opened right now. . . . In the center section here, somebody has been healed of an ulcer. . . . Somebody has swelling in the glands of their neck, the Lord is healing that. . . . There are so many tooth and gum disorders, several here, their teeth are infected and the Lord is healing the teeth right now. I will pray for the gum diseases being healed by the power of God.

And the references to diseases and abnormalities of the mouth bring this elaboration:

Somebody's bite is not right, and God is actually manipulating the jaw right now so the teeth will hit the way they are supposed to, and you can almost feel something happening in your jaw. The Lord is doing a miracle in your life right now. . . . Thank you Jesus.

Robertson utilized the same sermon to attest that he has had personal conversations with the Lord. On one of these occasions, he asked God for $1,000, and after receiving the petition "the heavenly Father said 'all right.'" Robertson received the $1,000, and within a week had to come up with $1,000 to pay for unexpected dental expenses for his daughter. "The Lord knew the need before I called on him," he exclaimed, as his listeners applauded.

When the political going got tough in 1988, he tried to remove or separate himself from the political liabilities of his career as a pentecostal minister. But even the step of relinquishing his ordination, so that he was no longer a pastor, or a "reverend," in formal or official terms, could not remove the heavy baggage of his extensive involvement in charismatic and Pentecostal Christianity. Paul Weyrich, conservative political strategist, pleaded with the electorate to accept Pat Robertson as a candidate for whom religion is his field or profession, just as other candidates represent the fields of law, economics, international relations, and the like. But Weyrich's proposal was not convincing, for it was not Robertson's identification with religion per se that hampered him most, but his nearly life-long advocacy of a particular form of religion that deeply affects how its aspirants make decisions, view the destiny of the human race, and understand the role of the nation within the international community.

For instance, Harald Bredesen, Robertson's chief spiritual advisor, is not only a speaker in tongues, but is a neo-Pentecostal leader whose claim to be speaking Polish and Egyptian Coptic was disputed by a group of government linguists who listened to tape recordings of his "tongue speech." Bredesen's utterances were also analyzed by a conference of linguists in Toronto—specialists who had done field work in more than 150 aboriginal languages in more than twenty-five countries—who concluded that it is "highly improbable that this is a human language." This is not to discredit whatever spiritual value speaking in tongues may have, but simply to call attention to the rather exotic features of the Christian religion that Robertson and his friends and colleagues understand to be its defining characteristics. Pat Robertson, on the election trail, would like to give the impression of being somewhat less exotic than other born-again Christians. But his deep involvement in the charismatic movement—an involvement that is absolutely central to his understanding of what it means to be a Christian—is unmistakable.

It would have helped him had he been able to escape the negative images that have been attached to Jerry Falwell, say, because of the latter's unpopular and inflammatory remarks about Bishop Tutu, Ferdinand Marcos, Ted Kennedy, Eleanor Smeal, and many others. One would have thought that the debonair son of a highly respected Virginia Senator would not allow himself to get involved in scandals of any kind. Certainly he would not be foolish enough, for example, to take on *Penthouse Magazine* in a legal suit—as Falwell has done—over issues of pornography. He seems too cultured, too refined, too self-possessed, indeed too much of the Virginia gentleman to allow himself to be tarnished in any of these ways.

And yet, under the heavy media attention and the close national inspection that comes with running for presidential office, he did find it necessary to confess that he had misrepresented the date of his marriage in 1954 to conceal the fact that his son Timothy was born ten weeks after his and Dede's actual marriage date. It was a difficult confession for him, for he has desired to be regarded as a pillar of moral virtue. Moreover, he has frequently gone on record as being a staunch advocate of sexual abstinence before marriage. When making his confession, he tried to make no excuses for his action, but explained "the transgression" had occurred two years before he had converted to Christianity, and that he had "never maintained that he didn't sow some wild oats." In fact, he amplified that as a young man "I was engaged in wine, women, and song on a number of continents."

When he was asked about the incident, son Timothy Robertson, who had become cohost of the "700 Club," admitted that he "didn't exactly appreciate having the story told on network television." But he knew that his father's life had changed after he had had the born-again experience. Furthermore, Tim affirmed that his parents, from the very beginning, had surrounded him with love.

But it was an episode that was to haunt Pat Robertson. He appeared on Ted Koppel's "Nightline" on October 8, 1987, to answer questions about the incident, and to complain that too much was being made of something that happened over thirty years ago. "The sharks are in a feeding frenzy," he told Koppel, "but there's no blood in the water." He reiterated that much too much was also being made of the allegations that he had claimed combat experience in the Korean War when none existed, and that he had listed "graduate study" at the London School of Economics on at least one of his résumés when he had done no more than enroll in a non-credit seminar in art history that was organized for non-British students. Robertson called it "nitpicking," and explained that he had received combat pay, and had been awarded three battle awards, though he hadn't actually served in the frontlines. And the course he had taken at the University of London involved seminar discussions with the likes of T. S. Eliot, and considerable exposure to the art museums of the area. But by now, such clarifications could not erase the political damage that had been done.

But the most lasting political damage came from Robertson's association with the Bakkers, and also with Jimmy Swaggart. Here, too, it is not the literal interpretation of the situations that create difficulty for a presidential candidate, but the family likenesses. After all, the Bakkers received their start in Christian television evangelism under the sponsorship of the "700 Club." When the two of them left the CBN operation in Virginia Beach to establish their Christian amusement park, they left amicably, with Robertson's blessing. And, from all appearances, this friendly cooperative arrangement existed between the "PTL Club" and the "700 Club" until approximately March 1987, when PTL was scandalized by the disclosure of Jim Bakker's liaison with Jessica Hahn. Until then, the two Christian-television ventures in charismatic renewal understood themselves to be working partners. Pat Robertson had been pleased to acknowledge the mentoring role he had been playing with respect to the Bakkers, and the Bakkers, for their part, were always quick to voice their undying gratitude and devotion toward their former employer. And, though the "700 Club" was designed as a television talk show, and "PTL" was classified much more as television entertainment, the two programs frequently featured the same guest stars. Instead of being perceived as competitors, Robertson's and the Bakkers' respective operations were understood to be working two distinctive areas of a thoroughly harmonious and unifiable ministry.

Pat Robertson tried his hardest to keep himself out of the scandal. He had not been implicated directly, but the principals in the case were well known to him, and national interest in the financial organization of CBN activities increased exponentially, and became specifically focused. Voluntarily, Robertson published and distributed copies of information his organization had supplied to the Internal Revenue Service. Though the reports appeared to be complete, they did not demonstrate that there was no need to be suspicious. An examination of the public records, together with testimony from former top officials within the organization, confirmed that the Internal Revenue Service was examining CBN tax reports. Though the IRS would not comment on the audit, or the reasons for it, it became apparent that the organization had made "misstatements" to the tax authorities either from ignorance or through a deliberate effort to withhold significant information. At issue was the question of whether the religious organization had abused its tax-exempt status by spending money on political activities.

At the same time, it became demonstrable that one or more of Robertson's groups had been directly involved in providing assistance to the Nicaraguan freedom fighters, most commonly

called the Contras. While no charges of illegality were either filed
or even suggested, since Robertson's contributions came in the
form of private gifts of food and personal supplies, knowledge of
CBN's involvement in the Contra cause was circulated widely. In
addition, network television showed pictures of Robertson, during
a visit to Honduras, encouraging the Contra troops. And in direct
testimony before the Joint Select Committees of Congress, Oliver
North acknowledged that he had frequently asked Pat Robertson
for his prayers. There was nothing in any of this to condemn the
Virginia Beach television evangelist. There had been no proof that
he had violated any laws of the land. Even his skirmish with the
Internal Revenue Service might have been classified as a
misunderstanding about legal technicalities implicit in a highly
complicated tax-reporting system. On the other hand, none of this
enabled Pat Robertson to increase and expand his rather narrow
basis of national political support. The "true believers" within his
camp were pleased with the repetition of evidence that he was a
bona fide political conservative. But large sections of the rest of
the population read the same evidence as confirmation of his
political and ideological extremism.

Robertson valiantly tried to separate himself from the Bakker
elements within his own community of religious affiliation.
Appearing at the 1987 annual meeting of the Full Gospel Business
Men's Fellowship International in Anaheim, he sought to assist his
own cause by being sharply critical of the Bakkers. Trying to
encourage the several thousand charismatic Christians who were
present for the meeting, Robertson selected a text from the Acts of
the Apostles, and told the story of Barnabas, and the disciples'
commendation of him, because he had given all that he had to
them after selling some property. Contrasting Barnabas's action
with that of Ananias and Sapphira, Robertson emphasized how the
apostles responded. Ananias and Sapphira sold their property, but
"kept back some of the proceeds, and brought only a part and laid
it at the apostles' feet." Because of this deception, both Ananias
and his wife were stricken. They "fell down and died" because, as
the text portrays it, "they lied to the Holy Spirit."

As Robertson retold the story, he commented that what had
happened to Ananias and Sapphira "didn't hurt the faith of the
apostles." Rather, "they [Ananias and Sapphira] were dead, that's
all." Then posing this question for his audience—"and how do you

deal with someone who plays games with money?"—Robertson offered this simple solution: *"You pronounce them dead."*

The direct application to the Jim and Tammy story came next. "Today we've had in the papers things about money," he commented, explaining that today there is "corruption at the heart of the church," and there are "people who are trying to make believe they were something they are not." He said this to illustrate that what had happened should not be startling. "You know," he pleaded, "it didn't hurt the faith of the church to have somebody misappropriate money." Then, following a pause of several seconds, he added: "God killed them." Then came this series of comments:

> You know, that didn't hurt the faith of the apostles. They were dead, that's all. . . . How do you deal with someone who misappropriates money? You pronounce the judgment of God on them. You don't say, "Oh my, my faith is hurt because so-and-so mismanaged money." No, that doesn't hurt my faith at all. All that means is that someone is going to get it real good from the Lord one of these days, and it's up to God to decide when.

The intention was to distance himself from the situation he was describing. "I wouldn't be in the shoes of somebody who played games with God's money for anything in the world," he repeated. And he also prayed that those who had been bothered by what they had read and heard would not allow the event to have a negative affect on their faith. "So we don't have to worry about what this one does with money, or what somebody else does with money; that's God's worry!" he said. "In the early church, they left this to the Lord."

Then came the most dramatic statement of all: "All they did was say, 'you were wrong. You lied.' *Bang!* It was all over . . . ha, ha. It's very simple. Clean. Easy. It's all done." And, as the applause from the audience mounted, Robertson finished the sequence: "You drag them out. You keep on going, see. That's all you have to do." By now, the applause was so heavy that the preacher had to wait for it to subside. When it was quieter again, he said softly, "and the text says that great fear fell on all the people. . . . Well, well it should," he intoned, and tried to continue. But, again, the enthusiastic response from the crowd made it impossible for anyone in the auditorium to hear anything of what he may have wanted to say next. He had already made his point. And when they applauded him at the end of his address, he stood there, his arms stretched high, his face beaming, his eyes sparkling. "Thank you Jesus. Thank you Jesus," he repeated. "Thank you Jesus."

But while Pat Robertson may have convinced the members and guests of the Full Gospel Business Men's Fellowship International that they need not worry about being implicated in the negative impact of the PTL scandal, he was not successful in convincing those who look in from the outside. From the outside, the Bakkers, the Falwells, the Swaggarts, the Oral Roberts, and the Pat Robertsons of the world are of the same cloth, represent the same basic orientation and attitude to life, and are motivated by the same set of religious and political objectives. Certainly the Bakkers scandalized themselves, and the movement, by deviations from acceptable patterns of individual and institutional behavior that became so great—so gross and excessive—that they had to be ostracized. Certainly Jimmy Swaggart did the same when he fell victim to "moral failure" in connection with his involvement with a prostitute. Whatever deviations Pat Robertson is responsible for are manifestly minor in comparison to the Bakkers' and Swaggart's. Nevertheless, his identification with them remains solid enough for him to be adversely affected by the public's negative appraisal of them. It is not only that their fall brought all of the others down. It is rather that hosts of public suspicions and questions surrounded the movement even before the PTL and Swaggart scandals were brought to light. Such events are confirming evidence that all such suspicions and questions are well founded. For, in these terms, contrary to what Pat Robertson would like to believe, it did hurt the credibility of the movement that prominent leaders were implicated in sexual scandals. And it did have a negative impact on the faith of the followers that "the apostles" misappropriated money. "You drag them out, and keep on going," Robertson urged, or wished. But the incidents were remembered, and will continue to influence voter disapproval and public disinclination.

Consequently, while Pat Robertson enjoyed some surprising initial successes in the Republican primaries in 1988 (particularly in Iowa, Michigan, and Hawaii), and claimed success in influencing the Republican platform policy, his candidacy for the presidency was never able to generate sustaining momentum. It is to his credit, no doubt, that he was taken seriously as a legitimate candidate for office, on his very first election try. It is to his credit, too, that he proved himself to be a political force to be reckoned with. Yet, his presidential ambitions garnered most support following his unexpected success in the February 1988 Iowa primary. After this, when he came under more intense scrutiny and thorough investigation, collective enthusiasm for his candidacy diminished.

The truth is that the real Pat Robertson—like the real Jim Bakker and the real Jimmy Swaggart, but unlike the vast majority of citizens—is a sectarian Christian. The real Pat Robertson speaks in tongues and receives prophecies. The real Pat Robertson is quick to acknowledge that the most significant event in his life was his baptism in the Holy Spirit. The real Pat Robertson is a Pentecostal evangelist, who wishes all persons—regardless of race or creed—to come to a saving knowledge of Jesus Christ. And the real Pat Robertson believes that his vocation, in whatever form divine providence determines it should take, is directly and intimately tied to the expected return of the Messiah to establish his kingdom. All such beliefs and attitudes are protected by the Constitution and the Bill of Rights, so long as there is no infringement on the rights and freedoms of others. On this matter there is no dispute. But Robertson's religion does not translate into an attractive or effective basis on which to run for the presidency, or even to provide moral and spiritual leadership to a multicultural and religiously plural society.

Yet the Robertson candidacy assisted the electorate in deciding what to do with the Religious Right. With Ronald Reagan that decision could be postponed. No matter how often he supplied contrary evidence, one could still believe, if one wanted to, that whatever identification the President had with the conservative fundamentalist and Pentecostalist movement was relatively incidental, a matter of political convenience, more or less. With Pat Robertson there can be no mistaking it. He is the personification of the Religious Right, and by a process of elimination the most vivid and articulate expression of its enthusiasms and intentions.

Will the voting public ever elect to make such a viewpoint normative? Will they ever allow the Religious Right to play the leading role in composing the elements of their collective identity? Will they ever opt, as the critical words have it, for a "Christian nation" in the literal sense, designed according to the blueprint New Religious Rightists have advanced? When they really see it, will they ever really want it? Or has it all been predetermined? In the end, will the forces of history conspire to enable the Religious Right to help usher in the messianic age?

This latter possibility, in my judgment, is how Pat Robertson, deep down, reads the events of our time. He is tantalized by the prospect (of which he is by no means certain) that he may have been divinely chosen to help prepare the way for the coming of the Kingdom of God. Eagerly awaiting the return of the Messiah, he is anticipating the day when all of the kingdoms of this world will bow in acknowledging that Jesus Christ is "king of kings and lord of lords." He is confident that this is the way human history will culminate, which final disclosures are imminent. He is convinced, too, that the present generation will be alive to witness the beginnings of the culmination. He is spiritually intoxicated with the conviction that God, perhaps, may just want him to monitor portions of the events to come from that desk in the Oval Office in the house at 1600 Pennsylvania Avenue, if not in 1988, perhaps in 1992 or 1996. From this vantage point, his experience in 1988, yes, all of his previous experience, is merely preparation for the good things yet to come. But this is also what everything is about: preparation for good and decisive things yet to come.

I suggested in a previous chapter that the New Religious Right stands as a deliberate effort to identify what it is to be a *bona fide* American and what it is to be a bona fide Christian in terms that are thoroughly compatible with each other. I hinted that when the characteristics of both identities are one and the same, the product is religious nationalism. What has happened in the situation before us is that a salvation religion is being recommended to guide the affairs of the nation. To achieve this conjunction, the movement launched a bold attempt to recast American history in biblical terms, transpose Christian teaching into distinctly American terms, and to package the synthesis in the form of programs, candidates, and ideology to submit to the judgment of the voters. But the fundamental axiom is that salvation religion can effectively function as an operational civil religion.

If asked about this situation, Pat Robertson would no doubt

counter that he has never intended that the equation be tight, that is, that being an American and being a Christian are interchangeable identities. He has protected his flexibility, in this regard, by affirming the primacy of a secret invisible and transcendent kingdom in relation and contrast to which both salvation religion and the affairs of the civil order are to be judged. This transcendent grounding provides the occasion for whatever formula allows the Christian believer to be "in the world, but not of the world." Robertson is confident that the same formula safeguards individual faith while encouraging direct political involvement. He is certain that he has made the necessary distinctions with such circumspection that one and the same American can be an exemplar of a resilient patriotism a vital piety at one and the same time. Duty to country and devotion to God, while drawing upon many of the same human aspirations and energies, need not be equated, though they are frequently found together.

But the problem Pat Robertson spells for the nation is that the proposed blueprint that is to guide the future course of the nation has been supplied by a narrow Christian apocalyptic vision of how this present world will be given up, yes, sacrificed, to that higher, permanent reality. In this sense, the basic motivational energy of the religion is employed to save souls from the wrath to come, or, in other words, to make certain that the faithful are thoroughly protected when that transition time comes. I have proposed that, no matter what ostensible affirmation of the American way of life exists within this perspective, the fundamental orientation is other-worldly. The day-to-day activities within the civil order are directed and undergirded by a dualistic attitude that expects the entire civil order to give way, some day soon, to the reality of the other world. Implicit (and often dramatically explicit) in this attitude is the conviction that the power of the civil order (variously called the "state" and/or the "government") is itself the force, and, thus, the enemy, that keeps would-be citizens of the other world in temporary bondage. Consequently, the leadership that Pat Robertson offers would be directed toward progressively decreasing the reign of the civil order over the affairs of human beings so that "born-again" reality would triumphantly become sole reality. This is his basis for hoping for "a country governed by Christians." The irony, then, is that the head of state would be

CHAPTER SEVEN

DRAWING THE COMPOSITE PICTURE

The preceding chapters have been devoted to a series of portrayals of the life and practice of what is now generally referred to as the New Religious Right. I have offered studies of several of the primary figures in the movement—Jerry Falwell, Jim and Tammy Bakker, Pat Robertson, and Francis Schaeffer—and examined a set of celebrated legal questions that was taken all the way to the United States Supreme Court. I suggested at the outset that an examination of these examples and cases would enable us to gain a firm grasp on the aspirations and behavior of the movement. I elected to approach my conclusions this way, that is, by focusing on some specific situations, rather than by attempting to provide a more generalized and comprehensive characterization of the movement.

In proceeding in this manner, I wish to illustrate and underscore that the several topics that have been addressed, though belonging together, should neither be approached nor interpreted in the same way. Though it is accurate to say that each of the examples and cases is reflective of the movement, that is, when the movement is considered in its most generic terms, it is necessary to qualify that these are distinctive entities, representing diverse roots and orientations. Jerry Falwell, for example, is the minister of a Baptist Church; this is his primary occupation. He calls himself a "fundamentalist" Christian, which, by definition, distinguishes his specific religious identity from that, say, of Pat Robertson and Jim Bakker who call themselves "Pentecostal" or even "neo-Pentecostal" Christians. And neither Robertson nor Bakker were pastors of individual congregations, that is, at the time that each became well known. To make the matter somewhat more complex, though Falwell, Robertson, and Bakker are appropriately identified as representing evangelical Protestant Christianity (whether in fundamentalist or Pentecostalist guise), each would run afoul of the standards that any of the Bob Joneses would cite to certify legitimate and/or normative instances of the same. Similarly, while Jerry Falwell holds the teachings of the theologian Francis Schaeffer in highest esteem, the Jones family and Robertson would prefer to look to other teachers as having more intellectual and spiritual influence. I cite these differentiating factors simply to illustrate that what is commonly referred to as the New Religious Right—or even the New Christian Right—is in no sense a monolith. Internally considered it does not consist of elements and ingredients that are easily homogeneous with each other, though it may appear this way from the outside. Rather the movement is comprised of a rather loose coalition of entities, and is most accurately represented as an informal confederation of persons and institutions, brought together through the magnetism of Christian television evangelism. All generalizations about the meaning of the movement, and its possible consequences, need to be mindful of this factor of diversification and heterogeneity.

Nevertheless, there are some general convictions which most parties to the movement share. In this respect, it is necessary for us to identify these convictions while avoiding the rhetorical venom, political passion, and theological enthusiasm with which they are usually expressed. Note, for instance, that *the spiritual vitality of the nation* is the primary subject, the most prominent theme, and the fundamental objective of the movement. One finds this theme enunciated repeatedly in the sermons from Jerry Falwell's pulpit, the conversations on Pat Robertson's "700 Club," Jimmy Swaggart's traveling evangelistic show, Paul Weyrich's[1] op/ed pieces in the national press, and in virtually all of the literature and television products that the movement produces. In all of it, the inescapable and fundamental message is that the most distinguishing resilience of the nation, and of the American people, is its spiritual strength. The attendant corollary is that the nation suffers deplorably when that spiritual vitality is weakened. Under such conditions, such suffering is always severe, and sometimes it is even tragic. When the spiritual vitality of the nation is diminished—so New Religious Right teaching has it—the nation itself is made vulnerable to threats from the outside as well as to forces of decay and debilitation from within. All of this is accepted as a matter of diagnostic principle.

Second, the contention is that contemporary America finds itself languishing in a sorry moral and spiritual state, which state must be corrected in order to reattain the stature to which, by mandate and destiny, Americans can properly lay claim. And to make this point forcefully, the contenders offer what they regard as compelling examples of this deplorable condition. They note, for example, that the drug culture is prevalent among youth. They speak about the prevalence of sexual promiscuity, the frequency of teenage abortions, and the support such deviant behavior receives from both the schools and the courts—as well as from what Bob Jones III would refer to as "prevailing public opinion." They understand such decadence to symbolize that human life has been degraded and cheapened in contemporary American society. In short, when one casts about, one finds more than sufficient evidence, they say, to support the contention that our national life does not exhibit the moral character that previous generations of Americans claimed for their lives.

Third, the message is that this woeful situation can only be remedied if it is addressed in a thoroughly radical way, and this requires an effective challenge to its underlying motivational sources. Being offered by prophets and reformers, the message is cast as an indictment against the underlying worldview of liberalism, secular humanism, ecumenical Christianity, and everything else that can be associated with the philosophy of "one-worldism." Here the diagnosis reads that the errant philosophy—which, by now, has reached into all areas of our individual and public life—has led the nation to potential shipwreck because it has tried to establish and enforce an inaccurate and unrealistic conception of human capacity. By attributing too much to the possibilities of "human potential," the errant philosophy's "overly optimistic view of human nature" has led to gross over-expectations regarding the services of government. The sad consequence is that millions of Americans have been seduced into looking to the government to provide remedies for basic human ills and satisfactions for fundamental human desires. But government should not be expected to function this way. "It functions best," some New Religious Rightists say, "when it functions least." When expectations are heaped upon it— government proves to be much more a part of the problem than of the solution. Similarly, in ascribing too much to man, the liberals and secularists have also diminished man's dependence upon God. As a consequence, they have failed to offer a resilient and satisfactory vision of human transcendence. And in neglecting this indispensable societal motivational factor, the errant philosophy has found itself weak and ineffective in inspiring the collective public imagination in ways that are also morally compelling. The sorry consequences are to be seen everywhere in our social, political, cultural, and spiritual life. Our music has become full of noise. Our art has become angry. The resources for compelling spiritual strength have become severely marginalized. And character, integrity, and effective linkages with idealism have disappeared, because the conditions of their possibilities have been undercut.

At bottom, and in essence, New Religious Right advocates understand the quarrel to be about the definition of human nature. In their view, human nature can only be defined in relationship to the three spheres of appropriate authority. That is, human nature is to be understood in relationship to what can rightfully be expected regarding the status and function of government. Human nature, secondly, is to be understood in relationship to what the biblical tradition teaches regarding the status and function of God. And, thirdly, human nature is to be understood in relationship to what can be reliably known regarding the distinctive qualities and ontological characteristics of men and women (and the differences that pertain thereto). In all of these essential areas, prevailing "secular humanist" philosophy, according to New Religious Right instincts and analyses, has been offering up—and at bargain-basement prices—unreliable and destructive guidance.

The movement is dramatically charged because it knows itself to be in competition. Thus, it must find or create the ability to serve as a viable working alternative to whatever set of underlying philosophical assumptions belong to its competitors. Its strategy, in this respect, is to make its competitor an object of derision, by calling it "the permissive society," or "the godless society," or by denouncing it as being beholden to "near-beer theology and loose-leaf liturgy," in sharp contrast to such positive appellations as "the Moral Majority," or "God's people," or "the Christian nation," or even "all you good, God-fearing people." Such names are chosen further to legitimize the life-world of those who are diligently seeking to reestablish their more reliable orientation to reality. The prophetic spokespersons for the new movement understand that their task is to make certain that everyone recognizes that the differences between the two orientations to life are fundamentally and thoroughly axiomatic.

On occasion, New Religious Right advocates have tried to tackle the major philosophical issues and questions head on, and in deliberate and explicit philosophical form. Senators Jesse Helms and Orrin Hatch, with their conservative colleagues, work egislatively to outlaw and banish the "secular-humanist philosophy" by making it illegal for Congress to give anything associated with it any financial support. With like-minded motives, watch-dog groups have closely scrutinized the work of public-school textbook evaluators to call into question, and, if possible, to eliminate, books that tend, for example, to promote evolutionist thinking. When exercised in this manner, such critics have made it clear that they find it necessary to oppose the theories because they fundamentally disagree with the axioms about human nature that are implicit in the theories. Their intention has been to challenge and resist the teaching of such falsehoods, by endeavoring to interrupt and undermine the alien and erroneous philosophy.

But, most of the time, the specific issues on which New Religious Right advocates have elected to stake their claim are ones for which the fundamental underlying opposition is more implicit than explicit. Voluntary school prayer, for instance, is about the rights of citizens—even school-age citizens—to enjoy the protections of the First Amendment. But, at another level, it is about the primacy of divine (as opposed to human) authority. Being about the primacy of divine authority, it can also be employed as a judgment against the permissive society. And a judgment against the permissive society is a contention against its supporting and enabling philosophical assumptions. Thus, when all of the pieces are fitted together, one's position on voluntary school prayer reflects one's allegiance to some fundamental truths regarding the basic meaning of human life.

Similarly, abortion, the issue of greatest and most intense symbolic significance, is about the conditions under which it is appropriate or inappropriate to bring a pregnancy to term. But, at another level, it too is about the primacy of divine authority. It is about divine authority because it is about who shall be regarded as the ultimate giver and source of life. Being about the primacy of divine authority, attitudes to abortion can be utilized as bases for judgments against the permissive society. And a judgment against the permissive society is a rejection or repudiation of its underlying philosophical principles. A vote against abortion is a sign that one truly believes God to be the exclusive source and end of human life. What one understands regarding the source and end of human life is reflective of one's attitude concerning what it is to be a human being.

When New Religious Right advocates state their case in these (their own) words, they say that contemporary American society lacks faith. The society lacks faith in itself, faith in its vocation and destiny, and faith in its God. As a consequence, societal motivation is unsure, people lack confidence in themselves, and the society persists without any clear sense of purpose or direction. At another level of generalization, the same diagnosis implies that contemporary America lacks access to meaningful transcendence, at least of the kind that must have pertained during the time of the nation's founders. A clear sign that such transcendence was effectively in place was the relative ease with which the citizenry could acknowledge authority, even to the point of confessing its dependence upon God. The fact that such expressions are difficult to come by in the contemporary world signifies that meaningful transcendence has become collectively—if not individually— inaccessible. The only solution is a repudiation of the philosophy that gives the permissive society license, and the reestablishment of the convictions and attitudes that might restore the nation's necessary spiritual vitality.

Thus, when denouncing "problem solving" and "social engineering," New Right theorists recognize that they are repudiating Enlightenment philosophy. In their judgment, the previous liberal consensus has failed dramatically because of its devotion to superficial and "overly optimistic" Enlightenment attitudes. Their assumption was that those who had accepted Enlightenment assumptions left too much to accident, chance, or unwarranted expectation. The educational incentives advanced by John Dewey and his disciples, for example, didn't bring any great educational successes, as conservatives analyze them, but only created chaos. Great Society legislation didn't stimulate its intended outcome, but only made the nation's social and economic conditions worse. Similar results describe the product of Enlightenment expectations throughout the nation's social, cultural, and economic life. Because the assumptions were wrong, the product, predictably, was disappointing.

A situation so dire requires remedies more radical than modest shifts in emphases. Rather, Enlightenment philosophy needs to be supplanted by a view of life that combines philosophical respectability and spiritual vitality. The new view, by definition, is identified as being antihumanistic, for humanism (a primary symbol of derision) is understood to be the underlying culprit. By contrast, the New Religious Right view openly and strongly champions *theism,* in opposition to both *humanism* and *atheism.* It bases its convictions on insights and truths that are not commonly accessible, but require the cultivation of spiritual insight. Such insights and truths are identified as being fundamental, and as being reflective of the "real world" orientation that pertained before the intellectual, social, and cultural damage was done. There is an inherent "back to basics" intention in all of it, and its influence is to be felt in every area of the nation's collective life. Francis Schaeffer's writings stand as the most prominent example of the conviction that Enlightenment philosophy has been superseded by an authoritative spiritually based orientation that makes true reality reliably accessible.

In most versions of New Religious Right theoretical reconstruction, Enlightenment philosophy is also replaced by an *apocalyptic* interpretation of the human situation. According to this rendition, something new and decisive has happened recently: the ongoing divine action in human history has entered a decisive phase. The temper of human life has been altered because God has disclosed his intentions for the world. This view understands the arena of human activity to be so dependent upon God's dominion that what transpires here below is a product and reflection of supernatural initiatives, which initiatives are being ordered by an absolutely trustworthy divine agenda. In the broad sweep of things—so this viewpoint would depict it—the human community is much closer to the culmination of history than it was when other guiding philosophies (including the Enlightenment perspective) were deemed to have been satisfactory. What is needed in these days immediately prior to the end are principles of life that are harmonious with God's present intentions for his creation. And it follows that those who are best able to fathom and interpret these principles are those who are most acutely and perceptively in tune with God's present will and ways.

This supernaturalist/apocalyptic reading of the dynamics of social and cultural change is particularly sensitive to the ways in which the direction of national life must be tailored to fit the requirements of a more comprehensive divine scheme. It is preoccupied, for instance, with "America"—its theological status, its place in God's providential plan, and its function with respect to the realization of these comprehensive intentions. Being so preoccupied, this view understands "America" to have a decisive role in the cosmic drama. At least, this is the hope, or, as some would say, the promise. And it encourages itself by having insights, from time to time, about divine action in history. It would be appropriate for one like St. Augustine to write a new version of *De Civitas Dei,* to describe the interaction between transcendent action and earthly occurrences. But this time, because the time is short, the drama about divine action in human history is occurring before our eyes—eyes that have been trained to perceive such marvels. It is a time of thorough and radical change because history itself is being prepared for a trans-historical set of circumstances. Indeed, from this vantage point, humanity is now experiencing "the last days" before the decisive action takes place. And this decisive action, which involves nothing less than divine intervention in history, promises to place the world on another foundation, that is, when the Messiah returns. The Messiah's return is demonstration that history is but one of the modalities within which human life is lived. Present occurrences in the world—which can only be seen, still, "through a glass darkly"— are preparatory to a series of continuing, decisive events through which a new theological age will be born. The world of human affairs is changing in response to compelling divine action.

Centuries ago, when St. Augustine tried to reconcile the events of his day with the broader, comprehensive divine plan, he took creation, humanity, and the Church to be his primary reference points. When New Religious Right theorists embark on their intellectual venture, by contrast, they link apocalyptic expectations more narrowly to the destiny of the United States. Then, since apocalyptic expectations are tied to national aspirations, spiritual vitalities are placed within the dynamics of patriotism. Personal religious faith is nationalized, and belief in the nation is made an article of faith. In the process, the dynamics of piety and patriotism are homologized.

Thus, in the America the Religious Right yearns for, the citizenry can look to God for support and protection of the national purpose. The resolute pursuit of that purpose offers access to the heroic ideal. And appropriate expressions of the heroic ideal, as well as firm dedication to the national purpose, mark out the characteristics of patriotism. In the world envisioned by the New Religious Right, such elements form a network of collective virtue. And warfare—especially warfare against an enemy who seems directly and blatantly to be challenging the nation's aspirations and sense of destiny—serves as the signal context within which such virtues are exercised most resolutely, compellingly, and intensely. Until patriotism is put to the test—as only war can do—there is no way of knowing whether it is vigorous or not. Until there is opportunity to contend against a real challenge to what one believes, there is no way of acting out the characteristics of heroism. Advocates of the New Religious Right philosophy covet a society that has no desire to argue about the rudiments of the heroic ideal. In their judgment, when a society exhibits such internal self-consistency there is no need to approach voluntary school prayer or abortion, for instance, as controversial issues. What is necessary is a return to the dependable values.

This is how the perspective of the New Religious Right can be portrayed, more or less, without rhetorical venom. It is a dialectical stance that has adopted an adversarial posture, because it offers its viewpoint in sharp contrast to what it understands to be the prevailing attitude. And, without venom, it asks that its set of convictions and proposals be taken with intellectual seriousness, even by those who are disposed not to agree.

Put the political rhetoric and religious passions back in, and one hears Patrick J. Buchanan, Director of Communications during the Reagan administration, talking this way. In a February

4, 1986, address, in Washington, to the National Religious Broadcasters, Buchanan blamed the recent failures of the nation on decisions by the Supreme Court:

> In the 1960s, prayer and Bible Study were driven out of the public schools of a nation whose institutions (even Justice Douglas had conceded) presupposed the existence of a Supreme Being. Postings of the Ten Commandments were torn down from classroom walls; athletes praying before a football game were told to cease and desist lest they violate the rights of unbelieving classmates, and our Highest Court deliberated over the great question of whether the gyrations of go-go dancers in New Jersey were a Constitutionally protected form of freedom of speech.
>
> At the end of the sixties, an impatient Supreme Court had ratified and approved the use of forced busing to overcome what it called racial imbalance in the public schools.

But the worst was yet to come:

> In 1973 came Roe v. Wade. Seven justices discovered within the Constitution a right to an abortion that neither the Founding Fathers nor any previous generation of jurists had known was there. As a direct consequence, in the land we call God's Country, four thousand unborn children are aborted every day—because their life has become an embarrassment or an inconvenience to the parents who bore them—and because their death provides a lucrative livelihood to those who destroy them.[2]

In Buchanan's rehearsal, there was only one thing for the virtuous citizens of the land to do: "Reacting first with astonishment, and then with direct political action . . . a handful of Americans began plotting and planning what has come to be called the Reagan Revolution." And in distinguishing the revolutionary disposition from the one that was responsible for so much debilitation, President Reagan's chief communicator employed phrases like "a New Nationalism," the "restoration of the spirit of Theodore Roosevelt," and "the new and refined America-First philosophy." Noting that "the future of America is still undecided," Buchanan stated that the only question is whether Ronald Reagan will have successfully charted a new course for the nation, or "whether history will see him as the conservative interruption in a process of inexorable national decline."

Patrick Buchanan's address was intended to encourage the

advocates of the conservative revival to press on, to bring their work to completion, to insure that the revolution would be successful. He wanted to be able to assure the movement's enthusiasts that, yes, "in the end, not they, but we shall overcome."

But the question he asked is an essential one. How will history judge the conservative revival? What will the movement eventually mean within the ongoing life of the nation? How will it be explained and interpreted?

For the final pages of this study, I have selected a few ways of responding to these questions. Specifically, I am advancing the thesis that, in formal interpretive terms, the New Religious Right stands as an example of American civil religion that wishes to function as a revitalization movement. However, since it aspires to be both civil religion and revitalization movement at one and the same time, and against uncommonly formidable obstacles, it has also acquired much of the character of a late twentieth-century American neo-nationalist movement. But I shall amplify this observation after exploring how the New Religious Right can be approached from each of these three interpretive categories.

ALTERNATIVE CIVIL RELIGION

From the first pages of this study, we have observed that the New Religious Right represents an Americanized version of the Christian faith as well as a Christianized version of the national creed. This equation was facilitated by the use of the Bible as the normative basis of reading and interpreting American history. The story of the founding of the nation, for example, is read in light of the dynamics of the biblical account of the exodus. The understanding of the status of the nation is conceived according to the biblical model of the covenant. The biblical account of the perennial cosmic conflict between the forces of good and evil is adapted to the contest between the United States and its foes, and, in particular, the threatening diabolical one that is currently represented by the Soviet Union. Biblical mythology continues to play a prominent role in expressing and explaining the nation's ultimate destiny. The examples of such cross-referencing are numerous.

All of this suggests that the religion of the New Religious Right represents an alternative version of American civil religion. I have already noted that Robert Bellah—and hosts of others—have employed this concept when describing the shape and comportment of American religion, particularly in those versions of it that exhibit a distinctly political cast. In his 1967 article on this subject, Bellah called attention to some of the prominent ways in which biblical motifs have been employed to help make collective sense of the nation's history.[3] He cited demonstrative statements from the speeches of presidents, proposing that many of these carry the force of creedal affirmations. He also pointed to the religious content of the ceremonies that occur on public holidays. He contended that the public school system was providing "the context for the cultic celebration of the civil rituals." He utilized such examples to demonstrate that civil religion is a dynamic reality in our national life, fundamental to the nation's collective behavior. And he urged scholars and interpreters to give this phenomenon "the same care in understanding that is devoted to religion in any other manifestation."

As might be expected, the article sparked continuing discussion and debate. Some agreed. Others disagreed. Some have offered additional confirming examples. A number of respondents have countered that Bellah's concept is so vague and abstract that it fails to be convincing, particularly in contrast to the explicit and established religion of the churches. Of course, the author was aware of the need for caution. He had warned that "in reifying and giving a name to something that, though pervasive enough when you look at it, has gone on only semi-consciously, there is risk of severely distorting the data." And yet he believed that his thesis stood, noting that when persons speak about "religion in general" or even about "the religion of the American way of life," they are pointing to a set of religious conviction and attitudes that reflects the experience of the American people.

In the seminal article, Bellah dismissed fundamentalist religion as having only a "tenuous" relation to "the civil religious consensus." However, in light of the developments I have chronicled in this book, Bellah's astute judgments need to be updated and amended. Falwellite religion has offered itself as an alternative American civil religion. In most respects, it exhibits the very characteristics Bellah isolated when making the original identification. In fact, in some ways, it even qualifies as the normative instance.

For example, Bellah noted that the creed of American civil religion is given expression, on patriotic and solemn occasions, through the speeches of the President of the United States. He cited John F. Kennedy's inaugural address on January 20, 1961. He referred to statements made by George Washington, and, most especially, by Abraham Lincoln. In the 1980s, however, the storehouse of illustrative materials had become resplendent with example after example from the speeches and addresses of President Reagan (who was attempting to form a civil-religious consensus from a very different point of orientation). Never before had there been a President who could speak as openly and freely about religion. Never before had an American President been as religiously and theologically explicit. And never before had a presidential administration given a higher priority to objectives that were identified as being religious, moral, or spiritual.

Accordingly, what Bellah had noted about the role of the public school in enunciating such religious teaching had become appreciated by practitioners of New Religious Right teachings. Their concern about voluntary school prayer, and about the role of the schools in moral and religious formation, is testimony to the fact that they recognized the school to be "the context for the cultic celebration of the civil rituals." So too with the employment of biblical motifs to explain the nature and destiny of the American people. Supporters and proponents of the movement have become adept at this, even to the point of claiming that the nation's Founding Fathers would have been advocates of the normative teachings of first-century Christianity, even as this is understood within Fundamentalist circles. It is as if the America they envisioned was an extension, in some direct ongoing succession, of the biblical community. They gave twentieth-century re-expression, or so they intended, to the biblical archetypes. They attempted to express their faith through a blending of religious and patriotic symbols. They were conscious of the fact that their religious tenets were identified exactly with the creeds or doctrinal statements of any single church or denomination. Indeed, though they tended to find their strongest sanctions within the Christian religion, they were pleased too that they had attracted the support of persons of other religious persuasions, and they were absolutely delighted that a significant number of Jews, both at home and abroad, were willing to identify with their cause. Theirs was (in

Robert Bellah's phrase) a collective religious consciousness that "actually exists alongside of and [is] rather clearly differentiated from the churches." It was also "elaborate and well-institutionalized," as Bellah's original description required.

In sum, the New Religious Right created or catalyzed a movement that is as graphic and explicit an example of civil religion as anything Bellah could point to when writing the seminal description. It was, and is, civil religion in the conservative key. From this perspective, what has been happening to a portion of American Fundamentalist Christianity is to be interpreted as a process by which it is striving to create a sanctioned form of public religious consensus.

CONTEMPORARY REVITALIZATION MOVEMENT

While assessing the possible identification of the New Religious Right as a contemporary instance of alternative American civil religion, we must also ask if it qualifies as a vivid example of a *revitalization movement*. We shall discover, as we compare example with interpretive nomenclature, that here too there is a useful interpretive framework to enable us to make the subject more comprehensively intelligible.

As early as 1958, the anthropologist Anthony F. C. Wallace described revitalization movement as "a deliberate, organized, conscious effort by members of a society to construct a more satisfying culture." The intention, Wallace stated, was to "innovate not merely discrete items, but a new cultural system, specifying new relationships as well as, in some cases, new traits."[4]

Instigators of revitalization recognize certainly that societies are perpetually undergoing change, most of it of a "gradual" or "chain-reaction" kind. They are interested in effecting a particular form of change—the kind that would not happen without deliberate action. Such change must alter the existing cultural system thoroughly and intensively, and it must accomplish its objectives in a single generation.

Observers and analysts of the work of revitalization movements report that there are a variety of debilitating experiences that might serve as sparks or catalysts. The society may have suffered troubling military defeat. Its people may have become victims of political subordination. They may be looking for safety valves under heavy pressure toward acculturation. It may be a time of severe economic distress. Or it may be all of these factors, or some combination of them. But the *pressure toward acculturation* appears to be the most common and frequent catalytic factor.

Wallace noted that the process occurs in stages. Under the pressure to conform, an individual is able to "tolerate a moderate degree of increased stress and still maintain the habitual way of behavior." However, after a while, "a point is reached at which some alternative way must be considered." Some persons, at this point, prefer to "tolerate high levels of chronic stress rather than make adaptive changes." Others, at this point, respond by effecting individual changes, still not attempting to alter the larger system of conditions and causes. Some resort to "psycho-dynamically regressive innovations"—examples of which are alcoholism, passivity, ambivalent dependency, altered sexual mores, and the like—usually to find that the remedies are temporary, and the stress levels continue to increase. And while such reactions are occurring—so the scholarship on the subject reflects—the process of social and cultural deterioration continues virtually unchecked. Eventually, the culture finds itself at manifestly low ebb, and, in most areas of activity, is subject to defeat or factional dispute.

The revitalization movement is designed to forestall or correct the downward cultural tendency. The availability of its instrumentality is brought to collective consciousness through the work of a prophet who needs first to get the people's attention. When he is listened to, the prophet identifies the failures of the society (sometimes by embellishing the significance of certain events), then explains that these troubles are due to the fact that the people have broken the rules. In breaking the rules, they have abandoned the conditions by which they were bonded to each other as well as to their higher sustaining authority. The prophet may point out that their recent defeat in a war they had every right to expect to win, for example, is an indication of their fallen state. Revitalization can occur, the prophet reiterates, if the foundational rules are reestablished, and the fundamental collective rituals are practiced again. The prophet claims authenticity and legitimation for the message by demonstrating that its contents are in full accord with the fundamental principles, convictions, and ideals upon which the society was originally founded. Characteristically, the prophet also casts about for demonstrable occurrences to confirm the authority of the traditional rules and practices. The intention is to illustrate that the old (but now revised) doctrine—the articulable side of revitalization—is commendable because it satisfies needs that are not being satisfied otherwise, and produces manifestly positive effects. Along the way, the prophet may need to modify the original doctrine to give it a better "fit" to the current situation. This recasting of the original creed can be expected to bring controversy: strict constructionists will be at odds with reconstructionists and with revisionist theorists within the community. When this happens—so the analyses from sociology and anthropology illustrate and confirm—counter-hostility develops in response to hostility, and internal tension abounds. Wallace notes, at this point, that "emphasis shifts from cultivation of the ideal to combat against the unbeliever." When there is great hostility and counter-hostility, the revitalization movement is challenged at two distinct points. It is obliged to continue its pursuit of the original cultural objectives, and, simultaneously, it is forced to do battle against the detractors both within and without. It can do both at once, of course, if it can find the means to demonstrate persuasively that its detractors are the real reason that the movement's goals are difficult to accomplish.

The description of revitalization movements that we have sketched here is applicable, both comprehensively and specifically, to the career of the New Religious Right. The movement came into being through deep and increasing dissatisfaction with a prevailing way of social and cultural life. Realizing that the source of the dissatisfaction was systemic, the advocates of deliberate cultural change contended that the entire social and cultural order needed to be revised. As they put it, the task was "to take back the land," or "to reclaim the dominion." They knew that if the necessary change was to come, they themselves would have to effect it. Their action would have to be deliberate. The change would need to be put in place within a single generation. Such objectives would not be met, they understood, unless the advocates of change submitted themselves to rigorous training, so as to acquire political sophistication and effectiveness. They felt compelled to take such action in order to cope, resist, and cultivate effective alternatives to the climate of adverse ideological opinion in which they suddenly found themselves.

Consider, for example, the changes that have affected traditional religion in the 1960s and 1970s. It was not many years ago that personal faith was talked about as involving choices between theism, atheism, and agnosticism. But in today's world there are new and multiform ways of being religious and/or irreligious. It can no longer be assumed that an interest in belief, or faith, is an effort to affirm the claims of Christianity. Nor should it be understood that those who continue to identify with the Christian religion do so in exclusive terms. The centuries-old fear of heresy or excommunication is hardly resilient any longer. Thousands of contemporary Christians also practice Buddhist meditation. Christian monastic communities join with monastic communities of Asian religious traditions to learn of the contemplative life together, from each other. Each year thousands of people from the Western world make visits to Hindu temples, and understand their journeys to be deliberate and authentic religious pilgrimages. Words and phrases, whose meanings and referents reside in the religious experience of Asian peoples, have been adapted to a Western vocabulary and show up frequently in everyday conversation. Many people, from a variety of traditional ways of life, are discovering the spiritual resourcefulness of native American insights and sensitivities, and claim these as belonging to their orientation to human experience. The modern world has become a global religious village within which, as Mircea Eliade eloquently taught, religion manifests itself as being a mode of consciousness alongside other modes or ways of apprehending reality. In this regard, what advocates of the various religious traditions share is much more extensive than the differences in attitude and belief that distinguish and separate them.

For Christians of traditional religious practice, the world has become much larger. They have been forced, by weight of circumstance, to think of life in more comprehensive and inclusive terms. But it is also true that the world has gotten smaller. In former days, Christians could take up collections for missionary work in "faraway lands," for example, and be reasonably confident that they would never directly encounter the recipients of such beneficence. Today the situation is markedly different. The person of another religion, culture, or race may be one's next-door neighbor. One encounters him in the marketplace, on the job, in the school, on neighborhood or citizens committees, in one's apartment building, yes, even in one's own family. The products of previous global missionary efforts are now enrolled in American colleges and universities.

Given the fact that recent social and cultural change has been dramatic, it is understandable that resistance to it would also become deliberate, determined and politically organized. It is also understandable that those who are able to assume leadership positions within the resistance movement are the ones who are best able to represent those who perceive themselves to have most to lose. And if this should happen, it wouldn't be the first time. In 1965, Jerry Falwell spoke out on behalf of those who understood themselves to have most to lose if Martin Luther King's civil rights movement were to become effective. In those days, the issue was racial equality. Twenty years later the same questions remain, but within the framework of enormous and expanding cultural diversity. Within this environment, the slogan "America is back again" can be taken as a rallying cry. The America that is longed for is the America that is thought to have existed before the period of destabilization. The "back to basics" movement can be understood in the same light, namely as an educational and intellectual effort that is designed to reestablish the resources that were normative before that the more recent stimulants were able to usurp their places. Such slogans are not simply descriptive, but are also declaratives and imperatives.

In other words, previous Falwellites may have been content to play a minor role in American society as long as it could be assumed that other segments of the society—minority groups, women, and special-interest advocates—would remain marginalized too. In fact, the early disposition of Fundamentalism was to accept the minor and marginal role, as long as one could count on the protections of the dominant society. But when that society became threatened by a new, revised order of things, that seemed to cater to the special interests of previously marginalized segments of the population, and when it became apparent that what had been understood to be the dominant society could no longer exercise effective majority control or provide appropriate protective guarantees, then it was time to take matters into one's own hands, as it were. And the reaction that seemed best able to achieve the desired results was one that reasserted the collective identity in effective political terms and with compelling religious sanctions. The conservative response came in the form of a deliberate attempt to breathe new life into traditional values while reestablishing a basis of national identity.

The first remedial steps in this process came through the work of the prophets—those, who were recognized as speaking with religious authority, who identified the people's failings and called them to repentance (that is, to turn from their errant ways), and pointed out the pathway of constructive resolution. After capturing the people's attention, the prophets acknowledged the extraordinary misery of the nation's fallen state. They utilized such acknowledgments as the basis for counseling a return to obedience to guiding laws and principles. They pleaded for individual and collective behavior that is harmonious with the original ideals.

This interpretation of the role of the prophet in a revitalization movement helps describe Jerry Falwell's vocation: to unmask the nation's collective moral decadence. Pat Robertson's work can be explained this way; so too the other spokespersons for the revitalization movement. Each has denounced the nation's manifest unrighteousness. All of them are enunciating a "back to basics" theme. All of them are advocating a thorough and decisive revitalization of the nation's spirit.

Because they had the prophet's nerve to challenge the status quo, these leaders of the New Religious Right invited controversy and hostility. Such hostility has been met by counter-hostility—the two forms of mounting hostility being so intense that the original revolutionary goals have, at times, become obscured. But the increasing opposition served to make the practitioners more resolute. Their goal, as we have noted, is nothing less than "to change the face of America," to restore the banner of the resuscitated vision of the nation's founders. They understood that the nation's ills are systemic. Nothing short of a complete revitalization of the entire way of life would provide appropriate remedies.

The career of the New Religious Right fits the classic description of revitalization movements in minute detail. Indeed, Protestant Fundamentalism is itself a vivid example of revitalization. Thus, the movement contained the appropriate ingredients even before it was applied to the present social and cultural situation. The story is that Christian fundamentalism offered its revitalizing services to a nation in a state of rather marked social and cultural distress. It felt itself qualified to do so because it had experience in this area. The moral and spiritual status of the nation provided good breeding ground for a fresh burst of revitalization religion.

RELIGIOUS AND POLITICAL NEONATIONALISM

In considering the theoretical and categorial possibilities that New Religious Right religion can be understood as civil religion and as revitalization movement, it is important to recognize under what sociopolitical conditions it came into prominence. As we have seen, during the Reagan administration much that it stands for has been blessed by no less an instrument and standard of legitimation than the office of the presidency. In these terms, no matter in what other ways the movement deserves to be judged, its ability to attain such large national prominence so quickly, and to gather and sustain religious and political momentum during the Reagan years, must be regarded as a significant accomplishment. On the other hand, in defining itself as favored civil religion and as authoritative revitalization movement at one and the same time, the movement reached too high, ventured too far, sought too much, and thus was forced to exercise its self-appointed national role in terms that were not always consistent with each other.

We recognize that in important respects the careers of the New Right and the Reagan presidency mirror each other. The movement came to power when Reagan was elected in 1980. In his first term, when he was strong, the movement was strong; when he experienced trying times, the movement experienced trying times. In the second term, when his administration was involved in questionable activities so was the movement subjected to a kind of national trial. For him, the occasion was the selling of arms to factions in Iran, to help secure the release of American hostages in Lebanon. As elements of the story became known, it was revealed that money from the weapons sales was employed to assist the Contra forces in Nicaragua during the period of time when Congress, following its approval of the Boland Amendment, forbade governmental involvement in the efforts of the counter-revolutionary military forces. The President's credibility was questioned, and though he appears to have been remarkably successful in making the case that responsibility for the episode lay elsewhere, for a time, at least, the damage was extensive.

For the revitalizationist movement, the severest crisis came through a disclosure of another kind, namely, the Bakker scandal that destroyed the PTL ministry. The immediate effect was a devastating loss of much of the national respect the television evangelists had previously claimed. This consequence was confirmed by the reduction in revenue that each of the television ministries experienced. PTL faced bankruptcy, and was saved—though only temporarily—by Jerry Falwell's declaration of a "May Emergency." Pat Robertson found it necessary to close down the Washington, D.C., office of his presidential-campaign committee, and laid off 500 employees of CBN in Virginia Beach. Jimmy Swaggart complained that his own ministry had "lost millions." And Jerry Falwell, who was trying to raise money to keep PTL alive, also suffered serious losses in volunteer income for his "Old Time Gospel Hour."

When it happened, some New Religious Right advocates wanted to blame external forces, including the devil. And yet, there was an admission that it was a matter of disintegration from within rather than destruction from without. Each of the precipitating events involved scandals that were virtually impossible to cover up or explain away.

The fact is that the movement had significantly overreached itself, a result of excessive and extravagant expectations mixed with an undereducated and only modestly trained leadership. Under such circumstances, it was impossible for the movement to fulfill everything to which it aspired. It was unrealistic to expect simultaneously to be a religion of individual salvation, a national faith, and a highly competitive political philosophy. It was unrealistic to expect success at all levels at once, for the several objectives were not and are not consistent with each other.

Both in theory and in fact, it is apparent that the revitalization of the nation cannot be effected or accomplished resourcefully and genuinely from fundamentalist and Pentecostalist Protestant Christian bases. To be sure, the desire for such revitalization can be expressed in these theological terms, and the expression can be supported by emotional fervor and patriotic eloquence. From this vantage point, the achievement of the Jerry Falwells and Pat Robertsons of the world is the acquisition and cultivation of the "know-how" to get their own conservative brands of Christian conviction into the national political discussion. But whatever achievements there may have been within this micro context did not (and do not) translate into macro political or spiritual effectiveness. Furthermore, an ability to participate in the discussion is no guarantee that one's opinions and convictions will be accepted, or that the conversation will proceed in the direction that one might choose, or even that the position one is advancing will be respected or accepted by the others. The problem with New Religious Right aspirations lies in the misperception that terms of entry and principles of resolution are identical. It wished to function as a revitalization movement not once, but twice: both as an instrument to revitalize Christian fundamentalism, and as the catalytic force to revitalize the life of the nation. But it was too much to expect that both objectives could be met simultaneously. The overreaching lay in the expectation that one and the same instrument could achieve both ends.

It might have been sufficient for the movement to have taken on the first of the two tasks, and to have done it well. For the New Religious Right did find success in this respect. Post-revitalization fundamentalism does have a fresh look. Its educational centers, together with the curricula that belongs to them, have been updated. The movement has experimented with new art forms and with modernized styles of music. It has involved itself in social and political issues of global scope. In the process, it has attained a greater intellectual respectability and political effectiveness. But the problem has come in the movement's audacity to attempt a full-scale revitalization of the culture, by trying to remold that culture into its own image of what is good, right, and proper. Fundamentalist revitalization will not be able to serve such purposes effectively. The need of a nation for cultural revitalization cannot be accomplished from such a narrow religious and spiritual base. And, certainly no matter how well intentioned, such a religious and philosophical base is not resilient or elastic enough to meet the profound needs of a multicultural society. Even a radically revised and updated fundamentalist posture will not be able to serve as the chief instrument in revitalizing the spiritual character of the nation. The task is too large and cumbersome for the instrument.

In summary, assessed according to its ambitions and intentions, the movement has attempted to perform double duty: it wished to be a revitalization movement, and it aspired to be the civil religion. It promised, both at the same time, to revitalize the culture and to serve as the mechanism by which such a revitalized culture would be sustained. It has offered its revivifying services because it claims to know the shape and character of the idealized nation whose construction is the ambition of revitalization. It has found courage, in this respect, since, from about 1979 forward, it has enjoyed some temporarily favorable political circumstances. But even under these circumstances, it has not been easy. And the situation cannot be expected to continue.

It is important to remember that when the New Religious Right came into being in August 1980, at a Dallas meeting of the Religious Roundtable, it was a coalition of elements. Representatives from religion, politics, and corporate finance declared their willingness to pool their resources for the sake of some common aspirations. Remove any of these essential ingredients, and the New Religious Right cannot remain what its founders wished it to be. Remove any of these elements and the movement may continue to prove itself effective in narrow working contexts and may be able to keep its voice alive, but it will not be able to realize its larger ambitions. To be specific, fundamentalist Christianity was not out there on its own, but became party to a more comprehensive reform movement. It was a coalition of elements, a blending of ingredients, that became something much more than simply Christian fundamentalism joined to effective political agency.

This is another way of saying that the effectiveness of the coalition was made dependent upon its ability to keep all of the constituent elements in a working relationship of mutual support. Should any of the essential ingredients be removed or be made ineffective, the coalition itself is threatened. In the long run, such disintegration could surely have been anticipated. It was to be expected because the effective interworking of component parts was ordered on the basis of a series of reciprocal working agreements, but not on anything more integral organically. That is, the New Religious Right stands as a coalition of elements. It qualifies as a movement, and as a thrust within the society, but was never able to lend itself easily into becoming an institution. And, in the long run, it could not be effective as a substitute, say, for the church. Take any of its key elements away—including its outstanding personalities—and the edifice itself will come tumbling down. Remove its strategic political function, diminish its voluntary financial support, or take away the requisite degree of good will and legitimacy it received from the public, and its days are numbered. The threats to the coalition's stability could come from within as well as from without. Allow its component parts to be out of harmony with each other, and the damage is as great as if the coalition were being severely challenged by external forces. What can happen to it—indeed, what did happen to it—is identical to what can and will happen to any coalitional entity. Its durability is dependent upon its remaining exactly what it is, or in its effectiveness in keeping its coalitional ingredients intact should it be called upon to alter its course or function. This is the reason that the several "Great Awakenings" that have occurred in American history tend to be one-generational phenomena. It is difficult, if not impossible, to institutionalize the occasions through which such developments receive their nurture and sustenance. It is difficult, if not impossible, to institutionalize religious and political movements whose *raison d'etre* is provided by revitalization inspiration.

For all of these reasons, the New Religious Right is most accurately understood as a neo-nationalist movement that came to prominence in the United States in the last quarter of the twentieth century. It is nationalistic in intention before it is religious or even Christian. To be sure, the objectives of the movement have been formulated in distinctively Christian terms, and a few Christian theologians are included among the movement's most trusted theoreticians. But the venture exhibits much more interest in revitalizing the life of the nation than in having an impact within the church and/or the religious community. What it counsels is loyalty and devotion to the nation. What it strives for is a sense of collective consciousness that exalts the nation. In wishing to "take back the land," the movement also desires to "bring America back again," that is, the America that enjoys the favored status among all of the nations of the world. Consequently, the movement pays much greater intellectual homage to the Founding Fathers of the nation than it does, say, to John Calvin, Martin Luther, Jonathan Edwards, or even J. Gresham Machen, or to any other figureheads within ecclesiastical history. As a neo-nationalist movement, the occurrence of a New Religious Right within the United States is no more surprising than are the occurrences of its counterparts and companion movements in Japan, Israel, Iran, and elsewhere. The function of each is to effect an unabashedly chauvinistic solidarity—in monolithic terms, if possible—among the citizenry.

The problem is that the United States can never again be considered or conceived as a monolith, if ever it was. Thus, a strictly defined basis of identity and solidarity functions as a limiting rather than as an inclusive principle. In this regard, it is telling that the limiting principle has been employed as a corrective, and has been asked to do its work, at the very time that the pluralistic character of the society is increasing dramatically. Nevertheless, regardless of the eventual outcome, it will always remain an intriguing story that, in the 1980s, within and on behalf of the most influential national power on the face of the earth, a strong but measurable portion of the national will was dedicated toward asserting a sense of national identity and destiny on the basis of a religious outlook that previously had belonged rather exclusively to primarily marginal segments of the society.

This, of course, is both the challenge and the dilemma. A vital sense of the American dream, can perhaps be conceptualized in literalist biblical terms. But the product promises to be an exclusive rather than an inclusive dream. The experience of having been "born again" can perhaps be reckoned as that which most singularly defines the meaning of human life. But one can hardly expect a program for the "revitalization of the nation" to become operational in such terms. A conservative version of the Christian faith can perhaps be demonstrated to be compatible with the ideals and aspirations of a democratic society. But being compatible with is not the same as being identical to. Redesigning traditional patterns of religious belief and practice may represent important theological work for those who are affected by the outcome, but such theological shifts and adjustments do not necessarily carry compelling prescriptive functions beyond the circle of their inherent sponsorship. In all of these areas, the New Religious Right has sought to nationalize—and then to internationalize on a nationalistic basis—its own aspirations and ambitions.

The truth is that the movement has not yet offered a constructive program that is able to rekindle a vital sense of the American dream in terms that are broad, resilient, expansive, and inclusive enough to meet the expressed needs and challenges of a pluralistic society. It has offered no impressive evidence that its desire is to build the kind of community that honors and protects such diversity, and recognizes that its long-term greatness lies in this direction. Instead, New Religious Right theology functions to encourage conformity, to instill and protect some monolith, and to reinforce the desire for a monochromatic society, even if these are not its declared objectives. Its political program, as Paul Weyrich likes to put it, is "to Christianize America." But such an ambition, were such an assemblage ever constructible, would do enormous violence both to the religion as well as to the nation. And because it cannot be successful, no matter how tenaciously committed its advocates remain, New Religious Right incentives register as a thoroughly defensive posture. Whatever more positive, constructive objectives may have been intended from the beginning, New Religious Right strategy is obliged to concentrate most of its effort on identifying and repelling real and perceived threats to its prescribed ideological tenets. And when the movement gets postured this way, it arouses comparisons to McCarthyism and "Gantryism" that justifiably strike fear in the hearts of the citizenry.

RELIGION IN A DEMOCRATIC SOCIETY

The moral of the story?

It is an ironic one. For it is not a story about the successful creation of a Christian America, or an account of how it happened that the United States was transformed into some desecularized theocratic state. Rather, we expect it eventually to be an exhibit regarding the continuing triumph of First Amendment sensibilities. And the story line goes something like this, namely, that approximately two hundred years after the Constitution was signed and the Bill of Rights was drafted there was a crisis in the land regarding the status of religious freedom. The President of the United States, Ronald Reagan, invoked the First Amendment in support of his view that Thomas Jefferson's famous "wall of separation" between church and state was designed, as he put it, "to protect religion from the tyranny of government." And he was supported in this view by millions of evangelical Christians, large numbers of whom had been incited to action by a recognition that the spiritual vitality of the nation had been adversely affected by pervasive moral degeneration. To recover from this condition, this reconstituted conservative evangelical force offered a vision of what could (and should) obtain on the basis of biblical images that were allegorically derived but presented with literal explicitness and dogmatic authority.

For a time the effort was remarkably successful. For a time the movement's leaders did secure the attention of the people. For a time it even appeared that this reconstituted religious and political force might make some headway, because its leadership seemed to comprehend something of the nature of the challenge. But in formulating their response they betrayed the constitutional principle that religious pluralism is the primary protector of religious freedom.

That same Thomas Jefferson whom the President loved to cite wrote same sobering, clarifying words in the opening paragraphs of the Virginia Statute of Religious Freedom in 1779 (passed by the Virginia Senate in 1786). In this document Jefferson asserted that "Almighty God has created the mind free so that all attempts to influence it by temporal punishments or burdens . . . tend only to beget habits of hypocrisy and meanness, and are a departure from the plan of the Holy Author of our religion." He also rebuked some legislators and rulers for presuming that they enjoyed "dominion over the faith of others, setting up their own opinions and modes of thinking as being true and infallible," and he suggested that this is the process through which "false religions" have been "established and maintained" throughout the world. He asserted that "our civil rights have no dependence on our religious opinions," and that "all men shall be free to profess, and by argument to maintain, their opinion in matters of religion, and that the same shall in no wise diminish, enlarge, or affect their civil capacities." In the final paragraph of the statement Jefferson asserted that these religious freedoms belong to "the natural rights of mankind," so that "if any act shall hereafter be passed to repeal the present, or to narrow its operation, such act will be an infringement of natural right."

In deciding whether the Board of Education in Cincinnati, Ohio, had the right to suspend the reading of the Bible at the beginning of the school day, the Supreme Court of Ohio, in 1869, supporting the board, provided the following description of the status of the Christian religion within the United States. The court observed that the only basis for invoking the words "a Christian country" is that "its constitutions and laws are made by a Christian people." But the court explained that such laws "do not attempt to enforce Christianity, or . . . place it upon exceptional or vantage ground." The court reiterated that "true Christianity asks no aid from the sword of civil authority," for "it began without the sword, and wherever it has taken the sword it has perished by the sword. . . . " Commenting directly on the sanctity of the First Amendment, the court concluded that "a man's right to his own religious convictions, and to impart them to his children, and his and their right to engage, in conformity thereto, in harmless acts of worship toward the Almighty, are as sacred in the eye of the law as his rights of person or property."

When then candidate John F. Kennedy was standing before Texas clergy (many of whom were critical of his being a Catholic) on September 12, 1960, he explained the separation of church and state to mean that America is "officially neither Catholic, Protestant nor Jewish," and "where no public official either requests or accepts instructions on public policy from the Pope, the National Council of Churches or any other ecclesiastical source." In Kennedy's America "no religious body seeks to impose its will directly or indirectly upon the general populace or the public acts of its officials," and "there is no Catholic vote, no anti-Catholic vote, no bloc voting of any kind." Speaking directly of the requirements of the elected office he was seeking, candidate Kennedy described the presidency as representing "a great office that must be neither humbled by making it the instrument of any religious group, nor tarnished by arbitrarily withholding it, its occupancy, from the members of any religious group." He affirmed that the President's views on religion "are his own private affair, neither imposed upon him by the nation or imposed by the nation upon him as a condition to holding that office." In sum, Kennedy said:

> I want a Chief Executive whose public acts are responsible to all and obligated to none—who can attend any ceremony, service or dinner his office may appropriately require him to fulfill—and whose fulfillment of his Presidential office is not limited or conditioned by any religious oath, ritual or obligation.

In his classic *Democracy in America*, Alexis de Tocqueville observed that only in close allegiance with the dictates of democracy will religion declare "all persons equal in the sight of God" and "all citizens equal before the law." By any other formula, de Tocqueville attested, religion will be "brought to rebuff the equality which it loves and to abuse freedom as its adversary, whereas by taking it by the hand it could sanctify its striving." Such statements suggest that the genius of the American dream lies in its inviolable affirmation of religious pluralism. Pluralism allows each of its constituent faiths to take itself with utmost seriousness so long as it not try to legislate its convictions in laws that are binding for everyone. From Alexis de Tocqueville's vantage point, when God blesses America it is religious pluralism that is being affirmed, and not one or another prescribed theological interpretation of the nation's nature and destiny.

It is important to recognize that *democracy* (defined as "government by the people" and/or as "rule by the majority") and religious *fundamentalism* have never been good candidates for partnership. The way each is structured makes them always somewhat suspicious of each other. For fundamentalism advances a dualism—an absolute distinction between the saved and the lost, a cosmic battle between good and evil—that is impossible to reconcile satisfactorily with the inviolate democratic conviction that the basic fact about the human condition is equality. At one level, democracy and fundamentalist Christianity have made their peace, for the latter is certainly included within the range of religious attitudes that is protected by a democratic form of government. However, fundamentalism's perennial preference to exist at the margins of the society, and to adopt a posture that has been described as apolitical and anti-intellectual, is not simply a matter of institutional strategy. It has remained on the margins because much of its deepest motivational energy involves instincts and impulses that run contrary, and are antithetical, to the spirit of democracy. An operational, functioning civil religion is fostered when the shared ideals and aspirations of a people are identified, and can be accorded some national creedal legitimation. It is not easy, therefore, to nationalize a religious perspective that is motivated to rescue a select minority of people, a group within a group, from the wrath that will be visited upon the others. The major obstacle is that such religious motivation is not easily homologized to cherished constitutional principles safeguarding "equality of conditions."

In this light, the unexpected achievement of the New Religious Right was to devise ways to effect some working accommodation to the ways of democracy, or at least to give the appearance thereof. However, in wishing to become a more vital and politically responsible element within democracy's religious pluralism, the Religious right was obliged to pay a significant price. To have working compatibility the movement was required to excise all elements of incompatibility, and/or to effect major revisions, adjustments, and transformations. And the only way this could be achieved, since there could be no modification of an absolutistic dogmatic faith, was for democratic principles to be refashioned, made over, or reinterpreted in light of the sanctioned religious perspective of the adherents of the movement. This required a deliberate and thorough revisionist program. Pat Robertson, for example, tried to make the case that those early Virginia settlers, the ones who landed at Jamestown, would have felt no discomfort in identifying themselves with the religious viewpoint that is being championed at CBN University. For his part, Jerry Falwell offered evidence that the signers of the Declaration of Independence would have felt at home in Thomas Road Baptist Church. Francis Schaeffer rewrote Western intellectual history to illustrate that the viewpoint he called normative was simultaneously representative of the teachings of the New Testament, the most edifying theology of the Reformation, the convictions of the Founding Fathers, as well as the philosophy that motivates the New Christian Right today. Other examples of revisionist American and Western intellectual history were crafted and offered to demonstrate that personages such as George Washington, if given the opportunity, probably would have been among the first to support an effort like that represented by the Moral Majority.

What such contentions overlook is that the religious viewpoint of the founders of the nation—never a consensus— is much more aptly expressed in the expansive categories of Enlightenment-philosophical rather than in Christian-fundamentalist terms. For among the Founding Fathers were deists, Masons, freethinkers, atheists, agnostics, as well as members of the various churches of Christendom, the overwhelming majority of which did not—and do not—require a "born again" experience as the indispensable criterion of authentic religious experience. Because they themselves represented such religious diversity, the Founders insured that such diversity would be protected. The irony is that most of the Founding Fathers espoused attitudes to life that contemporary New Religious Right advocates would wish, with passion, to displace, or, at least, to refine. In fact, in contending against a misnamed "secular humanism," the contemporary New Religious Right has established itself as an alternative to a set of convictions that looks remarkably like the very sense of life the Founding Fathers affirmed and espoused. In other words, to make a compelling case, New Religious Right theorists would be forced into quoting the Founding Fathers against each other. And, irony following irony, the set of religious attitudes of which the movement is deeply and incontrovertibly suspicious constitutes the very safeguards and protections that enable the New Religious Right to state its case.

But the problems and confusions are internal too. We have noted that when Jerry Falwell enticed his followers into political activism, he became a controversial figure for many of them. When Pat Robertson make the decision to run for the presidency, he also became a highly controversial figure, even within the community of faith he understood himself to be championing. By taking these adventurous steps, both Falwell and Robertson adopted a role in the world that could not enjoy the unqualified support of their faith, for the foundations of that faith are manifestly dualistic. The Bob Jones community, by contrast, had no such problem, for its commitment to the underlying dualism (as in "being in the world, but not of the world") remained absolute. Even Francis Schaeffer, for all of his vitriolic railings, committed no large transgression against the ontological structure. While he acknowledged that Christians were "at war" with the prevailing earthly powers, and, therefore, had every reason to commit acts of civil disobedience, Schaeffer, unlike Falwell and Robertson, did not talk of "winning" or of long-term positive outcomes. For all of their animated, enthusiastic talk, the Joneses and Schaeffers in the group do not expect to witness the occurrence of the "Christian nation," at least not this time through.

When contrasted with other leaders within the evangelical community, both Falwell and Robertson have been manifestly more enterprising. Each has worked diligently to transpose a form of the Christian credo into prevailing opinion in the United States. Each has given enormous effort to equip Christians institutions to be fully competitive with all other contenders. But when Falwell and Robertson embarked on these adventures, they could not assume that their actions would carry the support of their own institutions. Thus, each found it necessary—by direct-mail advertising and by recurrent television appeals—to develop auxiliary and independent financial support groups. Secondly, having moved out beyond the circle of activity for which there are sure protections, they lost the benefit of some of the built-in safeguards against excessive personal ambition. The mistake was to presume that a larger portion of the life of the nation could be ordered on their terms. But the fear was that unless they took such venturesome steps—that is, unless they took some of these matters into their own hands—the way of life they cherished would once again be relegated to insignificant sideshow status amidst the cacophony of competing philosophies and ideologies in contemporary American life. When pressed they defended their actions on grounds that if the very first Christians hadn't been similarly zealous, the world may never have known correct religious doctrine.

I have called it overreaching and overstepping, for the Christian faith was never intended to be a blueprint by which present society should be governed. I have also called it misadventure, for the intention was to insert a salvation religion into the heart of government. This, of course, is what fundamentalist religion is currently attempting throughout the world. In Christian America, the instrument of incursion is the Moral Majority and its like-minded religiously sanctioned political action groups. In Islamic Iran, zealous militant forces with parallel intentions brought the Ayatollah Khomeini to power. And, as the study of fundamentalism at the University of Chicago makes apparent, the phenomenon carries vivid but startling counterparts throughout the contemporary world.

Within the United States, Falwell, Robertson, and their associates remain resolutely committed to the biblical insight that "where the spirit of the Lord is, there is freedom." But tested American religious and political experience has been that the most specific as well as the most expansive application of this affirmation are both enunciated most fully by the genius of democracy, as protected by the Constitution. And that genius has dictated that the principles implicit in what Alexis de Tocqueville called "equality of conditions" be applied to all spheres of the society's life, and, most explicitly, to matters pertaining to religious belief and practice.

In the beginning of my description and analyses, I indicated that this story is important because the movement has found encouragement and has drawn spiritual and intellectual nourishment from resources lying deep within the American soul. The other side of this observation is that the story is important because the movement has also encountered discouragement and has met spiritual and intellectual resistance from resources lying deep within the American soul.

Will the story have a salutary ending? Can the story have a salutary ending? The answer to such questions lies less in the eventual successes and failures of the New Religious Right movement than in how the nation chooses to respond to the episode. Thomas F. O'Dea believed that potentially salutary resolutions of such dilemmas are implicit in the observation that conservatives exercise powerful diagnostic functions within the society, driven by an instinct that senses what is necessary to keep the social and cultural cohesiveness intact. O'Dea chided liberals for failing to recognize that such diagnoses are called for, and, when offered, carry important implications for all segments of the society. But he wanted conservatives to recognize that diagnoses are not prescriptions, and that an exercising of a critical intelligence does not necessarily translate into blueprints for constructive action.

Thus, the presence of the New Religious Right in twentieth-century America vividly illustrates that the vitality of the society is dependent upon compelling moral authority. In the discussion that needs to continue, the one side must acknowledge that the society's grip on such authority can no longer be assumed, indeed, that, in abundant respects, Enlightenment guidance is insufficient. For its part, the other side must agree, if, indeed, it can, that neither is such authority satisfied or circumvented by the availability of a functioning salvation religion.

We can hardly predict the outcome. But the discussion can be challenging if both sides realize that they share keen interest in learning how the pluralistic world (not only the theocratic world) is constituted by moral principles and religious convictions. The discussants must know too that the continuing conversation, as it was for the Founding Fathers, is fundamentally about democracy and only secondarily about religion.

NOTES

CHAPTER 1

1. See Mary Douglas, "The Effects of Modernization on Religious Change," in *Daedalus. Journal of the American Academy of Arts and Sciences,* Winter 1982, pp. 1–19, who observes that "events have taken religious studies by surprise. . . . If the renewal of right-wing political values in the West surprised all political scientists, it is natural that those who least welcomed it would have been the most surprised. Similarly, certain religious forms might have a natural appeal to intellectuals if they are going to be religious at all. People whose occupations do not require submission to authority or conformity to outward forms, and who are paid to ask searching questions and to take an independent stance, are likely to be more drawn to a personal style of religious worship than to a publicly conforming one."

2. The intellectual trajectory that would lead from the 1960s into the 1970s and 1980s and would give compelling place to developments in the third world has roots in the philosophy/theology of hope launched through the proposals of Jürgen Moltmann and Johannes B. Metz, in Germany, both of whom were inspired by the philosophy of Ernst Bloch. Hope theology helped inspire liberation theology, as enunciated by G. Gutierrez, L. Boff, J. Sobrino, and others, which derives from and applies directly to third-world dilemmas and challenges. In all such versions of a liberating outlook on contemporary human events, salvation is understood to have necessary collective implications, and cannot be restricted to individual experience. Thus for salvation to occur it is

necessary that the bonds of hunger and poverty be broken. The prime examples and instances are drawn from third-world experience.

3. Note that some of the early literature on the subject carried titles like *The New Subversives: Anti-Americanism of the Religious Right,* by Daniel C. Maguire; *Holy Terror,* by Flo Conway and Jim Siegelman; *The Fear Brokers,* by Thomas J. McIntyre and John C. Obert; *The Battle for the Mind,* by Tim LaHaye; *Meanness Mania,* by Gerald R. Gill; *The Politics of Doomsday,* by Erling Jorstad; "When the Self-Righteous Rule, Watch Out!," by Charles V. Bergstrom; *Thunder on the Right,* by G. K. Clabaugh; *Thunder on the Right,* by Alan Crawford.

4. Religious studies scholars pride themselves on being able to practice such methodological rigor and hermeneutical objectivity. See the discussion of this fundamental professional obligation in Donald Wiebe, *Religion and Truth* (The Hague: Mouton, 1981); P. Joseph Cahill, *Mended Speech: The Crisis of Religious Studies and Theology* (New York: Crossroad Publishing Company, 1982); Robert D. Baird, *Category Formation and the History of Religions* (The Hague: Mouton, 1971; Ninian Smart, *Worldviews: Crosscultural Explorations of Human Beliefs* (New York: Charles Scribner's Sons, 1983); Smart, *Religion and the Western Mind* (Albany: State University of New York Press, 1986); Smart, *The Science of Religion and the Sociology of Knowledge* (Princeton: Princeton University Press, 1973); Jonathan Z. Smith, *Imagining Religion: From Babylon to Jonestown* (Chicago: University of Chicago Press, 1982); Jacques Waardenburg, *Classical Approaches to the Study of Religion: Aims, Methods and Theories of Research* (The Hague: Mouton, 1973); Jan de Vries, *The Study of Religion,* translated by Kees W. Bolle (New York: Harcourt, Brace and World, 1967); Walter H. Capps, *Ways of Understanding Religion* (New York: Macmillan, 1972); Eric J. Sharpe, *Comparative Religion: A History* (London: Duckworth Press, 1975).

5. Thomas F. O'Dea is known for several books: *The Sociology of Religion* (Englewood Cliffs: Prentice-Hall, 1966); *The Mormons* (Chicago: University of Chicago Press, 1957); *American Catholic Dilemma* (New York: Sheed and Ward, 1958); and *The Catholic Crisis* (Boston: Beacon Press, 1968).

6. See Max Weber, *The Theory of Social and Economic Organization,* translated by A. M. Henderson and Talcott Parsons (New York: Oxford University Press, 1947); *The Sociology of Religion,* translated by Ephraim Fischoff (London: Methuen, 1956); *The Protestant Ethic and the Spirit of Capitalism,* translated by Talcott Parsons (New York: Charles Scribner's Sons, 1958); and Emile Durkheim, particularly his *The Elementary Forms of The Religious Life: A Study in Religious Sociology* (London: Allen and Unwin, 1915).

7. Among Clifford Geertz's published writings on this subject, his "Religion as a Cultural System," in Michael Banton (ed.) *Anthropological Approaches to the Study of Religion* (New York: Praeger, 1966), remains seminal.

8. Mircea Eliade's *Myths, Dreams, and Mysteries: The Encounter Between Contemporary Faiths and Archaic Realities,* translated by Philip Mairet (New York: Harper and Row, 1960), deals specifically with this subject. See also his *Cosmos and History* (New York: Harper and Row, 1959); *Myth and Reality* (New York: Harper and Row, 1963); *Rites and Symbols of Initiation* (New York: Harper and Row, 1965); *Patterns in Comparative Religion* (New York: World Publishing Company, 1958); and *The Quest* (Chicago: University of Chicago Press, 1969).

9. Alexis de Tocqueville, *Democracy in America,* edited by J. P. Mayer (Garden City: Doubleday, 1969).

10. See the discussion of this transposition in Colin Wilson, *The Outsider* (London: Victor Gollancz, 1956). See also Sidney Blumenthal, *The Rise of the Counter-Establishment: From Conservative Ideology to Political Power* (New York: Time Books, 1986).

11. Richard Hofstadter's most comprehensive statement on this subject is his *Anti-Intellectualism in American Life* (New York: Random House, 1962), especially Part 2, called "The Religion of the Heart." Here Hofstadter asserts and/or observes that "enthusiasts did not commonly dispense with theological beliefs or with sacraments; but, seeking above all an inner conviction of communion with God, they felt little need either for liturgical expression or for an intellectual foundation for religious conviction" (p. 56). Hofstadter cites the practice, among some evangelicals, of employing an allegorical illustration, in place of empirical evidence, to explain contemporary events. For example, believing Dwight D. Eisenhower to be a "dedicated agent of the international Communist conspiracy," some evangelicals took the next step and saw him mythologically and allegorically as "a kind of fallen angel." See also Hofstadter's *The Paranoid Style in American Politics, and Other Essays* (New York: Alfred A. Knopf, 1963).

12. The significance of this fact is explored in Ben Armstrong, *The Electric Church* (Nashville: Thomas Nelson, 1979); Martin E. Marty, *The Improper Opinion: Mass Media and the Christian Faith* (Philadelphia: Westminster Press, 1961); Jeffrey K. Hadden and Charles E. Swann, *Prime Time Preachers: The Rising Power of Televangelism* (Reading, Mass.: Addison-Wesley Publishing Company, 1981); and William C. Adams, *Television Coverage of the 1980 Presidential Campaign* (Norwood, N.J.: Ablex Publishing Corporation, 1983). See also Todd Gitlin, *Inside Prime Time* (New York: Pantheon, 1980).

13. The most comprehensive analysis and interpretation of the influence of theater and his background as a movie actor on the style of the presidency of Ronald Reagan is Michael Rogin, *"Ronald Reagan," The Movie and Other Episodes in Political Demonology* (Berkeley: University of California Press, 1987).

14. For analyses of fundamentalist principles of biblical interpretation, see the extensive discussion in George M. Marsden, *Fundamentalism and American Culture: The Shaping of Twentieth-Century Evangelicalism,* 1870–1925 (New York: Oxford University Press, 1980); especially see chapter 5, "Two Revisions of Millenialism," pp. 48–55, in which the implications of a fundamentalist reading of the Bible are explored at length, and chapter 6, "Dispensationalism and the Baconian Ideal," pp. 55–62, which explains typical fundamentalist attitudes toward the Bible. The work and influence of C. I. Scofield figures prominently in both chapters.

15. Robert Bellah, "Civil Religion in America," in *Daedalus.* Vol. 99, 1967, pp. 1–21.

16. A. James Reichley, *Religion in American Public Life* (Washington, D.C.: Brookings Institution, 1985).

CHAPTER 2

1. Liberty University published *The Liberty Way,* which is described as "the official LU Student Handbook," and requires that "each student will hold watchcare membership with the Thomas Road Baptist Church upon moving to the College." Students are enjoined to "become involved in the total ministries of Thomas Road Baptist Church, to learn to do by doing, and to go out with a valid degree and HEARTS AFLAME to win a world for Jesus." The handbook also makes clear that "ATTENDANCE AT LIBERTY UNIVERSITY IS A PRIVILEGE, AND THIS PRIVILEGE MAY BE FORFEITED BY ANY STUDENT WHO DOES NOT CONFORM TO ITS TRADITIONS AND REGULATIONS, OR WHO IS NOT WILLING TO ADJUST HIMSELF TO ITS ENVIRONMENT." Among the requirements listed under the Honor Code is this: "Students are not permitted to miss Sunday services for the purpose of going away for the weekend more than twice each semester. Students must also attend all chapel sessions." There is a prescribed dress code requiring all men to wear neckties on the campus until 4:30 **p.m.,** and forbids the wearing of shorts. Hair must be cut so that "it does not come over the ear or collar," and "beards or mustaches are not permitted." Women cannot wear skirts or dresses "with slits shorter than two inches from the middle of the knee." Furthermore, "anything tight, scant, backless, and low in the neckline is unacceptable." Also, "no skin should

show at the waist at any time or at any position." Students are not permitted to leave the campus on weekends unless they have the permission of the Dean of Students, and "students of the opposite sex may not go home together unless they have written permission from both parents involved." No one is allowed to listen to "rock, disco, country and western, Christian rock, or any other music that is associated closely with these types." Of course, the use or possession of alcohol or illegal drugs is forbidden, so too "visiting residence room of opposite sex" and "spending the night in a single person's apartment of the opposite sex." *THE LIBERTY WAY,* published by The Office of Student Affairs, Liberty University, Lynchburg, Virginia.

2. Carol Flake has explored the modeling of religious zeal to athletic competition within the fundamentalist community in her book, *Redemptorama: Culture, Politics, and the New Evangelicalism* (New York: Penguin Books, 1984), in the chapter "The God Squads." Among the subtopics covered and/or cited are the frequency with which the words of Vince Lombardi are quoted, the film version of Elmer Gantry in which Burt Lancaster bragged that Jesus Christ was "the greatest quarterback who ever lived," the interest in Roman gladiators as models for the Christian life, the establishment of groups like the Fellowship of Christian Athletes, institutional intentions to make Christian schools fully competitive with other schools, and, if possible, even more successful in competition, fondness for movies like *Chariots of Fire,* approaching the deity in robust masculine terms, et al. Flake also identifies and explores correlations between athletics, patriotism, and personal faith, and supplies a number of bibliographical references that would enable the interested inquirer or researcher to take this subject further.

3. Falwell cites such Founding Fathers in his book, *Listen America* (New York: Doubleday, 1980), pp. 30–45. Significantly, it is the same list of personages from which President Ronald Reagan drew when writing his article "What July Fourth Means to Me" for publication in *Parade* magazine June 28, 1981.

4. Though Falwell frequently provides autobiographical details in his sermons and addresses, the fuller account of his life is presented in his *Strength for the Journey* (New York: Simon and Schuster, 1987). See also Gerald Strober's and Ruth Tomczak's biography, *Jerry Falwell: Aflame For God* (Nashville: Thomas Nelson Publishers, 1979). In my judgment, the most perceptive analysis of Falwell's life and work is Francis Fitzgerald's "A Disciplined, Charging Army," in *The New Yorker* (May 18, 1981), pp. 54–59, 63, which is also a chapter in Fitzgerald's book *Cities On a Hill: A Journey Through Contemporary American Cultures* (New York: Simon and Schuster, 1986).

5. Falwell has made a point of criticizing the feminist movement. See Falwell, *Listen America,* pp. 150–64, for example. At the same time, he has aligned himself with Phyllis Schlafly in helping to identify "superior rights for women." See discussion of this subject in Flake, *Redemptorama,* p. 282ff., and in Carol Felsenthal, *The Sweetheart of the Moral Majority: The Biography of Phyllis Schlafly* (New York: Doubleday, 1981).

6. Daniel Yankelovich has explored this topic in his book, *New Rules: Searching for Self-Fulfillment in a World Turned Upside Down* (New York: Random House, 1981), especially pages 5–6 which deal specifically with the Moral Majority.

7. Fitzgerald, "A Disciplined, Charging Army."

8. As I shall illustrate in the next chapter, Falwell's critique of humanism—which he calls "secular humanism"—is fueled by Francis Schaeffer's criticism, which, in turn, is the basis for Tim LaHaye's criticism in *The Battle for the Mind* (Old Tappan, N.J.: Fleming H. Revell Company, 1980). Schaeffer held that humanism was just as dangerous to Christianity as communism, and thus wrote *The Christian Manifesto* in opposition to *The Humanist Manifesto* and *The Communist Manifesto.*

9. Falwell's attitude toward Israel and his relationships with Jews is explored in "That Miracle Called Israel," in *Listen, America,* pp. 107–13, and in "State of Israel," in *The Fundamentalist Phenomenon,* edited by Jerry Falwell (New York: Doubleday, 1981), pp. 215–16. And, of course, this is a subject on which the Lynchburg pastor has preached frequently.

10. Whenever challenged, Falwell has stressed that he is not calling for a theocratic form of government, at least not before the Messiah returns. There is extensive literature on this subject: Martin Marty, *Righteous Empire* (New York: Dial Press, 1970); Robert Handy, *A Christian America* (New York: Oxford University Press, 1971); George Marsden, *Fundamentalism and American Culture* (New York: Oxford University Press, 1980); Michael Johnson, "The New Christian Right in American Politics," in *The Political Science Quarterly,* vol. 53 (April–June, 1982); Samuel S. Hill and Dennis E. Owen, *The New Religious Right in America* (Nashville: Abingdon Press, 1982); Richard John Neuhaus, editor, *Unsecular America* (Grand Rapids, Michigan: William B. Eerdmans Publishing Company, 1986); Mark A. Noll, Nathan O. Hatch, and George M. Marsden, *The Search for Christian America* (Westchester, Ill.: Crossway Books, 1983); Ernest Lee Tuveson, *Redeemer Nation: The Idea of America's Millenial Role* (Chicago: University of Chicago Press, 1968); Rus Walton, *One Nation Under God* (Old Tappan, N.J.: Fleming H. Revell, 1975); John F. Wilson and Donald L. Drakeman, editors, *Church and State in American History: The Burden of Religious Pluralism* (Boston: Beacon Press, 1987), and, perhaps, most perceptive of all, H. Richard

Niebuhr, *The Kingdom of God in America* (New York: Harper Brothers, 1937).

11. Falwell, *Listen America,* p. 18.

12. *Ibid.,* p. 19.

13. *Ibid.*

14. Falwell has been critical of Jimmy Carter, a fellow Southern Baptist, from the beginning of the latter's national political involvement. When Carter won the presidency in 1976, virtually as soon as the election returns were in, Falwell declared, "Jimmy Carter is now my President-elect, and he will have my respect and support. I will pray for him daily. But I will oppose him when he violates moral codes which in my opinion are in opposition to Scripture." Quoted in Strober and Tomczak, *Jerry Falwell,* p. 179.

15. Evangelism is at the center of Falwell's activities. Indeed, Liberty University was established to prepare persons "to win the world for Jesus." Falwell's attitude toward the other religions of the world is hardly intellectual and theoretical. Christians are enjoined to win others for Christ. Even Jews, in his judgment, are "spiritually blind and desperately in need of their Messiah and Savior" (*Listen America,* p. 113).

16. Cal Thomas wrote his own book on censorship, wishing to demonstrate that those who oppose the Moral Majority are often guilty of prejudice and intolerance. See his book, *Book Burning* (Westchester, Ill.: Crossway Books, 1983).

17. LaHaye, *Battle for the Mind.*

18. Thomas developed this attitude during the course of debating George Cunningham before community groups and on college campuses. Cunningham is a long-time associate of former Senator George McGovern, and, during the debates, represented McGovern's group Americans for Common Sense. Though Thomas and Cunningham were on opposing sides, they developed a strong personal friendship, and liked to talk about the fact that they were able to sit down to dinner with one another, and even have family picnics, after debating their differences with convictional intensity.

19. Though Falwell frequently describes the founding and mission of Thomas Road Baptist Church—see, for example, the treatment of this subject in *Strength for the Journey*—he portrays his conception of the role he wishes the church to play in the Lynchburg community, in his *Capturing a Town For Christ* (Old Tappan, N.J.: Fleming H. Revell Company, 1973).

20. It is appropriate to begin with family matters since "traditional

family values" are regarded as the source for the "back to basics" movement Falwell is leading. For example, when identifying the fundamental "social issues" that belong to the Moral Majority's attempt "to bring America back to moral sanity," Falwell lists "Dignity of the Family" first. He defines the family as "the God-ordained institution of the marriage of one man and one woman together for a lifetime with their biological or adopted children," and attributes to the family the status of being "the fundamental building block and basic unit of our society." See Falwell's "Future-Word: An Agenda for the Eighties," in *The Fundamentalist Phenomenon,* edited by Falwell (New York: Doubleday, 1981), pp. 186–223, especially p. 205ff.

21. Falwell has stated his own position on the last days quite succintly in his "Foreword" to H. L. Willmington's *The King Is Coming: An Outline Study of the Last Days* (Wheaton, Ill.: Tyndale House Publishers, 1983), as follows: " . . . the rapture of the Church will be premillenial and pretribulation." He adds that "no doctrine in the Word provides a greater incentive for witnessing and soul-winning than that of the imminent return of Christ," p. 7.

CHAPTER 3

1. Francis A. Schaeffer, *A Christian Manifesto* (Westchester, Ill.: Crossway Books, 1981). Page ii of this book lists *The Communist Manifesto* (1848), *Humanist Manifesto I* (1933), and *Humanist Manifesto II* (1973), to illustrate the intellectual environment that is being addressed.

2. Schaeffer, *The Church Before the Watching World* (Downers Grove, Ill.: InterVarsity Press, 1971), p. 65.

3. Schaeffer, *The Great Evangelical Disaster* (Westchester, Ill.: Crossway Books, 1984), p. 32.

4. J. Gresham Machen, *Christianity and Liberalism* (Grand Rapids: William B. Eerdmans Publishing Company, 1923), p. 2.

5. Schaeffer, *The Great Evangelical Disaster,* p. 23.

6. *Ibid.,* p. 90.

7. Machen, *Christianity and Liberalism,* p. 10.

8. Schaeffer, *The Great Evangelical Disaster,* p. 47.

9. Machen, *Christianity and Liberalism,* pp. 176–77.

10. *Ibid.,* p. 177.

11. Schaeffer, *How Should We Then Live: The Rise and Decline of Western Thought and Culture* (Old Tappan, New Jersey: Fleming H. Revell Company, 1976). See also Schaeffer's *An Escape From Reason*

(Downers Grove, Ill.: InterVarsity Press, 1968); *He Is There and He Is Not Silent* (Wheaton, Ill.: Tyndale House, 1972); *The God Who Is There* (Downers Grove, Ill.: InterVarsity Press, 1968); *The Mark of the Christian* (Downers Grove, Ill.: InterVarsity Press, 1970); *Who Is For Peace?* (Nashville: Thomas Nelson Publishers, 1983); and the book coauthored with E. C. Koop, *Whatever Happened to the Human Race?* (Old Tappan, N.J.: Fleming H. Revell Company, 1979). Dr. Koop was appointed U.S. Surgeon General by the Reagan Administration.

12. Schaeffer, *How Should We Then Live?* p. 17. Further page references are noted parenthetically.

13. Hal Lindsey, *The Late Great Planet Earth* (Grand Rapids: Zondervan, 1970).

14. Schaeffer, *A Christian Manifesto,* p. 61. Further page references are noted parenthetically.

15. LaHaye, *The Battle for the Mind.*

16. *Ibid.*

17. *Ibid.*

18. Onalee McGraw, *Secular Humanism and the Schools: The Issue Whose Time Has Come* (Washington, D.C.: The Heritage Foundation, 1976), p. 4.

19. *Ibid.,* p. 7. In support of her view, McGraw cites William B. Ball, "Implications of Supreme Court Decisions for Contemporary Church-State Problems," in *The Catholic World* (August 1963), pp. 2–10, which she calls "one of the best summaries of the judicial history of church-state relations and Supreme Court cases involving the First Amendment." Note: it is the same William Ball who argued on behalf of Bob Jones University in the case studied in chapter 4 of this book.

20. Betty Arras, *California Monitor of Education.*

21. *Ibid.*

22. *Ibid.*

23. For more information about the Gablers, see Flake, *Redemptorama,* pp. 39–40. See also William Martin, *Texas Monthly,* November 1982; Donna Hilts, *Washington Post,* April 19, 1981.

24. Phyllis Schlafly, "Textbook and Curriculum Mistakes," in *The Phyllis Schlafly Report,* vol. 15, no. 8, section 1 (March, 1982), p. 2.

25. *Ibid.,* p. 4. See also Carol Felsenthal, *The Sweetheart of the Moral Majority: The Biography of Phyllis Schlafly* (New York: Doubleday, 1981).

26. Information about Accuracy in Media is available from the office at 1275 K Street, N.W., Suite 1150, in Washington, D.C. Regular

publications include *AIM REPORT* and *CAMPUS REPORT,* the latter of which identifies institutions and faculty members who foster Marxist-Lennist attitudes. Robert Ehrlich has assessed the impact of the organization on contemporary college and university life in his "Accuracy in Academia: The Chief Thing to Fear Is Our Own Hysterical Reaction," in *The Chronicle of Higher Education* (May 21, 1986), p. 96.

27. Franky Schaeffer, *Bad News For Modern Man: An Agenda for Christian Activism* (Westchester, Ill.: Crossway Books, 1984).

28. Quotations are taken from public address given at Westmont College, April, 1985. An insightful portrayal of Franky Schaeffer's viewpoint and conception of his own vocation is presented in an interview, "Franky Schaeffer: Rebel, Crusader, Activist," in *Fundamentalist Journal,* January 1985, pp. 42–43. In the same issue, Franky Schaeffer summarizes his own views, "The Christian and the Future," pp. 14–16. It is not surprising that the younger Schaeffer, who refers to himself as a Christian activist, is editor of the *Christian Activist* newspaper.

29. Nicolai F. S. Gruntvig, the nineteenth century Danish bishop, poet, theologian, and student of Norse folklore, gave expression to this attitude both in his essays and in the hymns that he wrote. In particular, see his treatise, "The Innate and the Reborn Humanity," in *N. F. S. Grundtvig, Selected Writings,* edited and with an Introduction by Johannes Knudsen (Philadelphia: Fortress Press, 1976, pp. 74–79). For a perceptive description and appraisal of Grundtvig's life and work, see Kaj Thaning, *N. F. S. Grundtvig,* translated by David Hohnen (Copenhagen: The Danish Institute, 1972).

CHAPTER 4

1. A brief history of the institution is available in tract form in B. K. Johnson, *Miracle From the Beginning* (Greenville: Bob Jones University, 1971), and in commemorative anniversary form in *Bob Jones University, 1927 to 1977, Fifty Years Under God* (Greenville: Bob Jones University, 1976).

2. *Bob Jones University, 1927 to 1977,* (no page number).

3. The court case is summarized, from the Bob Jones University perspective, in *Religious Freedom Imperiled: The IRS and BJU* (Greenville: Bob Jones University, 1982).

4. *Ibid.,* p. 6.

5. Ian Paisley has been a friend and coworker of the Bob Jones community for a considerable length of time. Bob Jones has written about him on several occasions. See "The Further Erosion of Liberty in the

U.S.," in *Faith for the Family,* vol. 10, no. 5, May/June 1982, p. 30; and "Reagan Administration Again Denies Paisley's Visa," in *Faith for the Family,* vol. XI, no. 5, May/June 1983, pp. 3, 9–11. Paisley has summarized his own position in *Who's Who in this Apostate Age* (Belfast: Puritan Printing, no date).

6. Many of these accusations are communicated through the "Editorial," in *Faith for the Family.* See particularly Jones's accusations against the United States, the Papacy, and Pope John Paul II specifically. "Editorial," in *Faith for the Family,* vol. IX, no. 10, December, 1981, p. 2. See also Avro Manhattan, "Pope John Paul II: Actor and Demagogue," in *Faith for the Family,* vol. XI, no. 2, February, 1983, pp. 26–27.

7. *Faith for the Family,* vol. IX, no. 10, December, 1981, p. 2.

8. Jones, "Editorial," in *Faith for the Family,* vol. X, no. 5, May/June 1982, pp. 2, 22.

9. The Jones's clash with Billy Graham is amply documented, beginning with Ian Paisley's critique of Graham: *Billy Graham and the Church of Rome* (Greenville: Bob Jones University Press, 1972). When I visited the campus, I was given a packet of anti-Billy Graham literature, within which I counted more than twenty entries, some of them authored by Bob Jones and Bob Jones III, but the majority of them having been written by pastors, occasional writers, editorial writers, and the like. In 1962, there was extensive correspondence between the two organizations in connection with Graham's visit to Greenville for an evangelism rally. Students at Bob Jones University were not allowed to attend the rally. Graham is accused of being sponsored by "modernists, infidels and unbelievers," for forming alliances with religious leaders who have sharply departed from fundamentalist doctrine, for being soft on communism, and for giving the impression, at least, that he favors a "one-world church." Harry Ward, representing the Bob Jones University community, has issued a summary of complaints concerning Graham, in his tract, *Why We Do Not Support Billy Graham,* Greenville: copyright Harry Ward, 1975.

10. Bob Jones, "The Impossible Dream," in *Faith for the Family,* vol. X, no. 1, January 1982, p. 13.

11. Bob Jones III, "The Issue Is Religion, Not Race," *Washington Post,* January 24, 1982, p. 18.

12. *Religious Freedom Imperiled: The IRS and BJU,* p. 41.

13. *Ibid.*

14. *Ibid.*

15. *Ibid.*

16. *Ibid.*

17. Testimony of Bob Jones III before United States District Court, Greenville, South Carolina, May 10, 1978.

18. *Ibid.*

19. *Ibid.*

20. Bob Jones, Sr., "Is Segregation Scriptural," Address given over Radio Station WMUU, Greenville, South Carolina, July 17, 1960, included as *Plaintiff's Exhibit No. 1* in *Bob Jones University v. the United States,* Case No. 81-3, October Term, 1981, United States Supreme Court.

21. Testimony of Director of Admissions, Goldsboro Christian Schools, in the United States District Court for the Eastern District of North Carolina, Wilson Division, filed July 14, 1975, and included as *Plaintiff's Answer to Interrogatories and Request for Production,* in Court Records.

22. *Proceedings of United States Supreme Court Case No. 81-3,* October Term, 1982, transcribed by Alderson Reporting Company, Washington, D.C. All further quotes from *Bob Jones Univ. v. the United States* are from this source.

23. Bob Jones III, "Chapel Address of May 24, 1983," in *Faith for the Family,* vol. XI, no. 1, July/August 1983, pp. 1A–8A.

24. *Ibid.*

25. *Ibid.*

26. *Ibid.*

27. Bob Jones, Jr., "Editorial," *Faith for the Family,* vol. XI, no. 1, July/August 1983, pp. 2, 20.

28. *Ibid.*

29. William Ball, "Reaction of William Bentley Ball," in *Faith for the Family,* vol. XI, no. 1, July/August 1983, p. 4A.

30. William Rehnquist, statement included in *Proceedings of the United States Supreme Court, Case No. 81-3.*

31. Bob Jones III, "Ramifications of Court Ruling, as Stated in Chapel, May 26, 1983, in *Faith for the Family,* vol. XI, no. 1, July/August 1983, pp. 5A–7A.

CHAPTER 5

1. For the information for this account, and for much of the information summarized on subsequent pages, I am indebted to the library staff of the *Charlotte Observer.* I also consulted numerous

newspapers, television newscasts, and documentaries, while interviewing persons close to the scene on my visit to Heritage USA in September 1986.

2. William Michael, "Oh, to Be Rid of TV Evangelists," in the *New York Times*, April 2, 1987, p. A27.

3. *Ibid.*

4. Falwell has provided a retrospective chronicle and analysis of his involvement in PTL in the final chapter (entitled "The PTL Scandal") of his autobiography, *Strength for the Journey*, pp. 400–441.

5. Taken from Falwell's report at a televised news conference, May 27, broadcast over CNN.

6. For example, the daily schedule of events included such items as a Holy Spirit Workshop, Pastors and Spouses Workshop, a discussion session for Nurses and Hospital Personnel that focuses on "healing the whole person," a training program for counselors, as well as frequent opportunities for Bible study, prayer and worship. Musical groups (such as the "Praise Dancers and Singers") would appear frequently on Main Street, as in Disneyland and Disneyworld, and there were regularly-scheduled pony rides as well as opportunities for children to play with zoo animals.

7. Jim Bakker has recorded this portion of his life in two books: *Move That Mountain* (Plainfield, N.J.: Logos International, 1976), and *The Big Three Mountain Movers* (Plainfield, N.J.: Logos International, 1977).

CHAPTER 6

1. Pat Robertson, with Jamie Buckingham, *Shout It from the Housetops* (Plainfield, N.J.: Logos International, 1972).

2. Dede Robertson, with John Sherrill, *My God Will Supply* (Lincoln, Va.: Chosen Books, 1979).

3. For summaries of and commentaries upon the Robertsons' biographies, see Erling Jorstad, *The Politics of Moralism* (St. Paul: Augsburg Publishing House, 1981), pp. 31–37; and Dick Dabney, "God's Own Network: The Electronic Kingdom of Pat Robertson," in *Harper's*, August 1980, pp. 33–52.

4. For perceptive analyses of the relationship between pentecostalist theology and the role assigned to television, see Dabney, "God's Own Network"; Ben Armstrong, *The Electric Church* (Nashville: Thomas Nelson, 1979); and Jeffrey K. Hadden and Charles E. Swann, *Prime Time Preachers: The Rising Power of Televangelism* (Menlo Park, Calif.: Addison-Wesley Publishing Company, 1981).

5. It is significant that, in succeeding years, both Pat Robertson and Dede Robertson became directly involved in the work of the periodical *Christian Life*. Dede Robertson undertook to write a column for the publication under the title "All in a Woman's Day," and news about Pat Robertson has become a regular feature of the publication over the years. For example, one of the earliest descriptions of how Robertson was responding to questions about whether or not he would run for presidential office appeared in *Christian Life* in August 1986, under the title, "Pat Robertson and Politics," pp. 44–47.

6. Robertson records this event in *Shout It from the Housetops*, p. 60.

7. Harald Bredesen, with Pat King, *Yes, Lord* (Shreveport, La.: Huntington House, 1982), p. 157.

8. *Ibid.*, pp. 158–59.

9. Robertson, *Shout It from the Housetops*, p. 61.

10. Bredesen, *Yes, Lord*, p. 161.

11. Robertson records this event in *Shout It from the Housetops*, pp. 63–64.

12. Dede Robertson describes the experience of being filled with the Holy Spirit in *My God Will Supply*, pp. 99–100.

13. Robertson has addressed himself to the subject of the Holy Spirit frequently when preaching and when discussing the issues of our time on his "700 Club" television program. His published commentaries on the subject are recorded in *The Secret Kingdom* (New York: Thomas Nelson, 1983), *Beyond Reason: How Miracles Can Change Your Life* (New York: William Morrow, 1984), and in *Answers to 200 of Life's Most Probing Questions* (New York: Thomas Nelson, 1985).

14. Robertson summarizes this progression of insight in the "Introduction" to *The Secret Kingdom*, pp. 15–17, then spells it out in detail in the passage quoted, on p. 43.

15. *Ibid.*, p. 44.

16. *Ibid.*, p. 45.

17. *Catalog of CBN University*, Virginia Beach, Virginia, from statement of purpose.

18. Professor Titus shared this information with me during the interview, and provided me with a copy of an unpublished manuscript on which he has been working in which his commentary on Blackstone's *Commentaries on the Law of England* is a major part.

CHAPTER 7

1. Paul Weyrich is the highly regarded New Right political strategist who is head of the Committee for the Survival of a Free Congress, and is heavily involved in the work of the Heritage Foundation.

2. Patrick J. Buchanan, address to National Religious Broadcasters annual meeting, February 4, 1986, subsequently published as an op/ed piece in numerous national newspapers.

3. Robert N. Bellah, "Civil Religion in America." The bibliography on American civil religion is extensive. See, for example, subsequent Bellah analyses: *Beyond Belief: Essays on Religion in a Post-Traditional World* (New York: Harper and Row, 1970); *The Broken Covenant: American Civil Religion in Time of Trial* (New York: Seabury Press, 1975), and (with Phillip E. Hammond), *Varieties of Civil Religion* (San Francisco: Harper and Row, 1980). See also John A. Coleman, "Civil Religion," in *Sociological Analysis,* vol. 31, 1970, pp. 67–77; Martin E. Marty, "Two Kinds of Civil Religion," in R. E. Richey and D. G. Jones, eds., *American Civil Religion* (New York: Harper and Row, 1974); John F. Wilson, *Public Religion in American Culture* (Philadelphia: Temple University Press, 1979); and Robert Wuthnow, "America's Legitimating Myths: Continuity and Crisis," in Terry Boswell and Albert Bergesen, eds., *America's Changing Role in the World System* (New York: Praeger, 1987).

4. Anthony F. C. Wallace, "Revitalization Movements," in *American Anthropology,* vol. 58, 1956, pp. 264–81. See also Wallace's *Religion: An Anthropological View* (New York: Random House, 1966), *The Death and Rebirth of the Seneca* (New York: Knopf, 1970), and *Culture and Personality* (New York: Random House, 1970). Additional analyses of revitalization movements include Michael P. Carroll, "Revitalization Movements and Social Structure: Some Quantitative Tests," in *American Sociological Review,* vol. 40, 1975, pp. 389–401; Duane Champagne, "Social Structure, Revitalization Movements and State Building: Social Change in Four Native American Societies," in *American Sociological Review,* vol. 48, no. 6, December 1983, pp. 754–763; S. N. Fisenstadt, *Tradition, Change and Modernity* (New York: John Wiley, 1973); Eisenstadt, *Revolutions and the Transformation of Societies* (New York: The Free Press, 1978); Talcott Parsons and Neil Smelser, *Economy and Society* (Glencoe, Illinois: The Free Press, 1956); and Wendy Reich, "The Uses of Folklore in Revitalization Movements," in *Folklore,* vol. 82, no. 3, 1971, pp. 233–43.

BIBLIOGRAPHY

Adams, William C. *Television Coverage of the 1980 Presidential Campaign.* Norwood, N.J.: Ablex Publishing Corporation, 1983.

Armstrong, Ben. *The Electric Church.* Nashville: Thomas Nelson, 1979.

Bakker, Jim. *The Big Three Mountain Movers.* Plainfield, N.J.: Logos International, 1977.

——— . *Move That Mountain.* Plainfield, N.J.: Logos International, 1976.

Bellah, Robert. "Civil Religion in America," *Daedalus.* Vol. 99, 1967, pp. 1021.

——— . *Habits of the Heart: Individualism and Commitment in American Life.* Berkeley: University of California Press, 1985.

Bellah, Robert, and Phillip E. Hammond. *Varieties of Civil Religion.* New York: Harper and Row, 1980.

Benson, Peter L., and Dorothy L. Williams. *Religion on Capitol Hill: Myths and Realities.* New York: Oxford University Press, 1986.

Blumenthal, Sidney. "The Religious Right and Republicans." *The New Republic,* October 22, 1984, pp. 18–24.

——— . *The Rise of the Counter-Establishment: From Conservative Ideology to Political Power.* New York: Time Books, 1986.

Bredesen, Harald, with James F. Scheer. *Need a Miracle?* Shreveport, La.: Huntington House, 1983.

——— , with Pat King. *Yes, Lord.* Shreveport, La.: Huntington House, 1982.

Capp, Walter H. *The Unfinished War: Vietnam and the American Conscience.* Boston: Beacon Press, 1982.

Chapple, Steve. "Whole Lotta Savin' Goin' On," *Mother Jones.* July/August, 1986, pp. 37–45, 86.

Clabaugh, Gary. *Thunder on the Right.* Chicago: Nelson-Hall, 1971.

Conway, Flo, and Jim Siegelman. *Holy Terror: The Fundamentalist War on America's Freedoms in Religion, Politics and Our Private Lives.* New York: Doubleday, 1982.

Cox, Harvey. *Religion in the Secular City.* New York: Simon and Schuster, 1984.

Crawford, Alan. *Thunder on the Right.* New York: Pantheon Books, 1980.

Dabney, Dick. "God's Own Network. The Electronic Kingdom of Pat Robertson," *Harper's.* August, 1980, pp. 33–52.

Douglas, Mary. "The Effects of Modernization on Religious Change," in *Daedalus.* Winter, 1982, pp. 1–19.

———, and Steven M. Tipton, eds. *Religion and America: Spirituality in a Secular Age.* Boston: Beacon Press, 1982.

Falwell, Jerry. *Capturing a Town for Christ.* Old Tappan, N.J.: Fleming H. Revell, 1973.

———. *Here's How You Can Help Save America.* (Lynchburg, Va.: Old Time Gospel Hour, 1980).

———. *Listen America.* New York: Doubleday, 1980.

———. *Strength for the Journey.* New York: Simon and Schuster, 1987.

———. *Wisdom for Living.* Wheaton, Ill.: Victor Books, 1984.

Felsenthal, Carol. *The Sweetheart of the Moral Majority: The Biography of Phyllis Schlafly.* New York: Doubleday, 1981.

Fitzgerald, Francis. *Cities on a Hill: A Journey Through Contemporary American Cultures.* New York: Simon and Schuster, 1986.

———. "A Disciplined, Charging Army," in *The New Yorker.* May 18, 1981.

Flake, Carol. *Redemptorama: Culture, Politics and the New Evangelicalism.* New York: Doubleday, 1984.

Frady, Marshall. *Billy Graham: A Parable of American Righteousness.* Boston: Little, Brown, 1979.

Gebner, George. *Religion and Television.* Philadelphia: University of Pennsylvania, Annenberg School of Communications, 1984.

Geertz, Clifford. "Religion as a Cultural System," in Michael Banton, ed., *Anthropological Approaches to the Study of Religion.* New York: Praeger, 1966.

Gritsch, Eric W. *Born Againism: Perspectives on a Movement.* Philadelphia: Fortress Press, 1982.

Hadden, Jeffrey K., and Charles E. Swann. *Prime Time Preachers: The Rising Power of Televangelism.* Reading, Mass.: Addison-Wesley Publishing Company, 1981.

Hammond, Phillip E. "The Sociology of American Civil Religion: A Bibliographic Essay," *Sociological Analysis* 37, 1976, pp. 169–82.

Handy, Robert T. *A Christian America: Protestant Hopes and Historical Realities.* New York: Oxford University Press, 1971.

Hill, Samuel S., and Dennis E. Owen. *The New Religious Right in America.* Nashville: Abingdon Press, 1982.

Hofstadter, Richard. *Anti-Intellectualism in American Life.* New York: Random House, 1962.

――――. *The Paranoid Style in American Politics, and Other Essays.* New York: Alfred A. Knopf, 1963.

Hunter, James Davison. *American Evangelicalism: Conservative Religion and the Quandry of Modernity.* New Brunswick, N.J.: Rutgers University Press, 1983.

Jehl, Douglas. "Robertson Says He's Only 'Winnable' Candidate," in *Los Angeles Times.* February 11, 1988, pp 1, 24.

Johnson, Michael. "The New Christian Right in American Politics," in *The Political Science Quarterly.* Vol. 53, April/June, 1982.

Jorstad, Erling. *The Politics of Moralism.* St. Paul: Augsburg Publishing House, 1981.

Kantzer, Kenneth S. "The Charismatics Among Us," in *Christianity Today.* 22, February 1980, pp. 25–29.

Kurtz, Paul. *In Defense of Secular Humanism.* Buffalo: Prometheus Books, 1983.

LaHaye, Tim. *The Battle for the Mind.* Old Tappan, N.J.: Fleming H. Revell Company, 1980.

Lasch, Christopher. *The Culture of Narcissism: American Life in An Age of Diminishing Expectations.* New York: W. W. Norton, 1979.

Lejon, Kjell O. U. *Reagan, Religion and Politics: The Revitalization of "A Nation Under God" During the 80s.* Lund: Lund University Press, 1988.

Liebman, Robert C., and Robert Wuthnow. *The New Christian Right: Mobilization and Legitimation.* New York: Aldine Publishing, 1983.

Lindsey, Hal, and C. C. Carlson. *The Late Great Planet Earth.* Grand Rapids: Eerdmans, 1970.

Maguire, Daniel C. *The New Subversives: Anti-Americanism of the Religious Right.* New York: Continuum, 1982.

Marsden, George. *Fundamentalism and American Culture.* New York: Oxford University Press, 1980.

Martin, William. "Video Evangelism," in *Washington Post Magazine.* June 4, 1978, pp. 37, 39, 41.

Marty, Martin. "Fundamentalism Reborn," in *Saturday Review.* May 1980.

――――. *The Improper Opinion: Mass Media and the Christian Faith.* Philadelphia: Westminster Press, 1961.

――――. *Righteous Empire.* New York: Dial Press, 1970.

McGraw, Onalee. *Secular Humanism and the Schools: The Issue Whose Time Has Come.* Washington, D.C.: The Heritage Foundation, 1976.

McLoughlin, William C. "Is There a Third Force in Christendom?" in *Daedalus.* Vol. 96, 1967, pp. 43–68.

——— . *Revivals, Awakenings, and Reform.* Chicago: University of Chicago Press, 1978.

Mead, Sidney E. *The Nation with the Soul of a Church.* New York: Harper and Row, 1975.

Michaelsen, Robert S. *The American Search for Soul.* Baton Rouge: Louisiana State University Press, 1985.

——— , and Wade C. Roof. *Liberal Protestantism.* New York: Pilgrim Press, 1986.

Mooney, Christopher. *Religion and the American Dream: The Search for Freedom Under God.* Philadelphia: Westminster Press, 1977.

Moorhead, James H. *American Apocalypse. Yankee Protestants and the Civil War. 1860–1869.* New Haven: Yale University Press, 1978.

Murray, John Courtney. *We Hold These Truths: Catholic Reflections on the America Proposition.* New York: Sheed and Ward, 1960.

Needleman, Jacob. *The New Religions.* New York: Doubleday, 1970.

Nelson, John Wiley. *Your God is Alive and Well and Appearing in Popular Culture.* Philadelphia: Westminster Press, 1976.

Neuhaus, Richard John. *The Naked Public Square.* Grand Rapids: Eerdmans, 1984.

——— , ed. *Unsecular America.* Grand Rapids: Eerdmans, 1986.

——— , and Michael Cromartie, eds. *Piety and Politics: Evangelicals and Fundamentalists Confront the World.* Washington, D.C.: Ethics and Public Policy Center, 1987.

Noll, Mark A., Nathan O. Hatch, and George M. Marsden. *The Search for Christian America.* Westchester, Ill.: Crossway Books, 1983.

O'Dea, Thomas F. *The Sociology of Religion.* Englewood Cliffs, N.J.: Prentice-Hall, 1966.

Quebedeaux, Richard. *The Worldly Evangelicals.* New York: Harper and Row, 1978.

Paisley, Ian. *Billy Graham and the Church of Rome. Greenville, S.C.: Bob Jones University Press, 1972.*

——— . *Who's Who in this Apostate Age.* Belfast, Ireland: Puritan Printing, no date.

Phillips, Kevin P. *Post-Conservative America: People, Politics, and Ideology in a Time of Crisis.* New York: Random House, 1982.

Reichley, A. James. *Religion in American Public Life.* Washington, D.C.: Brookings Institution, 1985.

Ringer, Art. "New Right Mullahs," in *Playboy.* June 1981, pp. 36–41.

Roberts, James C. *The Conservative Decade: Emerging Leaders of the 1980s.* Westport, Conn.: Arlington House Publishers, 1980.

Robertson, Dede, with John Sherrill. *My God Will Supply.* Lincoln, Va.: Chosen Books, 1979.

Robertson, Pat. *Answers to 200 of Life's Most Probing Questions.* New York: Thomas Nelson, 1985.

————, with William Proctor. *Beyond Reason: How Miracles Can Change Your Life*. New York: Bantam Books, 1984.

————, with Bob Slosser. *The Secret Kingdom: A Promise of Hope and Freedom in a World of Turmoil*. New York: Thomas Nelson, 1983.

————, with John Sherrill. *Shout It from the Housetops*. Plainfield, N.J.: Logos International, 1972.

Rogin, Michael. *"Ronald Reagan," The Movie and Other Episodes in Political Demonology*. Berkeley: University of California Press, 1987.

Sandeen, Ernest. *The Roots of Fundamentalism*. (Chicago: University of Chicago Press, 1970).

Schaeffer, Francis. *A Christian Manifesto*. Westchester, Ill.: Crossway Books, 1981.

————. *An Escape from Reason*. Downers Grove, Ill.: Inter-Varsity Press, 1968.

————. *The God Who Is There*. Downers Grove, Ill.: Inter-Varsity Press, 1968.

————. *The Great Evangelical Disaster*. Westchester, Ill.: Crossway Books, 1984.

————. *How Should We Then Live? The Rise and Decline of Western Thought and Culture*. Old Tappan, N.J.: Fleming H. Revell Company, 1976.

————. *Who Is For Peace?* Nashville: Thomas Nelson, 1983.

Schaeffer, Franky. *Bad News for Modern Man*. Westchester, Ill.: Crossway Books, 1984.

Shriver, Peggy L. *The Bible Vote: Religion and the New Right*. New York: Pilgrim Press, 1981.

Strober, Gerald, and Ruth Tomczak. *Jerry Falwell: Aflame for God*. Nashville: Thomas Nelson Publishers, 1979.

Thomas, Cal. *Book Burning* Westchester, Ill.: Crossway Books, 1983.

de Tocqueville, Alexis. *Democracy in America,* ed. J. P. Mayer. New York: Doubleday, 1969.

Tuveson, Ernest Lee. *Redeemer Nation: The Idea of America's Millenial Role*. Chicago: University of Chicago Press, 1968.

Wallace, Anthony F. C. *Religion: An Anthropological View*. New York: Random House, 1966.

————. "Revitalization Movements," in *American Anthropology*. 58, 1956, pp. 264–81.

Walton, Rus, *One Nation Under God*. Old Tappan, N.J.: Fleming H. Revell, 1975.

Wilson, Bryan R. *Religion in a Secular Society*. London: Watts, 1966.

Wilson, Colin. *The Outsider*. London: Victor Gollancz, 1956.

Wilson, John F., and Donald L. Drakeman, eds. *Church and State in American History: The Burden of Religious Pluralism*. Boston: Beacon Press, 1987.

INDEX